A Walk Along Land's End

A Walk
Along
Land's
End

DISCOVERING
CALIFORNIA'S
UNKNOWN
COAST

JOHN
McKINNEY

HarperCollins*West*
A Division of HarperCollins*Publishers*

Some selections in this book were previously published in the
Los Angeles Times Magazine, Santa Barbara Magazine, and *Unknown
California* (Macmillan).

A WALK ALONG LAND'S END: *Discovering California's Unknown Coast.*
Copyright © 1995 by John McKinney. All rights reserved. Printed in
the United States of America. No part of this book may be used or
reproduced in any manner whatsoever without written permission
except in the case of brief quotations embodied in critical articles and
reviews. For information address HarperCollins Publishers, 10 East
53rd Street, New York, NY 10022.

Book design by George Brown
Illustration on title page by Paul Buckley

FIRST EDITION

Library of Congress Cataloging-in-Publication Data
McKinney, John.
A walk along land's end : discovering California's unknown
coast / John McKinney. — 1st ed.
p.   cm.
ISBN 0–06–258530–4 (cloth : alk. paper)
1. Hiking—California—Pacific Coast.
2. Pacific Coast (Calif.)—Description and travel.
I. Title.
GV199.42.C22P336   1995   94-43000
796.5'1'09794—dc20   CIP

95 96 97 98 99 ❖ RRD/H 10 9 8 7 6 5 4 3 2 1

This edition is printed on acid-free paper that meets the American
National Standards Institute Z39.48 Standard.

What can we ever hope to do with the western coast, a coast of three thousand miles, rockbound, cheerless, uninviting, and not a harbor on it? What use have we for such a country? Mr. President, I will never vote one cent from the public treasury to place the Pacific coast one inch nearer to Boston than it now is.

DANIEL WEBSTER
from a speech to Congress, 1832

Contents

Acknowledgments

To the many Californians who provided encouragement, directions, and hot coffee while I was wayfaring up the coast, I thank you. For inspiring guidance along the sometimes perilous paths of publishing, I salute HarperCollinsWest editor Shirley Christine and literary agent Julie Castiglia. I thank my wife, Cheri, a native Californian, for her unwavering belief in me and this coastal narrative, and I thank my parents, Helen and Jim McKinney, who had the good sense to raise me near land's end.

Prologue

MY FAVORITE COURSE at the University of Southern California campus, "The West as an Idea in American Literature," was taught by an innovative, somewhat absent-minded professor named Patrick Morrow. Dr. Morrow's required reading list included all the classics of the Western genre: *The Virginian, Roughing It, The Big Sky*. But as I scanned the list on the first day of class, I noticed, at the very bottom of the page, a most peculiar title for a course on Western literature, *One Flew over the Cuckoo's Nest*. Overcoming my sophomore shyness, I raised my hand. The professor acknowledged me with a tip of his beard. "Dr. Morrow, as I understand it, Ken Kesey's novel is about crazies in an asylum. What's that have to do with the American West?"

"At the end of the West is insanity," Professor Morrow intoned. He said the words without rancor, without condescension. He mouthed them as if they were an oft-repeated mantra: At-the-end-of-the-West-is-in-san-i-ty.

I stared in disbelief at this totally hip professor. My mind raced for a rebuttal. Did he mean insanity was the last frontier? Was he suggesting everyone on the West Coast was a little insane? "You're speaking strictly metaphorically, aren't you Dr. Morrow?"

"No," he replied. "I'm not."

Two decades later, as I walked 1,700 miles along the edge of California, I began assessing the considerable insanity at the end of the West. I experienced firsthand confirmation of architect Frank Lloyd Wright's now legendary remark, "The continent is tilted and everything loose rolls into California." However, as I bushwhacked along the Golden State's overgrown historical trails, I realized that immigrants, both sane and insane, did not simply, as Wright put it, "roll into California"; they made a tremendous effort to get there.

In the last century, those dreaming of California left Eastern ports by steamer for a voyage to Panama, then trekked overland across the jungle to pick up another steamer for San Francisco. Other immigrants struggled westward in wagon trains. In this century came the Arkies, the Okies, and waves of Mexican nationals. And today, thousands of immigrants from the Near East, Middle East and Far East, Central America and South America, Asia, Indonesia and Micronesia pour into the state. And, despite severe setbacks in economics and race relations, immigrants and most natives still believe California to be the perfect place to pursue the American dream.

Few of these dreamers or doers realize how profoundly they are influenced by the land: redwood forests, earthquake faults, High Sierras, and the most influential force of all: the coast. Other states have snowy peaks, great deserts, and tall forests, but only California has a coast of such length and diversity; this coast exerts a powerful force on the spirit of the state.

When I started my walk, I was not out to interpret the California dream; my purpose was strictly pedestrian. On behalf of the nonprofit California Coastal Trails Foundation, it was my job to create a temporary route for the new California Coastal Trail (CCT). My assignment was to design a 1,700-mile system of interconnecting beach and mountain range routes—to guide the ambitious hiker from Mexico to Oregon and the less ambitious hiker to some weekend exercise spots.

For several decades, hikers and horseback riders have dreamed of a continuous trail along the beaches, bluffs, and coast ranges of California. Although many governmental officials and conservationists had championed the idea of a coastal trail, no one had ever walked the state to determine if such a trail was even possible. Were the beaches passable at low tide? Could the bluffs be traveled without arrest for trespass? Could a trail be found through the rugged coastal mountains?

During the past half-century, proposals for a Pacific Coast Trail and a Mission Trail surfaced, only to be buried in bureaucracy. (It would have been better to have blazed the California Coastal Trail decades ago, but better now than later.) My task was to outline a temporary route for the CCT, something to trek right now, a way along the coast providing a maximum of enjoyment of natural features and a minimum of hassle with private property owners.

But I must admit the idea of the California Coastal Trail, noble cause that it is, was not what kept me walking. After taking several hundred mile's worth of detailed trail notes, full of route descriptions and coastal access suggestions, my spirit rebelled. I had already written a half-dozen hiking guidebooks; I did not want to write another.

In fact, trail descriptions are wearying. For years, with my weekly *Los Angeles Times* hiking column, I've sent innumerable hikers tramping through California's parks, preserves, and hidden places. I tell my readers—the largest audience of walkers in North America, if you believe the *Times'* advertising-sales staff—where and when to go, what they'll see, and what precautions to take, with the most exact instructions I can muster.

No more pedestrian prose, I decided. When I reached the Santa Barbara headquarters of the California Coastal Trails Foundation, I handed my good friends a stack of southern California trail notes, resigned the job, and walked on. And so the book you are holding is not a guidebook, not a guide to anything except the path taken by my feet and by my heart.

I must make a second admission: Before starting my coast walk, which I intended to do in fifty-, one-hundred-, and two-hundred-mile sections, I relished the athletic challenge that such a hike would present. Something of a wilderness jock, I've climbed High Sierra peaks, explored obscure canyons in the Land of Zion, and jungaleered across remote tropical islands. A walk up the coast would be a physical challenge of the kind I enjoy, I figured.

After trekking a few hundred miles, I lost some of my athletic fervor. California's coast worked its magic on me, my internal clock began ticking slower and the joys of creation displaced those of recreation. From a sportsman with something to prove, I evolved into a traveler with something to learn.

"Going to the mountains is going home," wrote John Muir. He was at least half-right. California's mountains feel like home, but so do the beaches. I am half mountain man, half beach boy. Give me mountains and ocean and a trail with a view. God's country. My country.

Surf and rock marry here. The Pacific batters the mountains, making small rocks out of large boulders and strewing them on the shore. Rivers rush from the flanks of mountains and deposit sand on the beach. Many mountains were once undersea; fossils are found on their slopes. Some mountain ranges march out to sea, their peaks appearing offshore as islands. Yin and yang, water and earth, the coast and I. I spent my youth on the shores of the sundown sea. I have California bloodlines in my heart.

The rocky San Simeon headlands, palm-lined Santa Monica Beach, Pismo Dunes, Lady Bird Johnson Redwoods, Carpinteria, Cambria, Cayucos, and Castle Rock. California's variegated coast beckons with tableaux of pine and palm and neon and stucco, and proclaims to all the world the beauty, the strength, the profanity, and the contradictions of America.

What's America coming to?

It's coming to California. And especially to California's coast. California is the nation's most populous state and 80 percent of that population lives within thirty miles of the coast.

Those pundits not predicting the state's collapse still believe California to be on the brink of a great destiny. Complex historical and social forces—forces related to geography, meteorology, and the westward movement of progress—are working to make California's coast the world's Tomorrowland. As an aftermath of Asian and Middle Eastern wars and the consequence of a shrinking globe, southern California is replacing Ellis Island as the port of entry to America. What was land's end in the last century for foreigners and Americans who came west, is today land's beginning for those arriving from the Far East. The last hundred years has seen California's coastline change from frontier to gateway, from a natural geographic boundary to an open door to the lands and peoples of the Pacific.

California's coast is fast becoming the communications and financial center of the Pacific Rim—a vast multinational and economic entity encircling the Pacific Ocean from Alaska to Tierra del Fuego to Australia to China to Siberia. By the year 2000 it is estimated that 60 percent of the world's consumers will live in Pacific Rim regions, which lead the world in new technologies and natural resources. If this is so, the face of the land and the faces on the land will soon change and this book will record the end of an era.

Regrettably, this high-powered economy (formidable even in recession) and the tremendous development pressure exerted on land's end is responsible for much coastal destruction. The coast has been oiled, sullied, paved, polluted. Nevertheless, I hope to not take the position of a coroner conducting an inquest on a mutilated corpse when describing some of California's more unnatural beachfront attractions. Though critical of the coastal strata quo, I have a stubborn faith that present disfigurements are no more than unpleasant symptoms of a passing epidemic. My hope is we're bound for a more mature civilization. California's coast has outlived the failure of all its conservationists' hopes, and will outlive mine.

If apology be needed for the dearth of statistical information in this book, let me say that my primary interest is not in the cities and industries of this state, and there are plenty of prognosticators working on the statistical side. Rather, I am interested in and fascinated by the less-covered, less-civilized edges of California. It seems to me we already spend too much time quantifying California and not enough time knowing it.

There will be those who say I deal too much with the surfaces of things, that I dwell on the face of the land rather than on the faces of its people, that I am biocentric, that I cover more of California's geography than California's sociology. Good.

This is primarily a book about walking, an account of an adventure of a lifetime, and of the happiness and heartbreak it brought to one of California's native sons.

I walked twelve to fifteen miles a day, sometimes more. I carried my provisions in a small-to-medium-size internal frame backpack. It's a bit too small for a weeklong, live-out-of-your-pack kind of trip, but it's ideal for coast walking, where you can replenish your supplies every few days, if not every day. Only when I hiked into the backcountry of Los Padres National Forest and traversed Humboldt County's Lost Coast did I look like I stepped from an advertisement in *Backpacker* magazine.

En route, I trashed three pairs of lightweight hiking boots. The boots, though light, were sturdy and had ample support. However, because they were low-cut, trail mud and dust dirtied my socks, and my legs would get filthy fast.

My best equipment investment was the small fortune I spent for a top-of-the-line waterproof parka; it kept me dry from head to hips. On the California coast, dry equals warm, so I wasn't often cold. I wore a pocket T-shirt, a button-down shirt, and a sweater or sweatshirt, depending on the weather. I almost always hiked in shorts.

I carried freeze-dried dinners: beef stroganoff, tuna casserole, chicken and rice, macaroni and cheese; trail mix, dried fruit, dried milk, instant coffee, instant oatmeal, and granola in plastic bags. My stickiest food problem was peanut butter in a tube—getting it in and out are equally messy operations. Sometimes I cooked over a campfire; more often, I fired up my trusty Svea stove. When dining alone, I ate out of the pot to save cleaning another item in my mess kit. And sometimes, if I was camped near a town, I simply ate at a restaurant.

Mornings I crave coffee. In camp, I boiled some instant. In town, I stopped at nearly every coffeehouse I could find for a cappuccino or latte. (The coffeehouse boom was a blessing for this caffeine-buoyed walker.) When good coffee was unavailable, I bought bad coffee—swill from mini-marts or fast-food joints.

Most of my health regimen consisted of protecting my fair skin against the sun. Every morning, I smeared sunscreen on my face and

neck and globbed on lip balm. I wore sunglasses on all but the gloomi-
est days, and when the sun was intense, I wore a purple baseball cap
with a hiker emblem stitched on it.

During the long walk, my body held up well. A trick knee played
no tricks. In southern California, blowing sand aggravated a minor eye
infection; in central California, I had a bout of sinusitis. A wretched
night in Santa Cruz after consuming an avocado burrito was my only
profoundly uncomfortable time.

My tent was my only equipment problem. Nothing was wrong
with the tent itself. It was the moisture—wet nights, wet mornings,
sprinkles, storms, and incessant damp. Old mold became one with the
tent's modern miracle fabric and I feared mushrooms would grow in
its corners. Getting started early, which I prefer, meant rolling up a wet
tent. Sometimes, at my noon lunch stop, I would unroll the tent to let
it dry out, but often I was too lazy to do so, or the weather was too
wet to do any drying. When a banana slug curled up with me in Mendocino, I knew I was becoming one with the slime.

Many nights were spent at state parks with walk-in campgrounds.
Sometimes I had to rent an entire auto campsite—or stay in a more
expensive private campground. North of Monterey, I often camped in
unofficial campsites—that is, wherever I stopped walking. I spent perhaps a dozen nights under a roof: friends' houses, a couple of hostels, a
handful of cheap motels, and two splurges—at a Marin inn and a
Mendocino bed and breakfast.

I walked all 1,100 or so miles of the California coast plus another
600 miles or so through the coastal mountains. I chose a south-to-
north route, the way Don Gaspar de Portolá explored the state by land
and the way Juan Rodríguez Cabrillo explored the state by sea, which
meant that I hiked into the prevailing winds, a decision I was to regret
more than once during my journey.

I spent many an hour planning the route of my trek by studying
county maps, Forest Service maps, and topographic maps. Old maps
are best; they have more of the places I like to visit. Newer maps tell of
bigger places, crowds and asphalt, geography I prefer to avoid. New or
old, the map is not the territory and I often found my compass and
intuition to be better guides.

And the best guide of all, my companion on the trail, was that old curmudgeon Joseph Smeaton Chase who, in 1912, rode the California coast on horseback and recorded his impressions in *California Coast Trails*.

I spent many a day with the spirit of Chase, walking on a trail bordering the ocean but suspended above it a thousand feet, clinging to the side of a coastal slope that fell at a dizzy angle of forty-five degrees to the frothing surf. On my right, bisecting the slope, were deep canyons, full of madrone and redwood, oak and sage, blue jays and quail, deer and rabbits, pools and waterfalls. And on my left, an inch closer to my heart, was the deep blue ocean stretching all the way to China.

JOHN MCKINNEY
Santa Barbara, California

ONE

Borders

THE CALIFORNIA COASTLINE. Even the name sounds a thousand miles long.

The California coastline is mountains and rivers and deltas and estuaries; rocky shore and sandy beach, coral bottom and mud bottom, blue, green, and red tides, plankton and gray whales, clear waters and muddy waters, pillars and stacks and blowholes; pickleweed and salt grass, palms and redwoods, all the different kinds of trees and shrubs and cockles and mussels and limpets that people have named and not yet named on its ever-changing shore—a thousand different yet interconnected things at the end of one continent and the beginning of another.

And I've got a job to do on this coastline—at least that's what I'm thinking about during the predawn hours of my first day on the trail. It's my job to pioneer a trail along land's end, to connect California's remaining coastal wildlands to one another and to those walkers willing to make an effort to visit them. I must select the best combination of cow trails, horse trails, and people trails; ranch roads, fire roads, logging roads, and mining roads. I must avoid, as much as possible,

towns, cities, military bases, nuclear power plants, and marijuana growers who shoot at hikers. I must figure out a route for the new California Coastal Trail so that hikers less experienced than I can follow in
my footsteps.

That a coastal trail may be hard to find and harder still to follow
becomes apparent to me early this morning when I roll out of my
sleeping bag to watch the sun come up over the Otay Mountains and
illuminate the beach at the California-Mexico border.

I wait.

And watch.

And wait some more.

But the sun does not rise where I can see it, and shines only
enough to chase away some gloom. A quarter-mile, maybe a half-mile
west of my camp is the beginning of my California Coastal Trail, lost
in the mist. I wasn't able to see much coast last night either when my
friend Susan drove me 130 miles from Los Angeles to the Mexican
border.

AS WE LEAVE Los Angeles, a heavy cumulus inversion layer
squats over the city, trapping the day's smog and denying Angelenos
their customary nightly reduction in airborne particulate matter. A
witch's brew it is—nitrous oxide, sulfur dioxide, carbon monoxide—
made all the more toxic by the wet heavy air. Liquid smog. We gulp
for air like a couple of gaffed bass.

Susan remembers a bottle of Vitamin B-C Stress Formula stashed
in the Mazda's glove compartment. We each pop a 600-mg tablet, not
so much for our health but as a kind of talisman against the evil spirits
of the freeway. Thus fortified, we join the southbound Hollywood
Freeway and motor into the twilight ozone.

Interchange. South on the Santa Ana Freeway to Interstate 5.

On clear nights on the freeway, I often fancy myself a pilot, flying
over the glow of the city and its hundred suburbs, swooping over the
endless sprawl of stucco. But Los Angeles is far more finite tonight. No
freeway flying for me; I'm grounded by poor visibility. The heat of the
traffic dissolves just enough of the smog and fog to permit safe passage,

giving me a mole's eye view from an asphalt tunnel. I feel a vague sense of suffocation, as if trapped in the claustrophobia and flatulence of a subway.

Bell Gardens, Downey, Norwalk, Whittier, the ersatz Matterhorn of Disneyland. The miles pass without words.

We hurtle on through the night. More cities, murky streamers of light, hyper home movies playing on the windshield. We follow the coast now. San Clemente, Encinitas, Del Mar, San Diego.

As the lights of Tijuana come into view, we exit the interstate and turn west toward Border Field State Park. Monument Road takes us coastward, into a heavy mist.

We pass a few stucco ranch houses, horse corrals, lots of fence. A rabbit scampers onto the road, then, transfixed by our headlights, freezes on the centerline. Recovering its wits in the nick of time, the animal bounds off the road into the brush.

"I hear when the Border Patrol gets bored with chasing Mexicans they shoot rabbits," Susan comments.

"Remind me not to hop across the border."

"Don't hop across the border. You have a wife and daughter waiting for you back home."

We arrive at a Spanish-English sign warning that Border Field State Park closes at sunset. Good, I'll have the whole park to myself. I want to get a crack-of-dawn start on the coastal trail—possible only with an illegal bivouac.

Susan stops the car at the park entrance. "You know," she says, frowning at the mist, "you could spend the night at a motel in San Diego and walk from there."

"You gotta start a trail at the trailhead," I reply.

Good God, what fortune-cookie philosophy! Did I really say that? My laugh is visible, a warm exhalation on a cold night. Susan laughs too. She knows me, knows trails. I heave my pack and give Susan the thumbs-up sign. She wheels the car around and heads back to I-5. I watch the taillights disappear around the first bend, shivering in the faint starlight. In the mid-40s, it's not cold by mountain standards, by most any standards, but it's a wet, bone-chilling cold that seeps through

my windbreaker. The stars shine only in the east; they are overwhelmed by the earthly lights of San Diego to the north, by Tijuana
to the south, and by the marine layer to the west. Only the eastern
heavens glow on this moonless night.

It's far too wet a night for sleeping on the beach, so I hike a ways
into the coastal scrub. By flashlight, I pitch my tent, unroll my sleeping
bag, pull off my clothes, and am soon asleep.

But not for long . . .

I awake at 3 A.M. to the sound of a four-wheel-drive vehicle labor-
ing over the nearby sand dunes. It's the Border Patrol, looking for
aliens. I remember reading that the Patrol uses infrared sensors planted
in strategic border-crossing areas. The sensors, perfected during the
Vietnam War, detect body heat and relay the information to a command post. Armed with a vector reading and coordinates, the United
States Immigration and Naturalization Service then scoops up the
would-be immigrant. I imagine my tent appearing as an A-shaped blip
on some video monitor in downtown San Diego. "Alien at G-26
south. Let's roll, George."

After this disconcerting thought, I sleep fitfully, haunted by paranoid infrared dreams, afraid that the gendarmes will bayonet me in my
sleeping bag before they notice my blue eyes and sandy hair or ask for
my ID.

IN DAWN'S GRAY LIGHT the marsh birds raise a racket.
A white-tailed kite circles over the nearby Tijuana Estuary. Gulls fly
oceanside to scavenge the tide's debris. As I walk oceanward, I dip into
a ravine and soon lose sight of the gray horizon.

"La Migra!" A woman's shout comes out of the mist.

In the bottom of the ravine I stumble upon a Mexican family—
mother, father, and little girl—ready to take flight. They are frozen, like
jack-rabbits caught in headlights. When I walk closer they determine,
after a hurried whispered conference, that my green button-down
shirt is not the uniform of a border patrolman. Panic gives way to uneasy smiles.

"Qué pasa?"

My question is answered with more uneasy smiles. Obviously it's not going very well or they wouldn't be stuck out here in this no-man's-land half a mile from the border.

I try English. "Where are you going?"

"Chula Vista," answers the man.

The little girl tugs at my shirt. *"Agua?"*

"Sí." I find my water bottle, hand it to her. She gulps furiously, water trickling over her chin and down her neck to her stained blouse.

"Maria!" her mother scolds.

"It's all right," I soothe.

Maria hands the water bottle to her mother. The woman hesitates, caught between pride and thirst.

"It's all right," I repeat.

She drinks, hands the canteen to her husband. When he tilts his head back to drink I see thirty hard years etched in his face, fifty in his hands.

The canteen makes another round and is returned to me.

An uncomfortable silence settles over the dunes. This gringo can do nothing more for them. After an exchange of *adioses,* I leave them to their fate—a successful dash under the cover of darkness to Chula Vista or arrest by La Migra.

"Dios consiente, más no siempre," the Spanish say. God provides, but not always.

As I walk toward the Pacific, the sun sneaks up behind me and enlarges from a tiny spotlight into a floodlight. I emerge atop the coastal terrace overlooking Border Field Beach as the foggy curtain parts and white light pours down over the Pacific and the borderland. I look to the limits of the clouds: Point Loma, Silver Strand, Tijuana River floodplain, the Coronado Islands.

A few million years ago the ocean inundated this land, wearing the peaks beneath into a nearly flat platform. This platform was later lifted out of the water by forces within the earth to form a coastal terrace. The remains of this terrace, battered by the ocean to the west and the Tijuana River to the east, resemble an immense flattop aircraft carrier listing to the starboard.

An empty parking lot sprawls across the stern end of the ship-shaped blufftop, ending at the chain-link fence separating Mexico and California. The flimsy fence surprises most Americans; before visiting Border Field State Park they imagine a more militaristic border—the Berlin Wall before its fall, a barrier topped with barbed wire and ground glass, guarded with mine fields and machine gun nests. ("They gotta lotta damn nerve callin' this a border, Martha. This fence would-n't hold chickens in a chicken coop.") The wire fence extends only a little past the low tide line and northbound migrants could easily wade around it. Yet few cross here. (The term "wetback," as applied to Mex-ican migrants, originated in Texas where they must cross the Rio Grande to enter America.) Here in southernmost California, undocu-mented aliens prefer chancing the unfenced desert border, the Tortilla Curtain, farther east.

Next to the fence is the graffiti-splashed border marker; from a distance, it resembles a 1/25th-scale model of the Washington Monu-ment. When California became a territory at the end of the Mexican-American War in 1848 an international border became a necessity. The Treaty of Guadalupe Hidalgo dictated the location of the boundary and survey parties from both countries were appointed to mark and determine the line. The federal government, anxious to secure its new border, quickly dispatched an American survey team from Washington. In the meantime, gold was discovered at Sutter's Mill and practically every Yanqui in Southern California headed north. The Gold Rush slowed American surveyors, first delaying them in the crush of forty-niners tunneling across Panama, then luring some of the team to the gold fields. The more sober civil servants, preferring government sinecure over speculation in precious metals, finished surveying the borderline. The spot where the monument now stands was used as the initial survey site. Chiseled out of Italian marble, the monument trav-eled by ship from New York and with great ceremony was carried to this spot by Army escort.

My trail begins at this monument, at the very southwest corner of America, on the border between the United States and Estadios Unidos Mexicanos. Truly, there are more inspiring trailheads. On the

other side of the fence is the gaudy, pink Tijuana bullring, surrounded by flophouses and cantinas. A tired Chevrolet Impala (old
Chevys never die; they simply migrate across the border and live forever as Tijuana taxis), its muffler dragging, trumpets an exhausted
reveille.

But just as one shouldn't judge a book by its cover, nor, I suppose,
should a trail be judged by its trailhead. In contrast to its departure
point, the trail north looks promising. Long, wide Border Field Beach
is bisected by the Tijuana River, which flows parallel to shore for a
mile or so, then makes an abrupt dog-leg turn into the surf. Beyond
the river is another beach, the Silver Strand, where a trillion seashell
fragments glint in the sun.

But I'm not fully concentrating on this panoramic view of golden
light showering on silver sand; my head is filled with trailhead
thoughts—of what lies ahead and what I left behind. I review a mental
checklist of my backpack's contents, attempting to now remember
what I forgot. Map? Poncho? Sunscreen? My neuroses are interrupted
by what sounds like the high, revving whine of a chain saw.

Motoring down the beach is a border patrolman astride an all-
terrain vehicle, a machine nearly as cacophonous as the unmuffled
Tijuana taxis. The balloon tires squirm through the sand, leaving
clouds of granules in the ATV's wake. Law enforcement does not as-
sume a low profile in these parts. Like the outnumbered frontier cav-
alry troopers who rode their horses in circles to stir up dust and fool
the Indians into overestimating their strength, the Border Patrol hopes
a show of force will slow the onslaught.

The force this morning is one frozen patrolman, who zooms up an
asphalt ramp to the top of the bluffs. He stops ten feet from me, cuts
his engine, and dismounts. He swings his arms, stamps his boots, and
arches his back, hoping these impromptu aerobic exercises will transfer
some thermal energy to his extremities. The patrolman removes his
crash helmet, revealing the visage of an aging surfer: thinning blonde
hair, deep sun-squint crinkles around the eyes, a forever-red nose.
"Morning," he greets. "Where you headed?"

"El Norte. Like everybody else."

He laughs. "Yeah, like everyone else. Actually, we had a slow night last night. You'd think more of 'em would go for it on a foggy night with no moon. But it doesn't seem to work that way. Slow morning too. Nobody out but me and the birdwatchers."

"Birdwatchers?" I envision twenty pairs of binoculars trained on the dunes where three frightened would-be migrants await nightfall and a second chance.

"More than a hundred kinds of birds hang out in the estuary," he relates, sounding more like a tour guide than a patrolman. "They migrate here from all over the world."

His mention of the estuary prompts me to think of the Tijuana River, which spills out of the lagoon and arcs to the sea. My Auto Club map paints the river as a wide blue swath and I wonder about a difficult crossing. "How's the river crossing?"

"Radical. Probably comes up to the middle of your chest—or higher. And we've had a lot of sewage spills from Tijuana. Toxic to the max. And you'd better watch out for the current at the river mouth—it's really tricky. Know about the current?"

I shake my head.

"The current along most of the coast runs north to south, but the way Point Loma sticks out it reverses things and sets up eddies. The eddies built up Silver Strand Beach up north and make the current supergnarly down here, especially at the mouth of the river. Sometimes illegals try to cross the river; sometimes they don't make it."

With a wave to the patrolman and a last look at the border monument, I tramp down the asphalt path to the beach.

"I'd detour back to the highway if I was you," the patrolman calls out.

I hike oceanside over the firmly-packed sand at the high tide line. The sun pokes over the low sand dunes and chases the last of the shadows from the beach. Anchoring the dunes are clumps of salt grass, verbena, and pickleweed. California poppies and sea dahlias splash orange and yellow on the sand. Behind the dunes is the estuary, one of the last in southern California, full of native and migratory waterfowl—and birdwatchers. Through a gap in the dunes I spot a party of

birders, their bright orange parkas as obvious as signal flares. Fortunately for the family in the dunes, the orange-breasted Auduboners
have their sights set on a blue heron.

A hundred years ago a city was planned for the beach on America's
southwest border. The railroad reached San Diego in 1885 and precipi-
tated a land boom. Developers lured prospective buyers from colder
climes by selling the weather, supposedly sure to cure rheumatic pro-
clivities, catarrhal trouble, lesions of the lungs, and various other ail-
ments. Settlers poured in, land companies sprang up, property values
rose. The rich got richer and the poor got lots on the installment plan
($25 down, $25 monthly) and soon new cities surrounded San Diego
Bay. The town of International City was planned for the area just
north of the border. But the boom went bust, particularly for settle-
ments located so inconveniently far from San Diego, and International
City never came to be.

The Navy gave Border Field its name. During World War II the
Navy used the area as an aircraft landing field. Pilots received gunnery
training, learning to hit steam-driven targets that raced over the beach
on rails called rabbit tracks. The Navy resisted multifarious real-estate
schemers, who desired to build an International City of condominiums, and in the early 1970s turned over their airfield to the state park
system.

Whether delineated by the Great Wall, the blue Danube, or a chain-
link fence, borders are what you make of them. They become what
you say they are if others are willing to accept your declarations. Three
miles out to sea is the established demarcation line for America. The
1932 bestseller *Boundaries, Areas, Geographic Centers and Altitudes of the
United States, Geological Survey Bulletin 817* states: "When the three mile
limit was adopted, it was thought that this was the extreme range of
cannon that could be used for coastal defenses. . . ." Considering the
kinds of "cannon" available to today's armed forces, the three-mile
rule, at least as a defensive measure, becomes a quaint leftover from
yesteryear.

A less precise line is the border between land and sea. The ocean is
wet and land is dry, but the line separating them is never the same

from one minute to the next. With every wave, boundaries change; with every rise and fall of the tide, the ocean surrenders or conquers some of its realm. The sands move in and out with the seasons—in summer people walk the beach with their feet higher than their heads would have been a few months earlier. The dividing line between land and sea then is not really a line at all, it is a dominion in its own right, an intertidal zone filled with unusual life forms. Partaking in some measure of both earth and water, it belongs finally to neither.

The border between natural and built environments is another that intrigues me. If I chose a place to walk and observe that was wholly civilized, I would be trespassing into the field of sociology. If I chose a place to walk and observe that was wholly wild, I would be beyond my depth as a naturalist. What absorbs me is California's borderland, that margin between a restless sea and a restless civilization.

"With regard to Nature, I live a sort of border life," said Henry David Thoreau, a man caught between the wilderness at Walden Pond and the society of Concord. "I live a sort of border life on the confines of a world into which I make occasional and transient forays only."

Human destiny is transience, thought Thoreau. We are travelers on a ceaseless journey from the known to the unknown and back. Encouraged by Thoreau, I shall wander the borderlands. Since no one else is filling out an application for the position, I appoint myself Ambassador to the Rocks, Minister to the Mountains, Envoy to the Sea. With trail mix and trail maps, pen and pack, I will live a border life, a life of quiet confrontation.

My first confrontation is not quiet.

Brown with silt (and hopefully not Tijuana effluent), the Tijuana River rushes out of its placid estuary with what appears to be unseemly haste. I have crossed rougher, far more dramatic rivers than the Tijuana, but these crossings were made through wilderness waters; never have I crossed a river so near civilization. Have migrants found a watery grave here or was the border patrolman attempting to scare me? The offshore current is reversed here so if I don't make it across at least I won't be carried off to Mexico; instead, my bloated, barnacle-covered body will wash up on a populated stretch of sand to the

north—Mission Beach or Pacific Beach or the dining terrace of the
Hotel del Coronado.

The river looks worse, not better, when I reach its southern bank.
At the mouth of the Tijuana, fresh water and saltwater collide in a
boiling cauldron of kelp and froth. I can't see the bottom beneath the
whirlpooling green, blue, and brown waters. The river spreads itself
wide, and hopefully shallow, forking into three small tributaries that
spill across Border Field Beach into the surf.

I have two options: a short, but no doubt deep, crossing upriver or a
dash across the shallows between the incoming sea and the outgoing
river. The first option appeals to my common sense, the second to my
spirit of adventure. Either option means getting wet. Very wet. I remove boots and pants, then hesitate for reasons of modesty. This is a
public beach, but no public is in sight. A moment later I stand in my
birthday suit and regard the river. If I can time my sprint just right the
waves won't crash over me. . . .

Off and running. Cold water and soft sand shorten my stride. I'm
running hard, getting nowhere. I'm through the first fork of the river
and splashing through the second when a good-sized comber strikes
me waist high. I crab sideways ten feet or so, trying to keep my balance. Seconds behind the first wave, a second advances. I wriggle out
of my backpack and hold it above my head. A wall of water strikes me
shoulder high. My feet slip out from under me.

Swallowing water, I struggle to keep the pack above the surge. As
the wave recedes, I sprint again, splashing through the last branch of
the river mouth. Kelp wraps around my legs, like the tentacles of a sea
monster, pulling me downward. Another wave, a huge one, rolls toward me. Up the river bank I scrabble, trailing ten feet of seaweed. I
reach safety just as the mammoth wave crashes ashore with enough
force to reroute the Tijuana River to Arizona.

I stand spitting, sputtering. Saltwater fills my every pore. I feel not
so much delivered as baptized. Shivering, with the roar of the breakers
and the rush of the river behind me, I feel a delicious greed wash over
me. I want to walk it all, feel it all, know it all, embrace the entire borderland with heart and feet, possess it like the missionaries who

claimed this coast for God and like the conquistadores who claimed this coast for their king. I will lay claim to all of it. A ridiculous desire? Probably, but at least no one is on Border Field Beach this morning to dispute my claim.

I disentangle myself from the kelp. Ahead lies the Silver Strand, sparkling with seashells and promise.

Two

Stop 'n Go in San Diego

T H E   B E A C H E S north of the border—Border Field and Imperial, Silver Strand and Coronado, provide a wide sandy trail along the west side of San Diego Bay.

Late in the afternoon of my first day, I reach Coronado Island, which is not an island at all, but a peninsula. On Coronado Beach I encounter human architecture at its worst—the cell-block style of Condominium Shores; then architecture at its most droll, the rambling red-roofed, queen of Victorian-era hotels, the Hotel del Coronado. From the ridiculous to the sublime to downtown Coronado.

Coronado, although a peninsula, had, because of its isolation, some claim to island status, until the completion of the Coronado Bay Bridge in 1969. Before the bridge, generations of San Diegans and visitors from all over the world took the ferry from San Diego across the bay to Coronado and flocked to the "Del," as the grand hotel was abbreviated. The bridge brought hustle to a place where there was no bustle and today the storefronts of the "island" are little changed from their boutiqued counterparts on the mainland.

What made Coronado unique, its *islandness,* was lost when the bridge opened. To appreciate a place one must pause between coming and going; such a pause is inevitable with a ferryboat, unlikely with an auto.

The Coronado Bay Bridge arcs across the water toward San Diego's skyline. NO PEDESTRIANS reads a sign at the beginning of the bridge, and since no sidewalks accompany the four lanes of highway borne by the bridge, I make the best out of a bad situation by walking flush against the right curb. Fortunately, traffic is light. I'm hardly a hundred yards from Coronado Island when a police car screeches to a halt beside me.

"You . . . the walker . . . "

The policeman's voice is broadcast over a loudspeaker, which assaults me from a distance of five feet. "Yes, *you.* With the blue backpack. Pedestrians are *not permitted* on Coronado Bay Bridge. Please turn around."

Turn around? I've covered but fifteen miles of coastal trail and I'm asked to retreat. No way. I squeeze by the front fenderwell of the police car and walk around to the driver's side. Air conditioned air escapes to cool my sweaty brow. Behind the wheel is another one of southern California's surfer cops.

"Good afternoon," I offer, observing my sunburn in his reflective sunglasses.

"Hitchhiking?" he asks.

"Nope, just hiking."

I hand him my little blue business card, which has printed on it: CALIFORNIA COASTAL TRAILS FOUNDATION, John McKinney, Executive Director.

This is my business card's first test. The board of directors of the California Coastal Trails Foundation figured I should look as legit as possible, as should the foundation, so they ordered a thousand of the little suckers. The word *foundation* has such a nice establishment sound, like *bank* or *bureau* or *administration.* Much better than the other contenders—Hikers and Walkers and Club—the board reasoned. Foundation sounds governmental, bureaucratic, and authoritative, a convincing cover for a small group of hikers and militant environmentalists. After

the board twisted my arm, I parted with my titles of choice—
Trailblazer and Trailmaster—in favor of Executive Director. When
ranchers catch me going over fences, when forest rangers discover me
in illegal campgrounds, when loggers find me among their trees, when
policemen dislike the unshaven looks of me, I am to hand them a business card.

The card seems to be passing its first inspection. The officer appears
to have exactly the right mixture of confusion and curiosity that we
wished to cultivate. "What's this outfit for?" he asks.

"We're developing a California Coastal Trail from Mexico to
Oregon."

"And what are you doing?"

"Walking from Mexico to Oregon."

"Right." He hands me back my card. "So where's this coastal trail?"

"You're on it."

"This is for cars."

"We're taking over one lane for pedestrians."

"You're pulling my leg."

I smile, tighten my pack's shoulder straps, and take a step toward
San Diego.

"Hold it!" He sighs mightily. "Hop in, guy."

"Am I under arrest?"

"Only until we get to the other side of the bridge. Then you're San
Diego's problem."

This cool cop deposits me on the east side of San Diego Bay near
Seaport Shopping Center, where I resume walking. I pass some Navy
ships at berth and a tourist attraction—The Star of India, built in 1863
and the oldest merchant ship afloat, but I find it hard to concentrate
on the sights. I'm a little rattled—with that funny feeling in the stomach one gets when the California Highway Patrol pulls you over for
speeding—but it's not just an encounter with the law that's unset-
tling; I'm upset because already, on Day 1, the coastal trail's continuity
has been broken. I'm not a pathfinder, but a poseur, bluffing my way
along.

As darkness falls, I walk through a zone of urban renewal to the San
Diego Armed Forces YMCA Hotel. The Y's lobby is full of clean-cut

young Navy men; a few Marines, discussing "where the action is in this town," huddle at the door.

For fourteen dollars a night I sign up for a private room. On the guest register form, next to the place for one's last permanent address, is a blank for branch of service. I write "public" and climb the stairs to my room.

AFTER A QUICK SHOWER, I venture out of my spartan, disinfectant-smelling quarters in pursuit of dinner (I'm famished) and something to read (I just knew I forgot something). Shunning what look to be expensive tourist trap eateries, I walk away from the lights of the waterfront into the city. I walk for blocks and find nothing but convenience stores. Finally, just as I'm reconsidering the edibility of two-for-a-dollar microwaveable hamburgers and the readability of a shoot-'em-up western offered by one of these stores, I stumble upon a block that offers everything I'm looking for: a used bookstore and a cheap Mexican restaurant.

I enter the bookstore first. It's a dusty, musty place piled floor to ceiling with old books. The books are mostly hardbacks, which is a little disappointing to me because I really want a paperback that I can carry in my backpack. Nothing in the modern novel section quite strikes my fancy and I follow a yellowing sign to the California section. I spot a few old acquaintances: *The WPA Guide to California* and Richard Henry Dana's *Two Years Before the Mast*, which I made a point of re-reading just before beginning my walk.

After some minutes of browsing, a gray spine catches my eye: *California Desert Trails*. It's a 1919 account by one J. Smeaton Chase of his horseback adventures through the California desert. There's a picture of Chase, a tweedy Victorian-looking fellow with wire-frame glasses, staring at cholla. Palm Springs, Imperial Valley, the land of the Joshua Tree. He really got around. I also love the desert. Oh, not as much as the forest or the coast, but I've hiked many a mile in southern California's two great deserts—the Mojave and the Colorado.

And then my heart leaps. There, next to the empty space on the shelf left by my removal of *California Desert Trails* is another book by the same author. I pull it slowly from the shelf. It's olive-green with a gold embossed shield on the front bearing the title: *California Coast*

Trails. Framed in a gold circle is a silhouette of a man staring out to
sea. He stands by his horse on the edge of a blufftop, framed by a
wind-blown cypress. For a moment I am reluctant to open the book. So many times I
have been excited by the word *trails* in a book title only to find that
the author is describing his motorhome trip or a lion hunt in Africa.
However, the subtitle—A Horseback Ride from Mexico to Oregon—
is encouraging, and the 1913 copyright date intriguing.

Next I dive into the table of contents, done in detailed nineteenth-
century style and complete with a dozen or more subheads for each of
the twenty-two chapters—Relics of Mission Days; A Hermit's Cave;
The Torrey Pine; Friendly Mexicans; Warfare of Sun and Fog; Fording
the Ventura River; Friendly Mexicans Again; Montecito and Millionaires; The Big Sur River; Gilt-edged Real Estate; Fog among the Redwoods—

"We're closing."

The voice of the proprietor, an older, bespectacled gentleman in a
rumpled cardigan, brings me back to the present. "Do you want that
book?"

"Uh—." I look inside the cover: the book is thirty-five dollars.
"Thirty-five dollars, that's a lot of money," I say slowly.

He smiles, takes the book from me, and walks me to the counter. "I
keep a close eye on my California section—it's one of my favorites.
Chase, J. Smeaton. Not one of our better sellers. I'll let you have him
for twenty."

"Deal."

"Are you a collector?"

"Not really."

"Good. Doubt Chase will ever be collectible."

But Chase is readable, quotable, and fascinating to me. The quiet
little restaurant serves me two huge avocado burritos, a platter of chips
and salsa and I wash it all down with a couple of beers. I'm far too en-
grossed in Chase to taste the food, and am surprised when the waitress
tells me, "We're closing."

I hurry back to the Y; apparently I walked farther than I figured and
I'm dead-tired. Still, the excitement of reading Chase, of finding a kin-
dred spirit, keeps the beside lamp lit until midnight.

After sampling a bit from each chapter, I return to the beginning of *California Coast Trails*. I want to know his impressions of all of the California coast, but right now I particularly want his observations on southern California, where I will walk first.

When he took his ride, southern Californians were industriously drilling for oil and planting orange trees, grading roads and paving them, selling real estate and then more real estate. Boomtowns and orange blossoms. This was the beginning of the California consciousness, though nobody had a name for it in 1911.

"The facts and beauties in nature and the humane and historic elements in life were his points of special interest," Chase writes of himself in the preface. How many of those beauties in nature did Chase find in 1911? And how many of those beauties in nature will I find on my walk tomorrow and the days after that? It's the question I'm pondering when I fall into a deep but troubled sleep.

I L E A V E , as Chase put it, "the mild and friendly air for which San Diego is renowned," hike across Point Loma, and cross the San Diego River to the Mission Bay resorts.

As I make my way toward Mission Beach, my thoughts are fastened on another time, neither the 1911 of Chase nor the present of mine, but the 1945 of my mother. It was a year, a time, in her life that makes her smile.

It's a time she has often told me about. So vivid was her description of that era that I have difficulty focusing on the scene before me. And quite a scene it is; Mission Beach is San Diego's answer to the New Jersey shore. Beach culture to the max. In front of the now defunct Belmont Amusement Center, the boardwalk boogies with roller skaters, inline skaters, bicyclists, and more health-food, seafood, junk-food, and boogieboard-renting establishments than anyone could desire.

"Mission Beach was crazy," Mother always begins her tale. She was Helen Gekas then, a Greek-American school teacher who in 1945 left her native state of Rhode Island and settled here. She arrived in June and although she had a teaching job lined up for the fall semester, she needed some money to see her through the summer. Walking along a boardwalk that in 1945 boogied to Tommy Dorsey, she applied for, and was hired for, the job of cashier-manager-cotton-candy-maker at

Harry's Sugar Shack, then located on the beachfront midway of the then very-much-alive Belmont Amusement Center.

Business was good. It was the last year of the war and San Diego was a Navy boomtown. The sailors hit the beach and boardwalk on shore leave and flocked to the Dipper roller coaster, the Ferris wheel, the giant indoor saltwater plunge, the Casino, the games of chance, and Harry's Sugar Shack. Helen Gekas was soon joined by another Miss Gekas, her sister Emily, and the two of them worked seven days a week that summer of '45 selling candy bars, chewing gum, root beer, Coca-Cola, and lots of their most popular cavity-creating product—cotton candy. The sailors and their dates stood in line (sometimes in formations one hundred feet long) while Helen and Emily poured the granulated sugar into the machine and enticed the warm spun sugar onto paper cones.

"I remember working in a cloud of sugar," recalls Helen. "I get a toothache just thinking about it. Emily's hair would get white with sugar dust. Good thing sugar isn't a toxic substance; we'd be dead."

Harry, proprietor of the beachside business, it must be said, was not much of a manager, but he made two smart moves that summer of '45. First, he left two pretty daughters of a Greek candy store owner completely alone in the booth. Second, during a period of ration cards and shortages, he managed to secure seemingly infinite supplies of black-market sugar.

"The boardwalk people were nuts then too," Helen testifies. "N-U-T-S. The sailors were either celebrating a last time before leaving for overseas or celebrating because they returned in one piece. A lot of them had never seen a beach before. They were always respectful to us, though sometimes they'd proposition the, um, ladies of the evening near our stand."

Mission Beach was not Helen's first impression of southern California. "When the train rolled into Riverside County and I smelled the orange blossoms I had the feeling I might become a Californian. And when I saw the water and all those miles of white sand I knew I'd never return east."

When business was slow, one or both of the Gekas sisters would slip out of their pin-striped aprons and into their swimsuits and catch a few rays on the nearby sand. When Helen began teaching the second grade at Jefferson Elementary, she continued at Harry's on the weekends, as did sister Emily, who had found employment as a social worker. Money was one reason Helen continued her Mission Beach work; a schoolteacher's salary in those days was minuscule. One of Helen's brainstorms—buying a truckload of watermelons and cutting them up into twenty-cent slices—netted Harry's a thousand dollars one Sunday.

The work was fun and the money good, but it was the view of long and wide and sparkling Mission Beach that intrigued Helen. When she wasn't working she took walks along many of San Diego's beaches, along Del Mar bluffs unconquered by condominiums, along La Jolla shores untouched by engineers, along a San Diego Bay that was still a wild estuary, filled with countless birds whose names Helen tried to learn. She took her second graders on field trips to these wild beaches and showed them the creatures the tides cast ashore.

Near the end of 1945 Helen quit her job at Harry's. ("The principal found out I was moonlighting and thought it undignified for a public school teacher to be selling cotton candy.") Five years later Helen met James McKinney, a fast-talking salesman who apparently had better opening lines than the sailors. They wed and I became part of the postwar baby boom. I made my first visit to Mission Beach boardwalk in a baby carriage.

A photograph that comes to mind as I walk along the boardwalk, a picture I will always treasure, is of my mother sitting on a wall bordering Mission Beach boardwalk. Clad in a stunning white swimsuit that highlighted her olive skin and dark hair, she looks demurely out to sea. A Greek maiden in the Land of the Lotus-Eaters.

During my childhood, my mother often took me to many of the same beaches she explored in 1945. She pointed out the tidepools and the shorebirds, the physical-culture buffs lifting barbells, the sand castle sculptors—all the sights and sounds and smells of a day at the beach.

But she never bought me cotton candy.

THREE

Palm and Pine

YOU DON'T NEED a weatherman to know which way the wind blows; you need a palm tree, preferably a young, supple palm that dances in the ever-changing light and breeze. Wind out of the north this morning; the palms stretch south. I hike up Black's Beach, which enjoyed notoriety in the 1970s when it was designated "swimsuits optional"; the ordinance was revoked after a few years but naturists are still the majority here. Not a nude in sight today, though. A twenty-knot northerly sandblasts me, filling my ears and nose with grit and hurling sand against my pants with an incessant sizzle like white noise on a long-distance phone call.

To escape the wind, I follow a surfer trail up the towering sandstone bluffs to a tiny cluster of palm trees. Not much of a windbreak, these palms. The wind dislodges dead fronds and I must keep an eye out for these unguided missiles. Some of the fronds weigh twenty pounds and could easily impair one's ability to think if they hit their target.

I don't know why this handful of *Washingtonia filiferes* are here. The trees may have surrounded a long-vanished hotel. Perhaps they were planted by a developer who landscaped his bluff but never built upon it. These palms are property improvement enough, I think, as I sit against the shaggiest of the lot in a vain attempt to get out of the wind.

Washingtonia filiferes (named after our first president), commonly known as the California fan palm, is the state's—in fact, the nation's— only native palm and is found naturally only in oases scattered in the Mojave and Colorado Deserts. It's also the coast's most popular planted palm. Compared to the redwood or ponderosa pine, the fan palm is a flimsy-looking thing, but it's a tough tree, resistant to both wind and fire. And it has been around a long time—about 10 million years. These relics of the Miocene once ranged as far north as Oregon, but climatic and geologic changes forced their retreat to southern California.

There's something undeniably silly about a palm tree and it's easy to see why Mark Twain described it as "a feather duster struck by lightning." Palms sway in the wind like beautiful but uncoordinated hula girls. The droopy, dead leaves form a ground-length "skirt" that distinguishes the native California fan palm from other varieties, and, depending on your point of view, makes them appear half-naked or half-dressed. I've always felt that the palm tree, not the redwood, should be California's official state tree, being a more fitting symbol of a state of instability.

Not everyone appreciates palms. Some of the first southern Californians, the Serrano Indians, believed the fronds harbored evil spirits. To drive away the demons, they periodically set the trees on fire. Nowadays, in San Diego County and other coastal counties, palms have fallen into disfavor among some very powerful people. Landscape architects and city planners say palms have no more charm than a flagpole, offer no shade, and get sick easily. They advocate uprooting them and replacing them with something sensible, such as fake gas lights.

I feel compelled to defend them, although they have plenty of friends, including several California chapters of the Palm Society. Motel and hotel owners can also be counted on to rush to the tree's defense, for they know that visitors come from all over the world to enjoy the palm's picturesque form silhouetted against the setting sun. Nurseries, although they charge a pretty penny for what they mistakenly label "indoor palms," also swell the ranks of palm fans. (Alas, many of these palms end up in bars where they somehow manage to survive the habits of insensitive lounge lizards who toss still smoldering cigarettes into their pots.)

Palm critics are correct in saying palms give little shade, though the contention that they are fragile or unhealthy is poppycock. A few years back southern Florida did lose thousands of coconut palms to a virus called Lethal Yellow that came out of the West Indies, but California palms did not catch this affliction. Except for the occasional case of pink bud rot, they are healthy trees.

Most any palm can and does grow along the California coast. Climatically, it is a "rare palm belt." Species of Hawaiian palms will grow here, but Hawaiians have a devil of a time growing the California fan palm in Hawaii. Sometimes I bring a palm handbook along on my coastal walks and try to identify the many species. Even the names of the palms sound exotic: Canton Fish Tail, European Fan, San Jose, Guadalupe, Sentry, Date, Canary Island, Pygmy, Shaving Brush, Puerto Rican Hat, Queen, Windmill.

Me, I have no favorite among palms, although I am partial to the native *Washingtonia*. If only they were a better windbreak . . .

A FEW MORE MILES of beach walking brings me to Flatrock, appropriately named. Legend has it that this gouged-out rock, also known as Bathtub Rock, was the luckless site of a Scottish miner's search for coal. I climb the crumbling sandstone bluffs to a line of Torrey pines that occupy the bold headlands atop the cliffs. Clinging to the crumbling yellow sandstone, these rare and beautiful trees thrive on foggy atmosphere and precarious footing.

Time to inspect the reserve. By reserve I refer to the three miles of bluff protected by Torrey Pines State Reserve. Atop its bluffs lies a microcosm of old California, a garden of shrubs and succulents, an enclave of the kind of native life that the real native Californians (i.e., Native Americans) subsisted on. I contemplate what California looked like before the arrival of Europeans: Paradise before the Fall.

A paradise, that is, if one admires shrubs . . . and few people do. Shrub is not a pretty word and few of the plants in the reserve are real lookers. Shrubs are plants with distinctly woody trunks arising from the ground (not spreading out all over the place). But shrubs must not rise too high above the ground; it's botanically *verboten* that they rise more than twelve or fifteen feet, because then they cease being shrubs and are classified as trees. These distinctions are of more than academic interest in southern California, where it's difficult to tell the difference between tree and shrub and scrub. Botanists are still debating "The Case of the Manzanita." Sometimes it's four to eight feet high, obviously a shrub. Sometimes it grows twenty to twenty-five feet high, obviously a tree. And to make matters even more confusing, on cold, high-altitude slopes, it sometimes creeps over the ground, like a vine.

What's the difference between a shrub and scrub? The dictionary isn't much help:

shrub: akin to scrub, a low woody plant with several permanent stems instead of a single trunk.

scrub: 1. scraggly, stunted tree or shrub **2.** Anything smaller than the usual or inferior in quality or breeding.

Therefore, a shrub can be a scrub and a scrub can be a shrub, but not all shrubs are scrubs or all scrubs shrubs. Confusing matters further are trees like the scrub oak, which can be classified as either shrub or scrub, although no poet is rushing out to rhapsodize:

I think that I shall never see,
A poem as lovely as shrubbery.

The vegetation here at the reserve has been called "degraded chaparral," but some experts classify it separately as Coastal Sage Scrub. It's softer and more aromatic than true chaparral, even though there are many chaparral plants in it. Especially aromatic is black sage. It's much stronger than those sissy supermarket brands designed to blend in with turkey stuffing. Native hunters slept with the leaves of this potent sage under their armpits to confuse their game's sense of smell.

Another scrubby plant is lemonade berry. It has fruit about the size of a large corn kernel, which is covered with a sour coating. You can dissolve this coating off four or five berries in a glass of water and have a passable lemonade.

Large sections of the reserve are blanketed with what looks like ice plant but is really sea fig. (True ice plant, an annual from South Africa, really looks icy.) Sailors ate sea figs, picked up in Cape Town, to prevent scurvy. Some of the leftovers were dumped on California bluffs and thrived. That's one story anyway. Some botanists think the story is reversed and that sea fig is the native plant.

Few visitors come to Torrey Pines State Reserve to view scrubs or shrubs. Their interest is focused solely on the Torrey pines. Conditioned by other parks to expect the oldest, highest, or deepest somethingoranother, they are often disappointed with the Torrey pine. They expect a freak of nature, a tree that's . . . well, more spectacular.

What they see is *pinus Torreyana* quietly going about the business of being a tree, like it has for two or three hundred thousand years on this stretch of coast.

Confronted with your basic conifer, visitors seem at a loss and resort to exaggeration, as if finding something botanically incredible about the Torrey pine will justify their presence in the reserve. Park rangers patiently rebut visitors' boasts:

"It's the rarest pine in the world."

"No, that honor belongs to the Dalat pine of Vietnam."

"Torrey pine cones are the largest of any pine in the world."

"No, California's sugar pine and Coulter pine have much larger cones."

"Torrey pines are the only five-needle pine."

"No, more than half a dozen five-needle pines grow in California and more than twenty throughout the world."

"Torrey pines are the oldest living things on earth."

No, that distinction belongs to those ancient survivors, more than two thousand years old, the bristlecone pine. Torrey pines rarely live more than a hundred years. The elder of the tribe, a contorted specimen atop High Point, is the oldest Torrey pine on earth; a dendrologist, who took a core sample, adjudged it to be one hundred and thirty years old.

As I begin walking through Parry Grove, the northwest wind fades to a whisper of its former blustery self. The Torrey pines cease their moaning and creaking and resume their Sumo wrestlers stance. This pine grove would certainly be a better place to take shelter from the wind than the palm grove I selected earlier in the day.

This matter of palm vs. pine has obsessed southern Californians for a century. Joseph Smeaton Chase reported that he and artist Carl Eytel often debated the issue: "I had frequently, in argument with him, urged the preeminence of pine over the palm, if only on the ground of the greater amount of drawing in it. But Eytel is a colorist, and when he takes the argument on to that ground there is no following him; for you cannot argue about color, which every man perceives differently according to his spiritual composition."

So each to his own arboreal passion. Most southern Californians admire both species. Sunday *Los Angeles Times* readers of the 1930s found the Motoring/Outdoor section full of articles about Sunday drives that would take the motorist on "A Great Circle Route" from palm to pine. Typically, a *Times* reporter would borrow a Nash, Buick, or Packard from a local dealer, fill "the *Times* expedition car" full of impressionable New Yorkers or other refugees from inclement climes, and drive from palm oases to pine-covered snowy peaks. These Sunday drives often ended with a final climatic coup de grace—Santa Monica Beach, where reporter and awed entourage would plunge into the surf.

It was not so much the pines or the palms themselves that intrigued natives and visitors, but their juxtaposition. What a miraculous climate! All the different landscapes of the nation within a two-hour drive from downtown Los Angeles! Nature is a botanic garden of earthly delights—and every Sunday drive a feast!

The Pines-to-Palms Highway (Route 74) was added to the state highway system in the thirties. This curvy two-laner leaves the town of Palm Desert, heads west across two pine-covered national forests, and ends up on the coast in San Juan Capistrano. Another palm-to-pine thriller, the Palm Springs Aerial Tramway, was built in the 1960s. Visitors are wowed by a seven-thousand-foot ascent from a Palm Springs palm canyon to the piney shoulder of Mount San Jacinto.

Me, I have no preference among trees as long as they're wild and free!

Parry Grove Trail, named in honor of Dr. C. C. Parry, takes me through a handsome grove of Torrey pines. Parry was a botanist assigned to the boundary commission that surveyed the Mexican-American border in 1850. While waiting for the expedition to start, Parry explored the San Diego area. He investigated a tree that had been called the Soledad pine for the nearby Soledad Valley. Parry sent samples to his teacher and friend, Dr. John Torrey of Princeton, and requested that if it proved to be a new species it be named for Torrey. It did and it was. The Soledad pine became *pinus Torreyana,* or Torrey pine, in honor of the famous botanist and taxonomist. The Torrey pine and the many plants with *parryi* in their Latin names are only a small sampling of the many discoveries made by Dr. Parry.

At the time he made his discovery, Parry did not realize the rarity of these trees. Torrey pines, other botanists later determined, grow naturally only here on these sandstone bluffs and on Santa Rosa Island far off the coast of Santa Barbara; nowhere else in the world. Recently botanists have concluded that the island species differs slightly from the mainland species, which means that the Torrey pines growing here in north San Diego County are the last stand on earth.

I reach a promontory, where a lone Torrey pine, wind-bowed but unbroken, clings to a rocky precipice. On the trail behind me are two Germans, consulting a guidebook. The young man and young woman wear new hiking boots and confused expressions. When they reach the promontory, they nod pleasantly. They look from their guidebook to the pines to the ocean to the west and to the suburban developments east, north, and south, and back to their book. I know what they're thinking. This little reserve of pine is not easily described. The cramped black-and-white picture shows Torrey pines, maybe even the very pine my pack leans against, but doesn't show the isolated nature of the reserve, an island on the land. I interrupt their thoughts with a *"guten Tag."*

Delighted to find someone who speaks German, they begin jabbering. The trouble is, "guten Tag" is the only German I know. Monika is appointed translator and she tells me that she and Hans have not come to see tourist California—Disneyland and Hollywood—but the real California: the California coast, Big Sur, the redwoods.

Monika points to my pack and to the trail and asks, "Vy do you go?"

"Why?" I repeat.

Monika and Hans nod, but I'm sure these practical Germans, who have seen eight national parks in three weeks, have their interrogatives mixed up and want to know where I'm hiking, not why. So I explain where I intend to walk.

Monika shakes her head. "Nein. Vy do you go?"

For a moment, I'm at a loss for words. Am I being asked to expound upon the joy of scrubs or am I being queried about essential reality and the nature of being by two metaphysical disciples of Immanuel Kant? *Why do I go?* A cosmic question, now that I think of it. But a cosmic answer escapes me so I tell them I came to get lost, lost in the palm and pine, lost for a time from metropolitan life, lost in the challenge of a long trail, lost in what remains of the wild California coast.

"Lost?" Monika smiles indulgently. *"Verlaufen?"*

Closing their guidebooks, the Germans march off down the trail. Another day, another sight, another lunatic American.

The wind has cleared the reserve of visitors. It's a perfect day to get lost, but I don't think I'll manage it today, not in the reserve anyway. The park service in its mandated mania to provide safe holidays has planted a forest of signs to keep everyone on the paths and out of the trees. This is a reserve, not a park. We are to keep moving in orderly fashion around the loop trails. We are not to molest scrub or shrub, pick wildflowers, or picnic. This is not a pleasuring ground for humans but a preserve for trees, patrolled by the grumpiest gun-toting rangers west of the Rockies.

Perhaps such vigilance on behalf of the Torrey pine is necessary. The pines look particularly vulnerable now that they are in full bloom. The female blossoms resemble miniature red cones. It's the mating season and the male blossoms are busy ejaculating clouds of yellow pollen, which settle on the female blossoms and fertilize them. Of the thousands of tiny red cones, only a few will mature. The cones that survive will be about the size of golf balls by next summer. During their second summer, the cones will grow rapidly to full size and be dark green and glued shut with rosin. The cones mature during the third summer. Normally they will open and begin dropping seeds in October, unless a freak Santa Ana wind comes along and knocks the cones around and scatters the seeds; if this happens, the woodrats feast on the seeds. Perhaps one seed in a thousand will survive rodents and summer droughts and land in a bare spot where it can germinate. If a seed does germinate, it has to survive assorted fungae, nibbling by brush rabbits, and wayward picnickers.

Insect enemies of the Torrey pine are many. Female Mexican bark beetles drill into trunks or large limbs and lay eggs. The larvae hatch and eat the growing layer of the tree. A healthy tree can fight off the beetles by encasing itself in rosin, but during a long, dry spell, a tree's resistance may be down. One beetle can't do much damage, but thousands can girdle a tree and kill it. The smaller Torrey pine twig beetles do much the same thing near the growing tips of branches. Since Torrey pines can't resprout the way peach trees do, these beetles can kill limbs or even whole trees. Spittle bugs suck the turpentine-flavored juice from the needles, but don't do too much damage. In past years, mite epidemics have turned every tree in the reserve a sickly yellow; nature, however, miraculously boosted the population of jumping spiders to bring the mites under control.

No insecticides are used in the reserve. State officials wisely concluded that Torrey pines survived several hundred thousand years without man's chemicals and can probably do without them for a few years more. The pines have the ability to repel rusts and scales and insects. Apparently, all the Torrey pines require from humans is to be left alone.

Time to hit the trail. A winding path through the pines deposits me back at the beach. I look back at the Torrey pines, a last stand in the midst of ever-more-urban San Diego County. Unlike islands, the reserve is protected on only one side by the ocean. And unlike most ecosystems, the Torrey pines are unguarded by a river, mountain, or other natural feature that might slow the advance of autos, asphalt and luxury housing. All the boundaries of the reserve—a highway, a housing development, a golf course and public beach—are artificial. For

better or worse, the destiny of the last stand of Torrey pines is wedded
to that of humans.

Vy do you go?

I ponder Monika's question. Maybe, Monika, I go, as you go, to
places like Torrey Pines State Reserve because they celebrate life, because an attempt, sometimes noble, sometimes clumsy, has been made
by humans to set aside a place where we can see, feel, and touch the
living remnants of a once wild coastline. Just as darkness makes a flame
seem brighter, encroaching civilization makes the Torrey pines seem
more dear.

Yes, that, Monika, is why I go.

I WALK UP Torrey Pines State Beach and in less than a mile
reach Los Penasquitos Lagoon. When Chase camped here in 1912, it
was quite a bit bigger than it is today. Today Los Penasquitos is one
of southern California's last remaining estuaries. Rimmed by housing
developments and a trailer park, the lagoon's very existence seems a
minor miracle; it lies like a pastoral island amidst a fast-growing suburban area.

As I walk around the lagoon, my attention is drawn to a woman
standing in the muck. Clad in bib overalls and hip waders, she is erect-
ing a gold chain-link fence around a couple of pickleweed islands.
From a distance, she appears to be the kind of handsome, mature
woman depicted on those pre-glasnost East European posters calling
upon workers to struggle for universal socialism. On closer inspection,
Christine Oatman is neither a model for, nor a practitioner of, East
bloc tractor art; in fact, I soon learn her environmental art is designed
to keep developers' tractors from wrecking Los Penasquitos Lagoon. I
ask the obvious question.

"What are you doing putting up a gold chain-link fence around
some pickleweed island in the middle of a lagoon?"

"Symbolic protection," she answers. "The fence is only temporary
and obviously can't actually protect the estuary," she explains. "But I
believe that a symbolic act has a power to exist permanently in the
universal collective memory and eventually effect some change."

"I see."

Dark clouds brood over Los Penasquitos Lagoon. Wind ripples the water and sways the pickleweed. The gold chain-link fence put up by Christine Oatman looks as fragile, as vulnerable, as this wetland. She says she'll leave her fence up a week or two, long enough to bewilder a few people and perhaps remind them that the remnants of this little lagoon and others like it are the last 5 percent of the great bogs and estuaries that characterized the coastal California of a century ago.

At the beginning of this century, civilization, southern California style, was clustered in small islands with the wilderness all around, but nowadays the geographic ratio is reversed; the last wild areas are islands surrounded by artificial works. A stand of Torrey pines and some lagoons are the only vestiges of the California coast of Chase's time, ragtag remnants of natural history.

FOUR

Marine March

IN NORTHERN San Diego County Chase found boomtowns that in a few short years had boomed and busted. Depopulated hotels testified to the fickleness of the seaside tourist trade. Riding past a boarded-up dry goods and notions store, he puns that evidently the fate of the dry goods had been to dry up, and the last and best of the notions had been to go away.

Only the little town of Del Mar, with its fine hotel and superb beach, caught Chase's eye. Especially Del Mar Beach. "I should like to hear a winter storm beat on this exposed shore of shingle, as I have heard them on the shingle beaches of England, the wild air ringing with the shriek of multitudinous pebbles as they are driven to and fro by the claws of the raging sea."

I walk over the sparkling sand and soft green limestone rock of Del Mar Beach. The greenish beds are part of the Del Mar formation and above is cavernous, weathered Torrey sandstone. At the base of the cliffs are fossil fragments in places where resistant sandstone forms an outcropping. With such geologic instability, it's a wonder that anyone would build a home atop the cliffs, but a lot of anyones have.

Along Del Mar Beach the power of the surf is awesome and cliff collapse unpredictable. At this beach, permeable layers of rock tilt toward the sea and lie atop other more impermeable layers. Water percolates down through permeable rocks, settles on the impermeable ones, and "greases the skids"—an ideal condition for collapsing cliffs. On New Year's Day in 1941 a freight train suddenly found itself in midair. Erosion had undermined the tracks. A full passenger train had been delayed and the freight crew of three were the only casualties.

While Del Mar reminds him of English beaches, Chase makes no mention of Cardiff-by-the-Sea, so-called by an Anglophile, who borrowed the name from the seaport of Wales. British place names are on most of the streets.

The afternoon passes as I compare my observations to Chase's. From the highway, to the motorist, the towns of Del Mar, Solana Beach, Cardiff-by-the-Sea, Encinitas, and Leucadia all look alike, though residents would be quick to dispute this and point out the superiority of their town and beach. North County, as it's called, is a mellow land, mercifully bypassed by the construction of Interstate 5 three decades ago, and quite a bit removed from the hustle of California's second-largest city.

And in truth, as I walk, as opposed to drive, through the towns, I discover each has a distinct personality.

What Chase found especially attractive in North County were the patriarchal Torrey pines clinging to the cliffs, the shoreline of sandstone bluffs broken up by scattered lagoons, and the thrill (which I too experienced a few nights later) of sleeping thirty feet from the railroad tracks and waking to the late night run of freight and passenger trains.

I begin to experience an inner conflict between the athlete in me that wants to use the beach as a track to race, and the traveler in me that wants to linger atop the blufftops and see the sights and smells of the cities.

And tastes, too. In the beach towns, I pass Italian, Hungarian, Armenian, Chinese, Japanese, and Vietnamese restaurants, plus scores of coffeehouses, juice bars, malt shops and fish taco stands. Thanks to those millions of tax dollars we Californians have granted the State

Coastal Conservancy, there are plenty of officially designated coastal accessways from which to reach—or retreat from—the beach.

During the first few chapters of *California Coast Trails,* Chase seems to be feeling his way along, in search of a purpose for his prose, even as he was searching for a purpose for his journey. Saddling up his faithful steed, Chino, he left his home in El Monte (about twenty miles east of Los Angeles) in midsummer 1911. With him was artist Carl Eytel, who rode an Arizona cow pony, Billy.

Chase and Eytel headed south from El Monte and seemed in no particular hurry to get to the coast; in fact, they didn't reach the Pacific until midway through Orange County at Laguna Beach. I wonder why he headed south, why he didn't head directly for the coast. And the biggest why of all: Why the hell did he take this trip?

As if self-conscious about the indefinite nature of his journey he confesses that he has a difficult time fielding questions from the strangers who see his bedroll and bulging saddlebags, tent and camera tripod, and ask where he's bound. A Spanish word, thought Chase, best summed up the spirit of his journey—*paseo,* which he defines as "a walk, a ride, an excursion, a picnic, in fact a going anywhere and anyhow, so long as it is leisurely, pleasurable, and unbusinesslike."

A *paseo* by horseback was, even in the year 1911, becoming something of a quaint and old-fashioned way to travel. Southern California was on wheels. Already, southern Californians were buying and driving (in higher percentages than any other region in America) Henry Ford's Model Ts. And Henry Huntington's Pacific Electric Company tracks reached to the limits of Los Angeles suburbs and beyond. Instead of *paseos,* the southern Californians Chase observed were riding what was then the world's most extensive system of rapid transit or speeding over the horrible roads in their motorcars.

So Chase was out of synch with his time, his place, his peers.

Like me.

A bit beyond Cardiff is San Elijo State Beach, the southernmost beach campground in the state park system. I pitch my tent at the hike-bike campsite here, and enjoy a mellow night.

Next morning I hike past San Elijo Lagoon, a long, low point in the cliffs, where the surf is quite active. North of the lagoon, the bluffs rise higher and higher. Soon I reach "Swamis" of surfing and Beach Boys fame, a city park and beach named for the lotus-shaped Self-Realization Fellowship Ashram Center on the bluffs. Established in 1937, the Center provides a retreat for members and a meditation area with panoramic coastal views.

Beyond Swamis is the town of Encinitas, "the place of little oaks." Past the small town of Encinitas, the cliffs open up and fill with sand, forming wide, sandy Moonlight State Beach.

Past Moonlight is Leucadia State Beach. On the bluffs above is the town of Leucadia, founded during the boom of the 1880s and named after a Greek island renowned for its beauty, fine wine, and olives. Greek and Roman street names—Hygeia, Eolus, Hermes, Vulcan—abound. Leucadia and its streets were named by a group of British spiritualists with a penchant for classical culture, who came to the United States seeking religious freedom. Leucadia Beach is wide and sandy, again the domain of the surfer.

Several more miles of beach walking and I am approaching what appears to be a giant lighthouse, but on closer inspection turns out to be the Encina Power Plant located at Aqua Hedionda ("stinking water") Lagoon. The no longer odiferous waters of the lagoon make it a popular spot for boating and bird-watching.

The resort town of Carlsbad, which in the nineteenth century attracted visitors to its healing sulfur springs, is today the largest of the coastal towns lining Old Coast Highway. Fortified by a slice of pizza, I walk on.

According to local tradition, Oceanside was a community that named itself; prior to 1884 it was the custom of many inland-dwelling families "to go Oceanside" here on outings. Today, Oceanside Beach seems populated mostly by Camp Pendleton marines on R and R.

Whereas Chase went inland at Oceanside, I stick to the coast, and in so doing come face-to-face with the first major barrier to my coast walk—Camp Pendleton Marine Base, which occupies fifteen miles of shoreline. The marines strongly discourage trespassing.

Where should I route the California Coastal Trail? How can I get to San Onofre State Beach, the first public land north of Oceanside? Heading inland around the base would require a one-hundred-mile

detour. Should hikers take the bus or train twenty miles to San
Clemente, then double-back to the state beach? Bicyclists are allowed
to pedal through Camp Pendleton during daylight hours, but hikers
are denied passage by the marines. What to do?

IN THE FOGGY predawn hours I double-time, make that
triple-time north, hoping not to encounter any land mines, booby
traps, or sentries with shoot-to-kill orders. The military base was
named after Joseph H. Pendleton, a veteran of the "banana wars" in
Central America during the 1920s. Just my luck if the marines decide
to stage a practice invasion of Nicaragua this morning.

Three miles north of Oceanside I encounter my first obstacle, not
the Pendleton marines, but the Santa Margarita Marsh. Visibility is
poor and I stumble through the muck of the marsh, taking a beating from iodine bush and alkali bulrush. I wend my way around the
mouth of the Santa Margarita River, sinking to my knees in the muck
for what seems like miles, but is probably only a hundred yards.

I alternate my route between the bluffs and the beach. The blufftops
are covered with sage, toyon, and scrub oak—good cover for this guerrilla's advance—but the beach is faster going. Half-track tracks, tank
tracks, and jeep tracks crisscross the sand, but the land (I was expecting
bomb craters, bunkers and spent shell casings everywhere) is not as bal-
listically brutalized as I had forecast, though fear of being caught by
marines out on maneuvers keeps me in high gear and I have little opportunity to contemplate the landscape. While speeding along, I realize
why so many servicemen who go on such forced marches with the
military never want to go camping or backpacking again.

Halfway through the journey I'm slowed by another wetland, Las
Flores Marsh, but the Las Pulgas River ("River of the Fleas") is way
down and this mostly freshwater marsh lined with cattails and bul-
rushes isn't as daunting a barrier as Santa Margarita Marsh. Once past
this marsh, I feel better. Even this the grayest of dawns is welcome, as
are the Atchison-Topeka and Santa Fe railroad tracks and Interstate 5,
which I can now see from my trail. Now if I'm caught by marines I
can say that I strayed from the campground at the state beach; no need
to admit to crossing all fifteen miles of their turf.

Finally, after almost four hours of dipping in and out of gullies and trudging through wet sand, I exit the base, climb a chain-link fence, and follow a stretch of Old Coast Highway, left behind when megahighway Interstate 5 was constructed. The old highway, now a campground road for San Onofre State Beach, is lined with large trailers and motor homes. Although this is the kind of campground I usually avoid, I feel a profound sense of relief to be back in the civilian sector. Dodged another bullet. The many times in my youth when I tempted fate—when me and the guys surfed Pendleton, surfed San Clemente in front of Richard Nixon's seaside hacienda and made both peace signs and obscene gestures at his security forces, all the risks, all the trespasses of my youth—come back to me.

But that was then and this is now. The adrenaline, the mad energy that carried me fifteen fast miles, deserts me, and I suddenly feel tired. Maybe I'm getting too old to be a rebel.

Maybe not. Why should sixteen be the only society-sanctioned age for rebellion? Like wine, rebellion tastes better with age.

SAN ONOFRE is a place of steep bluffs, overlooking a wide sandy beach and magnificent surf. Unfortunately, the peaceful ambience of this beach has been utterly destroyed by the giant twin spheres of the San Onofre Nuclear Power Plant situated on the beach and bisecting the state park.

I meet the state park ranger on her rounds. She's a cheerful sort and greets me as if I am the first hiker to ever trek across the vehicle-oriented park. But my northward progress baffles her. "South of here is Camp Pendleton and you couldn't have just hiked across . . ."

She rolls her eyes heavenward, points out a special campsite for hikers and bicyclists, and hands me a park map with evacuation instructions, "in case of a nuclear incident." In the event of atomic accident, we are to avoid panic and in an orderly manner pile into our vehicles and drive down Old Coast Highway to a breakaway fence that will do just that and allow us to reach Interstate Highway 5. Depending on which way the wind is blowing, we are then to drive like crazy down the interstate. State park authorities have no instructions for hikers, who will apparently receive full radiation doses before fleeing San Onofre Beach.

Echo Arch Hike-In Campground is too close to the Nuke for my taste. After cooking up some oatmeal and coffee, I resolve to continue north to the campground at Doheny Beach. However, the Nuke itself blocks my progress. A sea wall, constructed to prevent the reactor from washing away, is impossible to surmount, so I have to detour inland.

North of the nuclear power plant is famous Trestles Beach, one of the finest surfing areas on the West Coast. When the surf is up, the waves peel rapidly across San Mateo Point, creating a great ride. Before the area became part of San Clemente State Beach, it was restricted government property belonging to Camp Pendleton. For well over twenty-five years surfers carried on guerrilla warfare with U.S. Marines. Trespassing surfers were chased, arrested, and fined. Veteran surfers from the '50s, '60s, and early '70s tell dramatic stories about escapes from jeep patrols and guard dogs. Many times, however, the cool jarheads would charitably give surfers rides while out on maneuvers. During the days of dissent, I too encountered the marines—and the U.S. Secret Service—when we scruffy-looking anti-establishment types surfed a little too close to then-President Richard Nixon's San Clemente beachfront home.

San Mateo Point is the northernmost boundary of San Diego County and the southernmost boundary of Orange County. When the original counties were set up in 1850, the line that separated them began on the coast at San Mateo Point. When Orange County was formed from southern Los Angeles County in 1889, San Mateo Point was established as the southern point of the new county.

At San Mateo Point, I rest, lunch, and compare notes with Chase, who found a couple of ranch houses and a water tank on the county line. "Here we performed the feat of cooking our supper in one county and eating it in the other."

I do likewise. One county walked, fourteen to go.

FIVE

Orange County Dreams

I FIND RICHARD HENRY DANA'S memorial over-
grown with weeds and overlooked by motorists whizzing by on Highway 1. His little bronze plaque abuts a cyclone fence separating the
gated, guarded, residential community of Monarch Bay from the highway.

One October day in 1835, Dana, a young sailor on the *Alert*, lowered himself over the two-hundred-foot cliff that now bears his name
to retrieve some cowhides he and his fellows were attempting to toss
down to their ship. Later Dana described his adventures in *Two Years
Before the Mast,* one of the greatest books ever written about life on
the high seas, and a California classic.

I wonder why this memorial to Dana stands forgotten among broken bottles and burger wrappings. Why has he been marooned so far
from his beloved sea and more than two miles north of his famous
Point?

As I stand with Dana's memorial in the shadow of Monarch Bay's
walls, the sun that I cannot see drops toward the ocean that I cannot
see, showering golden light on sandstone bluffs, where I cannot legally

walk. I stare at California Historical Landmark No. 169 and review what has been a simply awful day of walking Orange County's coast, a day so disheartening I'm compelled to rethink my dream of hiking the entire California coastline.

The day's journey began at Doheny State Beach. Hiking up-coast along water's edge I soon reach the southern breakwater of Dana Harbor. On the cliffs overlooking the harbor, the bulldozers are busy, making building pads out of bluffs. Lantern Bay, the name of the development, consists of 198 expensive homes, two hotels, and a New England seacoast village shopping center.

I walk across the acres of hot asphalt comprising the Dana Harbor parking lot. The sight of the huge, charmless, condominium-surrounded marina takes the wind out of my sails. A favorite surfing spot of my youth has been totally destroyed. Before Dana Cove became Dana Marina, better surfers than I rode waves as high as twenty-five feet and called the place "Killer Dana." More often, though, the waves came in smaller, less radical sets. We surfers loved Dana Cove, for it had everything a beach should have: white sand, azure water, a lack of adult supervision.

The marina builders did not completely overlook Dana, however. Along the concrete promenade I discover a statue of young Richard Henry, bare-chested, notebook in hand, his back to the sea. The sculptor has captured him in midstride, making Dana appear to be struggling to loose himself from his pedestal and flee the marina.

Leaving Dana to his fate, I clamber up collapsing sandstone cliffs past a closed restaurant that is also collapsing with the cliffs to the beach. Atop these cliffs is supposed to be Dana Point. I seem to remember, from childhood, a little wooden observation tower, complete with ten-cent telescopes. The tower has vanished, which may be just as well, because if telescopes were up here today, all they would view is a wall of residences. Alas, even Dana Point looks smaller from an adult's perspective. Still, it's the largest chunk of rock for miles around and would provide an inspiring coastal panorama if a few houses were pushed off the cliffs.

I find a vacant lot between the expensive homes and squeeze through to the cliff edge. This is more like it. A superb view! I marvel at the severely deformed, light-colored shale and Monterey sandstone beds of the Point, the translucent Capri-like waters swirling below. My mind paints pictures of Dana and his fellows hefting those stiff, heavy hides stripped from the backs of tough Mexican cattle and heaving them over the cliff. I imagine other sailors on the beach, retrieving the plywood-like hides, balancing them on their heads, and fighting the surf to the waiting longboats, which delivered tall stacks of them to the Alert anchored a hundred yards offshore. For an instant history comes alive for me, and I smile at how these majestic headlands must have impressed young Dana. "The only romantic spot in California," he wrote.

A man walking a Doberman interrupts my reverie.

"This is private property," he announces.

"Yes, I know."

"Well, people around here don't like trespassers." The dog snarls. "You'd better move on."

I briefly contemplate how satisfying it would be to toss *his* hide over the cliff, but move on peacefully.

I N T E R S E C T I N G an eroded surfer trail, I switchback down the bluffs to the far side of Dana Point and to the sand. A little beach walking brings me to Salt Creek, or what used to be Salt Creek. The creek mouth is now a cement spillway, scrubbed clean of the salt bush that gave it its name, Salt Creek is now a drainage ditch for a new suburb. From Salt Creek Beach to Coast Highway and from Coast Highway a mile inland, the land is being torn and terraced by giant earthmovers. A construction worker tells me scores of villas and a luxury hotel will soon be terraced onto the coastal bluffs and a golf course will line Salt Creek.

I continue hiking north but am soon halted in my tracks by a mass of barbed wire and cement, a residential Maginot Line, defeating my best efforts to continue north. Monarch Bay is more impregnable to trespass than was Camp Pendleton Marine Base! I climb up the bluffs and over a wall, retreating along Monarch Bay's private streets, suffering the stares of wealthy homeowners and the hostilities of a security guard ("This is private property. . . . You're subject to arrest. . . . The public beach is located . . .") when I emerge at his outpost on Coast Highway.

Fifty yards south of the Monarch Bay guardhouse is the place where the powers-that-be installed Dana's memorial. As I stare at the brass plaque I feel unstuck in time. I glimpse Dana's 1835, but it is snatched from me. I feel, for a brief moment, Chase's 1911, and then it's gone. But what is even more disheartening is that my 1960s memories have no more relevance to the Orange County of today than Dana's or Chase's.

Walking north, I pass through Orange County as if in a dream, for the land I see now is not the land I have seen a hundred times before. I was brought up in Whittier, in Downey, two inland cities whose citizenry, while technically part of Los Angeles County, thinks, votes, and plays like Orange County. And it was to Orange County's beaches that we flocked to escape the summer smog and the awful heat.

But there is one Orange County place that will be as Dana saw it, as Chase saw it, as I remember it. It beckons to me like an oasis to a thirsty man. I think about it and I'm comforted: the Irvine Ranch south of Corona del Mar. It's one of those pastoral scenes that becomes forever imprinted in boyhood memory. On the inland side of the highway (no cars pass in this memory) cattle graze the hillsides and cowboys ride the range. On the ocean side of the highway, sails move slowly along the horizon and kids on horseback ride the blufftop above the sparkling beach.

For a few moments, I am again transported in time, back to the 1960s. I round El Moro, a rocky volcanic promontory of eroded lava, and walk beautifully-cusped El Moro Beach. At Reef Point I walk the coreonsis and black-sage-dotted bluffs. The bluffs are state parkland, the rolling hills east of the Coast Highway belong to Irvine Ranch. The San Joaquin Hills and the clifftops glow amber in the late afternoon sunlight.

But something is missing from the bluffs.

Horses. There used to be lots of them, I remember. The horse trails are still here, an old corral and some fencing still stand, but I can't spot a single horse or rider.

And something is missing from the hills.

Cows. Cattle grazed here when Mission San Juan Capistrano owned this land, when José Sepúlveda had his Rancho San Joaquin in 1837, when James Irvine purchased the rancho in 1869. And ever since. The horses and cows are gone from the land, but to my horror, the hills are not empty. Earthmovers, larger than the largest dinosaur, lumber over the hills. The yellow machines tear at the land, move over the hills, move the hills themselves, rearrange the range into suburban plots.

The hills the *vaqueros* rode are being ridden by dozer jockeys racing for the finish of the last stretch of undeveloped coast in Orange County.

I spot a hard-hatted construction worker sitting at the cliff edge, admiring the sunset. "Where are the horses?" I demand.

"Horses? The cows," he says, gesturing to the hills, ". . . I remember. But no horses."

Irvine Ranch cows are being replaced with two thousand homes, he tells me.

Running out of light, running out of energy, my fatigue made worse by this dispiriting development, I walk a mile to the outskirts of Corona del Mar and find a pay phone. I've got to be rescued from this madness. But no would-be rescuers—friends or family—are home, so I talk only to Angeleno answering machines. I buy a sandwich, beer, and flashlight batteries, and return to the Irvine bluffs.

It's a warm night. I lie atop my sleeping bag, reading more of *California Coast Trails*. I get the feeling Chase knew that Progress with a capital *P* was coming to Orange County. He saw California's Spanish heritage in jeopardy. The old adobes lay in ruins. He took pictures of the ruins and his companion Carl Eytel filled a sketch pad with drawings of the once proud haciendas. Chase notes: "We remarked again upon the discreditable feature of Western American life which is illustrated by the condition of these interesting and once beautiful monuments of our history. Perhaps it would be too much to expect that those who have succeeded to the ownership of the estates of the Spanish Californians should expend a fraction of their revenues upon the preservation of the old houses; but that is not our way."

You wouldn't recognize Orange County now, Joe. We lost a lot more than the old haciendas. We lost the whole damned rancho. The boom of the surf, the whoosh of traffic on Coast Highway, and some beer finally lulls me to sleep.

I'm awakened by hoofbeats. Soft hoofbeats, but hoofbeats nonetheless. Am I dreaming? Dreaming of the days of the *vaqueros?* Dreaming of the days when I saw horses ridden over these bluffs?

Naw, I can't be dreaming; I see Pacific Coast Highway and the occasional car, a star or two and half a moon. My watch reads 2 A.M.

I burrow deeper into my sleeping bag.

But the hoofbeats come closer. Closer.

A deer maybe, I think. Awfully heavy for a deer, though. And deer don't snort. Maybe I overlooked a stable, and a rent-a-horse has come for a visit.

I sit up and see him in the moonlight, a lone rider on a chestnut horse. He's traveling north. He stops not ten feet away and looks down at me. Now I know I'm dreaming.

"Where you bound?" he asks.

"Oregon."

"And me as well." The voice is British, educated. "When the curious ask me and I tell them 'Oregon,' they think I'm trifling with them."

"You're riding to Oregon?" My voice is hollow, distant, apart from me. I stand up, rub my eyes. Barefoot, clad only in T-shirt and briefs, I look up at the rider. He looks like a Rough Rider—broad-brimmed campaign hat, khaki pants stuffed into the tops of high boots, coat and kerchief. But the face, what I can see of it in the moonlight anyway, isn't rough. The face is that of a man of about fifty, healthy, but not ruddy or weather-beaten, more distinguished than handsome. Brown eyes twinkle behind what I at first think are wire-frame glasses, but on closer inspection determine to be pince-nez, connected to a thin chain behind his head. A thick mustache dominates his face. The mustache is salt-and-pepper; his hair, the little I can see under his hat, is more salt than pepper.

"Is riding to Oregon so surprising?" he asks.

"Most people don't want to take the time to travel so far, see the country. It's so . . . unusual."

"Many times in Los Angeles I have looked up at some amazing cloud formation or the purple San Gabriel Mountains above the city and realized I was the only one of thousands to take notice. The others were all looking in the shop windows or at the ladies' hats. There's something awful about this lack of perception. What can it mean?"

What can it mean? What it means is I've flipped out, traveled back in time, or am talking to a ghost. Or all three of the above. I rub my eyes, but he doesn't go away. I'm still face-to-face with Joseph Smeaton Chase.

"I don't know what it means," I stammer. "It means I've walked a hundred miles up this coast and I'm getting discouraged. I wanted to quit yesterday. I don't know how you—I'm reading your book—how you stay so enthusiastic. I can't follow your coast trail. I can't even follow the coast half the time."

"The beauty of the coast is there, waiting for us to discover it. You must continue to Oregon."

"I can't. The coast has closed up on us. There's no trail."

"There's always a trail."

"Where?"

"Wherever your heart leads."

"I can't just follow my heart. I mean, I need some practical advice here."

"Keep the ocean on your left."

"What?"

"Keep the ocean on your left."

He gathers his reins, digs in with the stirrups.

"Joe?"

"C'mon, Chino," he urges his horse. He rides north and in a moment horse and rider are swallowed up by the darkness, leaving me shivering in the moonlight.

CHASE PREDICTED that Orange County would one day live up to its name. He led his horse through bogs and estuaries, saw the many small streams running across a fertile basin to the sea, and noting the artesian water at shallow depth made a prediction: "I could foresee a time, not very distant, when the prairie-like landscape I saw would be chequered into hundreds of trim little farms, occupied by Farmers of the New Style, who, scientifically blending water and soil under the most generous climate in the world, would cover the great expanse with the choicest fruits of the earth."

But there's no escape for me now, not even into the memories of my youth. I walk through once modest Orange County beach towns that have been smothered by immodest developments. I walk past a Seal Beach without a seal, a Laguna Beach without a laguna, and a Crystal Cove without the slightest coastal indentation or anything crystalline, unless one counts the trailer park of glass and aluminum situated on the "cove." I walk the length of Orange County without seeing an orange.

Joseph, your prediction of an Orange County worked by farmers of the new age did come true, for a while anyway. For a generation the coastal slope was perfumed by orange blossoms. But the citrus growers wiped out the water table and soon changed the ecology of the entire south coast. If you hadn't recorded it, I never would have guessed that the countryside behind Huntington Beach was once lush with willows, springs, and peat bogs. A beautiful river rose a few miles inland and flowed southwest, sweeping along the base of Huntington Beach mesa and entering the sea through Bolsa Bay. During the 1920s, when the citrus boom you predicted filled the rich soil with orange and lemon trees, great numbers of artesian wells and drainage ditches were dug and the river disappeared. Good-bye to the river, good-bye to the citrus orchards, good-bye to the land.

Six

Whales and Trails

IT'S DRIZZLING on this gloomy Saturday. San Pedro Harbor is shrouded in gray. Bridgeworks, smokestacks, and oil tankers are penciled upon the near horizon as in a charcoal drawing. Mist softens the harsh lines of the harbor's superstructure, rendering the shoreline of steel more serious and less sinister than it appears on a sunny day. "Industrial drama" is how corporate architects might characterize this coastal scene. A perfect location, I imagine, for some expressionist filmmaker to remake Fritz Lang's *Metropolis.*

I join two hundred wet but enthusiastic souls on the dock at Catalina Terminal, embarkation point for passage to Catalina Island. But we're not sailing to Catalina this morning; we're heading out to sea in search of the California gray whale. Port of Los Angeles, home port for America's largest fishing fleet, leader in number of tuna canneries, shipping and receiving point for Pacific Rim trade, largest artificial harbor in the world, now has a new distinction: Whale Watching Capital of the World.

Yesterday I walked the docks, traveling from Long Beach to San Pedro via a ten-mile maze of berths, terminals, and cargo-loading facilities. I passed the *Queen Mary,* crossed the cement-lined Los Angeles River, and trudged through the huge Port of Long Beach and the gargantuan Port of Los Angeles. I felt so small, dwarfed by the ships, the cranes, a coastline of cement and steel. I wanted to get another perspective and turned to Joseph Smeaton Chase, but since we crossed paths in Orange County, he has left me. He notes that a great port is in the making at San Pedro, but elects to dodge it completely. No, I needed another perspective on the port that would shrink it down to human size, help me understand it. I wanted an offshore perspective, and when the opportunity came to hop a boat, I took it.

"Welcome aboard the *Princess.* Make yourself comfortable. We'll be casting off in five minutes."

The voice broadcasting over the ship's loudspeakers belongs to John Olguin, widely credited as founder of the spectator sport of whale watching. At his invitation I'm here to observe a phenomenon of California culture, and hope to take an oceanside look at both Los Angeles Harbor and the rugged Palos Verdes coast, where I'll soon be walking.

With a bellow from its fog horn, the *Princess* leaves its berth. Children, lots of them, play with the life preservers, run amok on the upper deck. Adults sip coffee and hot chocolate, swallow Dramamine, check the trans-derm patches behind their ears, and grouse about the latest weather report, which is discouraging, to say the least.

The ferry churns through the mist, running alongside the huge, federally-built breakwater providing the protection for San Pedro Harbor that nature doesn't. From San Diego to San Francisco, California has no natural harbor, a fact painfully evident to the Los Angeles boosters of old. The ambitious city planners knew their history: for want of an outlet to the sea, many of the world's great cities suffered decline and even fall. These early twentieth-century boosters were determined that Los Angeles would pursue a different course. Their boosterism and technological improvisation had in the past always triumphed over the shortcomings of geography, and they resolved not to let a little inconvenience like a lack of a natural harbor halt their city on the doorstep of greatness. Technocracy had solved Los Angeles's previous problems: a lack of water was mitigated by the construction of a great aqueduct from the High Sierra, distances and sprawl were conquered by the Pacific Electric railway.

True, as far as a harbor was concerned, nature offered little encouragement. In 1542, Juan Rodríguez Cabrillo sailed by and noticed only the slightest of indentations here. He called it "The Bay of Smokes," though no one knows why. (Smog would not be noticeable in the Los Angeles Basin for another four hundred years.) Quite possibly the Indians were setting the grass afire for one of their rabbit hunts and Cabrillo spotted the smoke. In 1835, Richard Henry Dana sailed by and reported it as being "universally called the Hell of California," adding that "this rascally hole of San Pedro is unsafe in every wind but a southwester, which is seldom known to blow more than once in half a century."

Four hundred years after Cabrillo, seventy-five years after Dana, the coastline around San Pedro still displayed only a small dimple, but this did not stop Los Angeles city fathers from annexing (read stealing) land from other municipalities, and Angeleno engineers from designing and dredging an immense harbor—twenty-eight miles worth of waterfront.

The *Princess* chugs through a maze of sea lanes, past huge auto transport boats unloading Nissans, Toyotas, Hondas, Mazdas, and Subarus. Other Japanese freighters load junk autos, which have been compressed into refrigerator-sized cubes by a huge stamping machine located on well-named Terminal Island. Steel from the old autos will be recycled and come back to these shores in the form of brand-new Japanese models. I wonder how many Japanese cars buzzing around Los Angeles today were 1971 Pontiacs in a previous life.

A fishing boat, heading for port, cuts across our wake. By looking at the faces of some of the passengers, I can imagine their thoughts. *If the weather is too awful for fishermen, what are we doing out on this pleasure cruise?*

Never mind, the fishermen are a poor barometer; no doubt they are returning from far away. Back when San Pedro was a sleepy fishing port, the fishermen did not have to venture far to spread their nets. Large commercial catches of halibut, yellow tail, and sea bass were made right in the harbor until about 1950. After the harbor was completed, water quality was deliberately allowed to deteriorate to protect wood structures from ship worms and other boring organisms. The reproductive habitat of the fish, polluted by bilge water, petroleum, and sewage outfall, was eliminated, and today's fishermen must travel great distances to gather the Pacific's bounty.

We spot a unique motor yacht, a converted World War II gunboat, once owned by John Wayne. It looks right at home in this unbeautiful setting. The *Princess* passes two dozen harbor seals, who lounge on the buoys and bark at the incessant fog horn. Finally the ferry churns into the open sea.

I find John Olguin on the top deck in the pilot's cabin. He directs his binoculars through the boat's busy windshield wipers. An old salt he is. Give his hands some more calluses and he could pass for a lobster fisherman. The skin on his face not covered by his salt-and-pepper beard and jaunty nautical cap is weathered and furrowed.

"*This* is southern California?" he greets me, as he buttons up a bright red windbreaker covered with whale-watch patches.

The heavy bow of the *Princess* plows through the whitecaps, tossing wavelets onto the lower deck to the delight of some children, who play chicken with the crashing water. Olguin hands his binoculars to the first mate, and with the captain's help works the ship-to-ship radio.

"*Princess* calling. You guys see anything?"

"Nothing, John," a hoarse voice responds through the static. "We got a lotta people upchucking. Roughest day of the year. How about you guys?"

"Nothing."

This is the second-to-last Saturday of the season, Olguin informs me. The spectator sport of whale watching extends from about the end of football season to the beginning of baseball season, or from mid-December through March, when the California gray whale returns from Alaska seas to its calving and mating waters in Baja, California, and passes the coast of southern California.

"In the early days, we used to watch whales right from the beach," relates Olguin. "Now we go right among them. I told everybody in the early 1970s that in ten years it would be a million-dollar business.

And it was. And today it's a fifty-million-dollar business along the coast of California. We started with one boat; now we have fourteen."

These days a whale-watching cruise is often sold-out, and customers are advised to purchase their tickets in advance from one of Los Angeles's computerized ticket agencies. Customers are not guaranteed a whale to watch, though John Olguin, captain and crew do their best to find one.

"It's a unique opportunity. People don't have the chance to see whales elsewhere on earth unless they go to Hawaii or Patagonia. You can see whales along other parts of the Pacific coast but you have to go way out in the open ocean to view them. For some reason, they come very close to shore in southern California."

An hour passes. The light rain gets lighter but the heavy wind gets heavier. Eric, age eight, his red curly hair a wet mop, tugs on Olguin's windbreaker for attention. "We gonna see a whale?"

"Plenty of whales out here, son."

Eric is dubious.

"Look for a spout. That means the whale is coming to the surface."

Eric is still dubious.

"Look for a heart-shaped spray about fifteen feet high," advises Olguin. "And if you see the whale spouting be sure to yell, 'Thar she blows!' Another way to spot a whale is to find a flat, swirling area on the water—that's the whale's footprint. And like human fingerprints, no two whale footprints are alike."

The first mate with the binoculars prances in place. "A gray at one o'clock!" she shouts.

Olguin seizes the microphone. "Whale on the starboard—that's the right side of the boat—at one o'clock."

The watchers hustle to the rail. The quick and keen-eyed catch a brief glimpse of a whale's fluke disappearing beneath the surface. That's it. Most miss even this little bit of action and huddle deeper into their rainwear.

Olguin smiles a weary smile. "We've been going out commercially for ten years and only failed to see a whale twice. We don't make guarantees, but the customer has a better than 99 percent chance of seeing a California gray whale."

Little Eric pops in again. "The whale didn't stay long," he complains. Olguin whisks him out. "Thee thith gray hair. I got it looking for gray whaleth." Under the pressure of the hunt, Olguin's slight lisp manifests itself. Suddenly he notices some splashing by the bow. He grabs the microphone. "Dolphin! Off the starboard bow!"

A nearly motionless school of about a dozen dolphins bobs in the water. The creatures watch our boat pass but do not swim alongside it.

Olguin switches off the mike. "I can't believe it. What's wrong with those dolphins? They're not doing anything. Sometimes the dolphins don't behave right. They won't jump; they give a bad show. They ride a few waves and that's all. Last weekend they were wonderful. Hundreds of them. What a performance!"

The captain of the *Princess* makes a slow U-turn and heads back to port. With the absence of any land or horizon, the passengers don't realize we've changed direction. If I wasn't leaning against the big ship's compass, I wouldn't know either.

Olguin takes a few deep breaths to relax his diaphragm and picks up his microphone. "Guess the dolphins are taking the day off, folks. You might be interested to know that dolphins have two voices: one is ultrasonic—it goes out at terrific speed. It's a series of clicking sounds: *Arrrrh! Arrrrh!* Some dolphins make noises like knocking on wood."

Olguin exhales mightily, then turns up the PA system. He fingers the mike like a nightclub comic. "Pilot whales also have two voices: one is like a squealing pig—*Wheeee, wheeee, wheeee, wheeee.* The second is *Rrrrrrggggrrrprggg!* Combined, they make a heckuva noise beneath the water."

The rain begins falling in heavy sheets, driving even the most hardy passengers inside. Olguin realizes he has a captive audience and continues with his cetacean impressions. "*Gotta-gotta-gotta-gotta.* That's the voice of the humpback whale. The second voice is very deep; it goes down to forty cycles. The human ear can go down to fifty cycles. The second voice sounds like this: *Rrrrraaaaaaooooohhhh.*"

In the enclosed second deck, some of the children begin to get sick. One kid vomits and starts a chain reaction of upchucking children.

"Now the finback whale was thought to be mute until scientists put supersensitive hydrophones in the water and recorded their call. The finback communicates below the forty-cycle range. Because its voice is so low, you don't hear it, you feel it. If one was calling below the ship, you'd feel the vibration. All the windows would rattle. *Mmmm,* it calls, like a foghorn. It's so powerful and so deep that the humpback whale would shatter the wood on this boat."

Olguin flicks off the mike and scans the horizon.

"Nothing, John," reports the captain. "Better keep talking."

"The show goes on," sighs Olguin, returning to his microphone. "Now the sperm whale is unique-looking; one-third of its body is nose. The nose is filled with spermaceti oil. It uses its nose as a vibrating tank for its call. This whale makes the loudest noise of any creature on earth. If it made its noise right next to you, the sound would tear the hair and skin right off your body. Scientists can't understand why a sperm whale doesn't tear off its own skin.

"Now listen to the sperm whale sound." Olguin puts the microphone between his knees and claps his hands. "Now multiply that sound by a thousand times and you'll get the idea."

Olguin's brow furrows as he checks his mental files. He is plainly groping for something more to say. "Normal cow's milk is $3\frac{1}{2}$ percent butterfat content. Whale's milk is $47\frac{1}{2}$ percent. It's incredibly rich, much more rich than whipping cream. On this milk diet, a baby gray whale gains weight by the hour. In one year it grows to twenty-seven feet long."

Exhausted, Olguin hangs up his microphone.

Little Eric pokes his head back into the cabin. "Last year we saw fourteen whales," he says accusingly. "And today, all morning and one stupid fluke."

"This isn't the zoo, son," says Olguin.

"And it wasn't so bumpy last year. My little sister got sick today. My mom, not too long ago, when I had my samwich, said, 'You got an iron stomach, Eric.'"

"That's what it takes, huh?"

For some passengers, the best part of the voyage is their first step back onto solid ground. Weak-kneed, they struggle up the gangplank. A few glower at John Olguin. Sales of whale pendants, patches, and pins at the souvenir stand are almost nil; the passengers stay away in droves.

"Well, we did see a whale," Olguin says defensively to a sodden elderly couple. "It's like rolling the dice at Las Vegas—you never know what you're going to get."

John Olguin heads for home. Home was, is, and always will be, the Palos Verdes Peninsula, a prow of land that arcs northward from the Port of Los Angeles. "I've worked at the Cabrillo Marine Museum for fifty years. I was born at Point Fermin, live at Point Fermin, work at Point Fermin. I've spent my whole life at Cabrillo Beach next to the harbor. When I can share my love for whales I want to do it. I love my work and get paid for it—it's hard to believe."

The rain is letting up, but Olguin's beard continues dripping water like a hedge after a thunderstorm. "About twenty years ago, my wife and I started sleeping outside. We pushed our bed out on the back porch, which overlooks the ocean. We're not on earth a very long time, and I like to be close to nature. I like to see whales spouting right from my bedroom. I want to see the stars, the moon, the sunrise. Our lives are so damn short. We're just passing through. And while I'm passing through, I don't want to miss one minute of it."

IN THEIR RED, white, and blue windbreakers, the Ghormleys by all appearances are the all-American family. Patches stitched on their sleeves read Beach Walk, which is how this family plays together, stays together. And beach walking is what the Ghormley family is doing this blustery morning on Royal Palms Beach, just north of the Port of Los Angeles. Carl Ghormley, patriarch of the clan, is in the lead. Moving slower is the rest of the family, which spontaneously breaks into song:

Back in nineteen sixty-four
Father thought we needed more
So we went down to the shore
To walk the beach.
Hey!

The Ghormleys have walked the entire length of the California coast, hiking one or two weeks a year for eighteen years. Persistence.

I heard about the Ghormley's Mexico-to-Oregon beach walk through the coast hiker's grapevine and gave Carl Ghormley a call when I reached his hometown of San Pedro. He was delighted to talk to a fellow coast walker and agreed to meet me on his home beach. To my surprise, he showed up with the whole family—wife Harriet, sons Miles and Justus, his son's wives, and a couple of grandchildren. The singing follows us:

> We're on the beach walk,
> We're on the beach walk,
> Walking to and fro.
> Hey!

Carl slows the pace, allowing his wife to catch up.

"When the kids were little, we used to take a month-long trip each summer—the Great American Vacation—usually a long drive to Key West or Maine or British Columbia. I wanted a trip to give us closeness, continuity from one year to the next. Anyway, one day when I was stuck in rush-hour traffic on Pacific Coast Highway, I got the idea for the beach walk."

He smiles at his wife, who has stopped to examine a piece of driftwood. "Actually, I began having doubts about the wisdom of my idea as soon as we drove up to the Tijuana bullring at the border."

"I don't think we thought beyond San Diego," confesses Harriet, as she catches up with her husband. "We just started in. We never imagined it would take us eighteen years and be such an incredible project."

"The eighteen years is a bit deceiving," says Carl, as he once again strides out ahead of the family. "We weren't trying to set a record. The idea was to enjoy some time free of distractions and to be with the children." He lowers his voice, taking me into his confidence. "I love having the family along, but I find it difficult walking at another person's pace. Know what I mean?"

"Exactly."

"Our boys brought their girlfriends, then wives, then suddenly we had grandchildren. . . . Each person you add complicates things a bit. Still, it's been a harmonious group."

I accelerate to keep up with Carl, who picks his way up the storm-battered coast, over exposed rocks and piles of kelp. "The coast, in my mind, runs south-to-north. For some reason, I can't imagine walking any other way."

"Me either, though it gets tiring always walking into the wind."

"My God, the wind! Some years we met right after Christmas—December 26. It's always windy and rainy then, but you appreciate the coast more in bad weather. I know the kids would sometimes say, 'Christmas! Oh, no, not the beach walk again.' Sometimes the thought of walking in another storm was dreadful. But once we got walking, the worries and agonies melted away. We lost ourselves in the daily adventure of being out on the coast."

Another benefit of the beach walk was an escape from routine. For Carl, it was a respite from corporate life; for Harriet a reprieve from domestic duties; for the kids, who grew up on the walk, a break from school and later from their own jobs. The Ghormleys walked away from cities and freeways to a California more profound and more beautiful than they had ever dreamed.

"In San Mateo County, at Cape Ano Nuevo, we came upon a giant sea monster—a two-thousand-pound creature with a huge bulbous nose. It was absolutely still. We thought it was dead. I figured maybe a little water would revive it, so I emptied a canteen on its head. It let out this great big roarrrr! Later we found out it was an elephant seal and that Ano Nuevo is a breeding ground for them. We had no idea the coast had a wild animal of that size and shape."

Still walking briskly along the water's edge, Ghormley lets the whole beautiful trip tumble out in a series of anecdotes that rise and fall like waves: white and black crescents of sand that no one to this day has named; sea otters bobbing off the coast of Monterey; driftwood bonfires and abalone roasts; crossing the Golden Gate Bridge; the family's Saint Bernard, who carried the lunches until he became an incorrigible swimmer and had to be relieved of that duty.

"We bought all kinds of books on shells and classified a few hundred varieties. I assigned everyone in the family an area of research—one was in charge of human history, another studied tidepools, another birds. Cormorants, teals, grebes, ducks, terns, gulls—we must've identified over a hundred kinds of shorebirds. We filled notebooks with our observations and took thousands of pictures.

"The beach walk gave our family a depth of appreciation for nature that's almost indescribable. It's so easy to walk down the beach and see nothing. You have to keep your senses open, seek it out, try to understand.

"Even this beach close to home, this beach beneath our feet, has a history and specialness all its own," emphasizes Ghormley.

Palos Verdes Peninsula is fifteen miles of reefs, tidepools, coves, and sea cliff caves. Indians, Spanish rancheros, and Yankee smugglers have added to the peninsula's romantic history. This rocky, fog-shrouded coastline has meant the death of many ships. A few miles north lies the rusted hulk of the Greek freighter *Dominator*, which ran aground at Rocky Point in 1961. Never mind the white-stuccoed, red-tiled mansions atop the peninsula's bluff; the beach below remains pristine.

We near White's Point, which once flourished as a Roaring Twenties health spa and resort. Ghormley points out the sea-battered ruins of a large circular fountain and some curious cement foundations. Lush overgrown tropical gardens highlighted by skewed palm trees decorate the bluffs above the beach. White's Point was originally settled by Japanese immigrants, fishermen who harvested the bountiful abalone from the waters off the peninsula. Tons of abalone were both shipped to the Far East and consumed locally in Los Angeles's Little Tokyo. In a few years the abalone was depleted, but an even greater resource was discovered at White's Point—sulfur springs. In 1915, a spa and large hotel were built at the water's edge. Palm gardens and a golf course graced the cliffs above. The sulfur baths were especially popular with the Japanese American population of southern California.

The spa boomed in the twenties, but the 1933 Long Beach earthquake closed the springs. White's Point became part of Fort McArthur during World War II, the Japanese Americans were incarcerated in internment camps, and the resort was soon overwhelmed by the crumbling cliffs and the powerful sea.

"Does anybody in California care about their history?" asks Carl Ghormley, posing his question to the bluffs above us. "History's being covered up by the ocean on one side and luxury houses on the other.

All along the coast it's the same. We can't even get California Historical Landmark status for White's Point, can't even get a little plaque installed."

I think of Richard Henry Dana's plaque in Orange County, his forgotten name, his violated Point. Dana threw hides from the Palos Verdes cliffs too, but nobody ever named a point there after him, perhaps because he wrote nasty things about Los Angeles in general and Palos Verdes in particular. The young author found the headlands stark and oppressive; doubtless it's difficult to appreciate nature when busily engaged in hide-loading. Dana complained, "The water and stones together would wear out a pair of shoes a day, and as shoes were very scarce and very dear we were compelled to go barefooted. At night we went on board, having the most disagreeable day's work that we had yet experienced."

The rocky beach that tortured Dana's feet now afflicts ours, even if ours are protected by hiking boots. It's like walking over a surface of broken bowling balls. From Dana's point of view, the top of the Palos Verdes Peninsula was drab and barren, and small wonder considering the conditions under which he worked. As he lugged cow hides over Rancho Palos Verdes, he could hardly have been expected to appreciate the desolate beauty or to see the purple sage, flowering prickly pear cactus, or tall yellow mustard as anything but impediments to progress over the rolling hills.

"History's being covered up all around us," Ghormley charges. "Like we were ashamed of it or something." He pauses. "We should turn around."

Above us are sheer cliffs, which rise nearly three hundred feet above the ocean. Thirteen wave-cut terraces testify to the sea level fluctuations caused by the formation and melting of glaciers. We hear, feel, and see the surf rolling in and know that today the waves, as they have for so many thousands of years, are actively eroding the shoreline, cutting yet another terrace into the land.

"Palos Verdes Peninsula is the roughest part of the coast until you get to Big Sur," Ghormley declares. "You following the beach all the way?"

Walking the broken beaches of Orange County and through the
Port of Los Angeles comes back to me like a bad dream. And I wonder
if walking the many beaches of Los Angeles County will be any better.
Twenty-five miles ahead are mountains, the Santa Monica Mountains,
and a trail through the mountains might be just the thing I need to
raise my spirits.

"I think I'll head into the mountains, soon as I get to Santa Monica."

"That's right. You were telling me you gotta figure out that California Coastal Trail and that it's not just a beach trail. A trail the length of
the coast would be great. It'd sure make the coast easier to walk,
though finding your own way is the best way."

Suddenly I feel uneasy. Deep down in my heart I have to agree
with Ghormley—finding your own way is the best way. Maybe the
coast should belong to those who can find their own way. But what
about those who can't find their own way? Shouldn't they have a
chance to see the coast's wilder places?

"John, you getting any help with your trail-finding?"

For a moment I feel very much alone. Carl Ghormley had his family on his beach walk. And even Joseph Smeaton Chase had the com-
panionship of his horse. "I did get some advice," I say slowly, "from a
man who traveled the coast a long time ago. He said, 'Keep the ocean
on your left.'"

Ghormley chuckles. "Great advice."

He picks up the pace as we head for a rendezvous with his family.
"Took us 177 days to get to Oregon. We filled everybody up with oatmeal in the morning and hit the trail. We walked six to twelve miles a
day. People's idiosyncrasies and character traits really come out on a
walk like this; we all have our own madnesses. When we finished the
beach walk at the Oregon border it was a very sad thing. We carried an
American flag and a California flag over the state line. Can't help feeling patriotic when you're seeing so much beauty. Harriet began crying. I began crying. When the walk ended, we really felt like we had
lost something."

Carl Ghormley and I say our good-byes. I head north as Carl
catches up with his singing family and turns south:

Lullaby
We bid you fond adieu.
As the years roll by,
I'll come back to you.
The sky will be more blue,
Walking the coast with you.
We'll return to see you now and then,
And walk the beach together once again.
Don't change, we love you so,
Until we meet again.

N O W *this* is southern California. A perfect Saturday morning: blue skies, flat water, a gentle breeze. The *Princess* gleams ivory and inviting at berth. On board, business at the whale souvenir stand is brisk. John Olguin is a happy fellow, either because a passenger just bought a copy of his glossy book about the gray whale, or because he is about to lead his last whale watch of the season.

"The whales are waiting for us," Olguin broadcasts over the public address system.

So are the dolphins. As soon as the *Princess* reaches the open sea, a school of dolphins surfaces near the bow. They comport themselves in a manner befitting their performing fellows at Sea World.

"Dolphins!" exults Olguin. "Off the starboard side and off the port side too—they're all around us. Leaping! Diving! They do this out of pure joy; no other reason. We're surrounded by dolphins. It's a wild animal show in our backyard in beautiful southern California!"

The dolphins deliver a perfect impression of an Olympic synchronized swim team. When they dive, their dorsal fins cut through the water like a row of buzz saws.

After the dolphins leave, the *Princess* heads north along Palos Verde Peninsula. Sunlight sparkles off the mansions on the peninsula bluffs and it's easy to agree with Louis Bromfield, who in 1930 wrote in *Vogue,* "In Palos Verdes, one has the impression of entering a paradise designed by the Spanish for the anointed of heaven."

Suddenly we come upon a pod—a group of seven whales swim-ming together. Binoculars are riveted to eyeballs, children shriek. "Thar she blows!" shouts Olguin. "Whales! What a show! Look at that one breach! And, oh, my God, there's one spyhopping!"

The spectator sport of whale watching, I realize, has a full lexicon of terms, as familiar to its fans as the quarterback sneak, sacrifice fly, and full court press are to the followers of more traditional sports. When a whale breaches, it comes out of the water and falls over to one side. Spyhopping means the animal rises head first out of the water, seemingly standing on its tail, and comes down slowly.

Busby Berkeley couldn't have choreographed a better show. The whales linger between boat and shore. Only a quarter-mile of Pacific separates them from exclusive Palos Verdes Estates. There's something funny about whales blowing spray in front of the huge haciendas.

Because the gray whale travels the length of the California coast, Californians call it the California gray whale. Provincialism, of course. No doubt, Mexicans could claim the species as the Mexican gray whale; after all, the grays are born in Baja waters. Scientists, with little success, insist on the Pacific gray whale, pointing out that the creature swims from the Arctic to Baja and back, the longest migration of any animal in the world. Any locality along its 14,000-mile journey could claim the whale as its own. But it's Californians who have made an in-dustry out of whale watching and Californians who have installed the whale as their official state marine mammal—not the best omen, con-sidering that the official state land mammal, the grizzly, is extinct in the Golden State.

The gray whale, by whatever regional appellation one chooses, was nearly exterminated twice. Twice it has been nearly wiped off the face of the earth and twice it has recovered. Shore whaling was carried out on California's coast in the 1850s when a string of whaling stations was established from Baja to Half Moon Bay. From my vantage point on the *Princess,* I can see the former location of one of these whaling sta-tions, Portuguese Bend, named for its many Portuguese whalers. Large iron kettles, used to boil whale blubber, have been found in the sea cliff caves of Palos Verdes Peninsula.

As recently as fifty years ago, whalers were harpooning whales along the Peninsula. When the killing finally stopped, fewer than six hundred grays remained. Left alone, the species displays a marvelous fecundity and increases about 5 percent a year. Today seventeen thousand whales pass by San Pedro without drawing pursuit, except by us ocean-going tourists.

"We've saved the gray whale, we meaning everybody in the world," relates John Olguin after the whales have moved south and the on-board excitement had faded. "People are more conscious now. The other kinds of whales will be saved if the Japanese and Russians stop hunting."

As our boat full of happy whale watchers returns to San Pedro Harbor, I begin wondering what effect human presence has on the whales. Maybe I'm guilty of anthropomorphism, but don't all these tour boats bother the whales? "Do the whales know we're following them?" I ask Olguin.

"Of course they know we're around."

"Don't we bother them?"

Olguin bristles, scratching his beard. "Whale watching is not harassing the whale. The whales are just passing through; we don't stop their migration."

Still, I have my doubts. "Could our whale watching be causing them psychological or physiological stress?"

"We adhere to the American Cetacean Society rules, which state that we must stay at least a hundred yards away from the whale. I'm sure that's an adequate distance."

"A hundred yards isn't much; maybe to avoid collisions, but not enough to keep the whales from knowing we're following them. Animals in zoos go crazy, you know. Too many eyes watching them."

"That's completely different. We're helping the whale survive in its own environment."

"Why should its environment include humans at all?"

"Believe me, humans are necessary to whale ecology; if there weren't whale watching, there would be no gray whales."

I figure he's talking in paradigms. "You mean, like if a tree falls in the forest and there's no one around to hear it, is there a sound?"

"No, no. I'm talking politics, not philosophy." And it's politics Olguin does talk: Creatures in this modern world need attention, or in the parlance of the politically astute conservationist, a "constituency." No doubt about it, whale watching trips build a constituency. Olguin alone has introduced one million schoolchildren to the California gray whale.

And Olguin talks economics. What killed the whale was economics; blubber was good business until the supply ran low. Now, ironically, economics is saving the whale: whale watching is good business. There's no chance that whaling will be revived along California's coast; everyone agrees the whale is far more valuable whole than dismembered.

The founding father of whale watching thinks the multimillion-dollar industry is a blessing, and not a mixed one, for the California gray whale and for people as well. "I started whale watching because it brought me closer to the whale; now I find it also brings me closer to people. Maybe I've been staring out at the horizon for too long, but I can't help thinking that what will happen to the whale will happen to us."

SEVEN

Exodus to the Promised Sand

FROM THE BLUFFTOP above Leo Carrillo State Beach, I watch a movie being filmed. Hollywood technicians have rolled in portable palms and constructed a thatched hut on the sand, transforming the state beach into the South Seas. Parked along Pacific Coast Highway are moving vans full of equipment and "honey wagons" full of primping stars. The film crew, clad in Polynesian print shirts, seems to be having a good time as they set up huge metal sun reflectors and the camera.

From Sequit Point, where I stand, I can also see another beach that marks the northern boundary of Los Angeles County, the southern boundary of Ventura County. County Line Beach, when the wind and surf are just right, is popular with windsurfers. The lightest of breezes and flat water means the beach is all but deserted today.

After beach walking the length of Los Angeles County, some eighty miles, I feel not so much exhausted as bedazzled. The five days of walking Los Angeles beaches from Rat (Right after Torrance) Beach to County Line Beach was a sensory assault, a lot of sun and little fun, a barrage of beach culture, a rock video of a trip played out before my eyes and two hundred million more eyes (a hundred million visits a

year to Los Angeles County beaches, that's what some beach bureaucrat figured), with most eyes, most bodies, clustering blanket-to-
blanket on a couple of beaches, mass use beaches—acres of hot sand,
with a lifeguard station every few hundred feet, a boardwalk full of
roller skaters, snack shoppes, revolting restrooms, and a thousand gaily-
painted trashcans (virtually unused) over which local rock radio sta-
tions fight for the right to paint with their call letters, and filled with
beachgoers who cast a remarkable amount of debris on the shore,
most of it, amazingly, scooped up by the huge mechanical sand rakes
that work through the night—and it's not just on one or two beaches
but two dozen, miles and miles of white sand warmed by golden sun
and cooled by the breezes off the big blue bay, and populated with
splayed or on-parade bodies—well-sculpted, well-oiled, with the scant-
iest of bikinis on the most beautiful women, all this beach and the
bodies on it making a scene pretty as a picture, sometimes anyway, a
scene every bit the southern California of the picture postcards; it
wasn't like this in Indiana, Iowa, and Illinois think the Indianans,
Iowans, and Illini, who've come to visit, and it sure wasn't like this in
Iraq, Iran, and Pakistan think the Iraqis, Iranians, and Pakistanis, who've
come to stay, and it's not like this anywhere inland, think the blacks,
Latinos, Asians, Anglos, and Arabs, who flock to the promised sand,
each ethnicity settling on its own stretch of shore (in this regard neither more integrated nor more segregated than their lives inland) with
their boom boxes blaring salsa, rock, rap and reggae, as well as including crooning in Korean, Armenian, Tagalog, and Farsi.

My Los Angeles County beach walk, miles and miles over wide,
sandy beaches, was far different than my Orange County beach walk.
While in Orange County, artificial obstructions kept me from seeing
the shore; in Los Angeles County, nothing kept me from seeing the
coast exactly as it is. I had the feeling I was walking into one of those
good news/bad news jokes: The good news is I had no trouble seeing
the coast; the bad news is I had no trouble seeing the coast.

Often, as I walked the beaches, I thought it would have been far
more enjoyable to visit them during another time, another era. I would
have enjoyed visiting Redondo Beach and its little harbor in the 1890s;
it was a busy little port then. Great vessels anchored offshore, goods
from Asia and the Pacific islands were unloaded at wharfs, and railroads

ran from Redondo docks to downtown Los Angeles. The U.S. Congress considered San Pedro, Santa Monica, and Redondo for federal funding to build a great seaport for emerging Los Angeles. San Pedro got the port, Santa Monica and Redondo became resorts. Maybe, like thousands of southern Californians, I would have enjoyed visiting Redondo during the Roaring Twenties when it boasted a big amusement park and saltwater plunge and the way to flaunt Prohibition was to take a water taxi out to one of the "entertainment" boats anchored offshore, just outside the three-mile limit. Redondo Pier today receives no goods from overseas; it's a pleasure pier with a displeasing number of junque shops and mediocre restaurants.

Hermosa, Redondo's northern neighbor, I would have liked to visit in the 1950s; that's when crowds of beatniks hung out in Hermosa Beach coffeehouses and bookstores, listening to jazz and poetry read to music.

Maybe I would have appreciated El Segundo in the 1950s too. Above the beach towers an astonishing "plumber's nightmare" of a structure—the Hyperion Waste Treatment Plant. It's fifties design all right, massive and heavy with miles of pipe; it would look right at home with a parking lot full of chrome-teethed Buick Roadmasters and Cadillac Coupe de Villes.

I would have liked to visit Venice of America in 1914, the hallucination of Abbot Kinney, the manufacturer of Sweet Caporal cigarettes. He was, as they say, a rich man with artistic impulses. He proceeded to drain the swampland here and build cottages connected by canals. He imported gondolas and gondoliers from that other Venice across the Atlantic, built arched Venetian bridges over the canals and even a St. Marks Hotel, and erected a cultural center for the education of the citizenry.

At least I did visit Venice in the 1960s and early 1970s when hippies made it their home. Poets, writers, artists, and political protesters called the funky neighborhoods home. It was easier living then. Most of the rage Venetians felt was directed at politics and government leaders, not at fellow Venetians.

But that was then and this is now, and Venice is about as now as now gets. The canal neighborhoods have been gentrified, fine restaurants opened, but all of this prettification hasn't quite reached the Venice Beach Boardwalk, which resembles a third world marketplace, a bizarre bazaar, full of mimes, jugglers, palm readers, sunglasses sellers, and frozen yogurt peddlers; but most of all homeless people, desperate people, burned out Vietnam vets who went off to war and never came all the way back, winos one drink from the grave, drug addicts with expensive habits, drug addicts who don't care what they swallow, shoot, or smoke just so it takes them somewhere else, anywhere else; crazies who go from the revolving door of mental institutions to Venice Beach and back over and over and over again. This is the Venice of America today, an American tragedy.

I smile only once as I walk Venice Beach boardwalk. Unshaven, with a backpack, it's the first time in two decades I've walked the length of the boardwalk without being panhandled.

Leaving Venice and heading into Santa Monica, I'm trying to reconcile the picture postcards of Venice, 1914, with the Venice of my youth in 1969 with the Venice of today when suddenly a car, followed by a speeding police car, spins out of control, skids across the beachfront parking lot toward the boardwalk, and comes to a halt not thirty feet from the lightpost I take refuge behind. The police car skids to a halt behind it.

I wait for a showdown, a shoot-out, angry words, for the cop to confront the man he's chasing. But then I hear someone shout, "Looked good!" and I realize that I have walked into a movie, into an episode of a TV cop show.

Shaken, I walk on, soon passing the portable dressing rooms where the young and muscled cast linger outside to watch the action. "You could kill somebody, you oughta watch where you're driving those cars!" I shout at them. Even as the words clear my lips, I feel self-conscious, unhip, twice my age, an eighty-year-old crank. The actors ignore me. Just another Venice Beach crazy.

Past the Santa Monica Pier, past the Playland Amusement Arcade, past Will Rogers Beach, I unwind a little. I turn west with Santa Monica Bay and walk into the sun; in fact, for the whole length of the Malibu Coast it seems like I'm hiking into the sun. Malibu has its moments, particularly when I reach Zonker Harris Memorial Beach,

honoring a character from the Doonesbury comic strip whose primary goal in life is to acquire the perfect tan. The infamous Zonker
Harris Accessway is a focal point of the ongoing debate between the
California Coastal Commission, which is determined to provide access
to the coast, and some Malibu residents who would prefer the public
stay out. I round Malibu Point and arrive at Surfrider Beach (Malibu
Lagoon State Beach). When natives say "Malibu Beach" this is what
they mean: the site of beach-blanket movies and Beach Boy songs.
Then I walk up the narrow and sandy beach lined by exclusive Malibu
Colony residences, home to many a movie star. Some of the houses
are built on stilts, and as the tide comes in I'm actually forced to walk
beneath a few of the houses. I must be getting sun dazed or just plain
crazed, I think, when I look up at a wide redwood deck above me and
see the cast of *Baywatch* sipping drinks.

Atop the Leo Carrillo Beach bluffs, I think: *I should have followed
Joseph Smeaton Chase.* When he left Los Angeles, he rode out through
the San Fernando Valley, then into the Santa Monica Mountains, without returning to the coast until the far reaches of Malibu. He took a
circuitous route to the coast, he says, because "I was willing to forego
the sight of that galaxy of pleasure towns, Santa Monica, Redondo,
Long Beach, San Pedro, and several more, which in the exuberant
metaphor of the real estate circulars, 'are flung like a tribute of gems at
the feet of Imperial Los Angeles.'"

Since we met in Orange County, our paths have not crossed again.
Without a word of guidance, he left me to travel the Los Angeles
County coast. He left the coast for the Santa Monica Mountains.

Having reached the end of Los Angeles County, I've covered about
two hundred miles, some good ones and some bad ones. But my goal,
unlike that of the Ghormley family, is not to walk the beach; my interest is all of the coast—the bluffs, the cliffs, the coastal mountains.
Maybe if I can devise a route, California Coastal Trail hikers will have
the option of a beach route along Santa Monica Bay or a trail through
the Santa Monica Mountains.

My mountains.

I was born on the other side of the Santa Monica Mountains, just
outside Griffith Park; these mountains are home for me. For many

years, I lived in Santa Monica and looked up from the beach at the mountains that beckoned from nearby. Then, as now, I never could decide whether the seashore or the peaks had the stronger pull, so I've always tried to live near one or the other. I've lived in the most urban section of the Santa Monica Mountains—the Hollywood Hills—and in one of the most rural parts—Topanga Canyon. Not even the awesome proximity of Los Angeles and its hundred satellite cities has succeeded in leveling the mountains.

A fella's home mountains are where he goes on his first overnight trip with the Scouts; where he learns to drive a car with a clutch; the isolated make-out spot where he kisses his first girl; and later in life, a meditation site for the great issues of his day.

A lot of people have an interest in my home. The Santa Monica Mountains are the only mountain range in the United States that bisect a major metropolitan area. Portions of the mountains are a near-wilderness within an hour's drive of 6 million people, and stretch all the way from Griffith Park in the heart of Los Angeles to Point Mugu fifty miles away. A lot of developers say the mountains' slopes and canyons are ideal for subdivisions, which could be connected by a trans-mountains freeway. And a lot of government agencies say they're committed to protecting the mountains—the Los Angeles County Parks Department, the California Department of Parks and Recreation, the Santa Monica Mountains Conservancy, and even the National Park Service, which says the mountains are ecologically important because they're an example of Mediterranean terrain, the only such terrain in the nation in their care.

I want to hike it all, the whole home range. So many times before the mountains' tranquility has cleared my head; they've helped me answer questions and helped me ask them.

EIGHT

L.A. Without a Backbone (Trail)

THE FOG LIFTS early this morning and our view from Inspiration Point is . . . well, inspiring. My friend Susan, who has joined me for the day, snaps a picture of downtown Los Angeles with snow-capped Old Baldy towering in the background. However, it's not the panoramic view of basin and range that captures our attention today, but the trail sign located just below the summit that reads:

BACKBONE TRAIL

TOPANGA STATE PARK 11
POINT MUGU STATE PARK 65

It's a sign as optimistic as this beautiful day. I have been warned by that grand old man of the mountains, Milt McAuley, the range's flora expert and author of a half dozen guidebooks to the mountains, that despite many years of effort by conservationists, the Backbone Trail is a long, long way from connecting Inspiration Point in Will Rogers State Park to Point Mugu State Park. My friend Milt gave me some topographic maps and trail hints to follow.

Trail signs usually measure what is, not what should be; they list miles, not wishes. But this is a very special sign, part of the propaganda war over the fate of the Santa Monica Mountains. Other signs posted in these mountains suggest different uses of the land: FUTURE HOME OF CARPETERIA and TWENTY ACRES FOR RESIDENTIAL DEVELOPMENT—CALL COLDWELL BANKER.

For two decades hikers have promoted the idea of a Backbone Trail that would travel east-west through the Santa Monicas. If completed, the trail will link the three large state parks of Topanga, Malibu, and Point Mugu, enabling Southland residents to spend days and weekends hiking and backpacking across the rugged spine of the mountains. Camps and hostels will eventually be established along the trail.

The project has moved along quite slowly for political and financial reasons, and each delay means that the private land that must be purchased increases in price. A trail corridor ranging from a hundred feet to a quarter-mile wide must be acquired in order to protect the ridges and canyons en route. State and national park planners say it is a "high priority" for them.

Backbone Trail takes us over hot, exposed ridges. To the east is Rustic Canyon, a beauty, lined with sycamores and blue Santa Monica slate. Depressing to know the Los Angeles County Board of Sanitation owns this canyon.

We pause at several inspiration points, each a little loftier than the last. Rabbits bound out of the bushes. A hawk circles the sandstone cliffs. An eleven-mile hike, with a nearly two-thousand-foot elevation gain, brings us to Topanga State Park. We look down upon imperturbable Topanga Canyon, surrounded by urban sprawl, yet somehow retaining its rural character.

Plenty of daylight remains and we're still feeling frisky, but alas, the Backbone Trail dead-ends in Topanga Canyon. Ahead are only plans. As planned, the Backbone Trail will cross the hamlet of Topanga through a wooded greenbelt, traverse rolling Topanga Meadows, and cross over into Hondo Canyon, where a trail camp will be located in a dense forest of bay trees. The trail will then climb to the crest of Saddle Peak, where a hostel will offer spectacular ocean views, then pass through more meadowland on its way to Malibu Canyon.

A nice plan.

Planning is something Susan knows well. A space planner by trade, she spends her days figuring out exactly how much space should be allotted to whom and for what purpose in new medical buildings. When I begin grousing about the bureaucracy blocking the trail, she will have none of it.

"This isn't the Old West. You can't just blaze a trail; you have to plan it. You have to conduct needs assessment studies and user surveys. You have to weigh the competing objectives of function, cost, and aesthetics. Have a little sympathy for park planners."

Maybe that's my problem; I understand where trails should go, but I just don't understand how to get them through the political process. I decide to take a few days off, get a hot shower, some good food, and try to understand the plans for my home mountains.

I spend a day reading the weighty *Santa Monica Mountains General Management Plan,* produced by the National Park Service. To the non-planner, it is a bewildering document—a catalog of flora, fauna, and good intentions. The Santa Monica Mountains are destined to become, in the parlance of planners, a collection of Native American Indian Cultural Sites, Watershed Buffer Areas, Wildlife Corridors, and Urban Landscape Areas, whatever those are.

I am overwhelmed. The park service has left no stone unplanned. And the park service sure has lots of plans for trails. Not only are recreation trails planned for the Santa Monicas, but so are sensory trails, leg-stretcher trails, self-guided interpretive trails, special event trails, and underwater trails.

The Backbone Trail is planned as an "expedition trail," one requiring more than a day to complete. An expedition trail, according to the national park service, offers "greater solitude and a means of getting away from the more intensely used areas of the mountains." One of the purposes of the Backbone Trail will be to "provide an opportunity for people to experience the relationship between the mountains and the ocean."

My sentiments, exactly.

AFTER I TELL HER about the Backbone Trail to nowhere, Alice Allen gestures to the gigantic subdivision maps covering the walls of her park office. "I guess this isn't what the public imagines when it thinks about a national park," the interpretive specialist admits.

Headquarters for the Santa Monica Mountains National Recreation Area is an industrial park located off the Ventura Freeway in the northern San Fernando Valley. The freeway is the busiest in the United States, but almost no would-be parkgoers drop in at the recreation area's visitor center.

Uniformed rangers and their pickup trucks are, to say the least, noticeable when they mingle on lunch breaks with the well-dressed workers from nearby office buildings. On a clear day the Santa Monica Mountains are within sight of park headquarters, though rangers must drive at least a half hour to visit the nearest national park properties. During smoggy days, the mountains might as well be a thousand miles away.

Alice Allen—a sensible, no-nonsense name for a sensible, no-nonsense woman. She's a brisk, by-the-book, keep-all-the-buttons-buttoned park employee; one imagines her dutifully putting her Smokey the Bear hat in a hat press when not in use.

She confesses to being a bit exasperated. Yesterday, she babysat a movie company that was filming a car chase on park service land. This morning she went back to the remote location to inspect for damages. "They left two wrecked cars," she reports with disgust. "They promised me they would tow them out of there and they didn't."

I think of all the filming I witnessed on my walk along Santa Monica Bay. And I think back at how often, during my many wanderings in the Santa Monica Mountains, I've observed a movie being filmed—picnic scenes at Point Mugu, *Mayberry, R.F.D.* in Franklin Canyon. For a decade, the *M*A*S*H* set stood in Malibu Creek State Park; now it's on display in the Smithsonian in Washington, D.C.

Illusion. The mountains double for the antebellum south and the Old West, South Carolina and South Vietnam, Greece, Italy, or the south of France. When a low fog seeps into the canyons and enshrouds the sycamores, the mountains are positively Gothic. Arid grass slopes could be the steppes of Asia, red-rock canyons the planet Mars.

Illusion. The cinematographer's lens is most selective. Kept out of frame are power lines, concrete creekbeds, and condominiums. The natural world is recorded at twenty-four frames a second, unhappy landscapes are edited out, and a kind of generic wildland appears daily on television. The Santa Monica Mountains appear in 50 million American living rooms and yet no one knows their name.

And as Alice Allen and I try to trace the route of the Backbone Trail on the wall map, and as we talk of lost canyons and lost trails, I get the funny feeling that the national recreation area, too, is an illusion, a collection of scattered locations, pieces of land standing in for the whole. Sizable portions of what is now Santa Monica Mountains parkland were donated or sold at below market value by movie people—the Twentieth Century Fox Ranch, the Paramount Ranch, the Bob Hope Ranch, the Ronald Reagan Ranch, the Will Rogers Ranch, the Peter Strauss Ranch, to name a half-dozen. Unlike two other government agencies—the state park system and the Santa Monica Mountains Conservancy—the national park service does not own significant portions of the mountains; it owns a pond, a peak, a couple canyons, all isolated from one another and from developments all around. It is not the mountains but the image of mountains, not a park but the image of a park, that the national park service is selling.

When the Santa Monica Mountains were set aside by Congress in 1978, the bill's passage was viewed by Los Angeles citizens as a triumph for local conservationists. They had, without the benefit of meaningful local land-use laws, succeeded in placing the mountains under the protection of the national park service, arguably the best stewards of scenery in the world. At last, thought preservationists, the mountains would have the national recognition they deserved. Obviously, the rest of the country agreed with Los Angeles and viewed the mountains as a national treasure of national significance.

But something happened.

Or didn't happen.

What there is of the national recreation area is widely scattered parcels held together by promises and red tape. Instead of park trails, the national park service brought paper trails; instead of park land, it brought park plans.

The large tracts of land in the Santa Monica Mountains still belong to the state park system, which has no intention of relinquishing title or authority. Few of the promised federal acquisitions were made.

Since the national recreation area is more a collection of plans than a collection of lands, rangers here have a different sort of schedule than their more rural counterparts. The nature walk has given way to the drafting of an environmental impact report. The nature talk has been replaced with meetings with homeowner associations. The ranger-led campfire program—that peculiarly American institution complete with off-key singing, corny jokes, and admonitions about skunks that delight the child in all of us—is not scheduled in the Santa Monica Mountains because the national park service has no campground or property where a campfire can be legally made.

It used to be that the worst fate a park ranger could suffer was transfer to one of the cannonball parks—Gettysburg, Appomattox Court House, Fort Laramie—or a sentence of ten years to life at the Carl Sandburg Home or William Howard Taft National Historic Site. Now a worse fate can befall a civil servant: life as a boulevard ranger, with assignment to a desk and computer screen. A terminal sentence. Certainly it's the same national park payscale, civil service requirements, and uniform allowance, though clothing suffers less from wilderness brambles and briars than from the shine caused by furniture rubbing against seats of pants.

But it's not all office work, Alice Allen assures me. She rushes to detail the park service's programs for the disabled, the elderly, and youth in trouble with the law. She explains how tired spirits are uplifted, cardiovascular efficiency improved, young delinquents steered away from a life of crime.

For a moment I'm caught up in the emotion of what she says; I too am a believer in the restorative power of nature. But then I think further: It is not that these goals are unworthy, it is that the park service is the wrong agency performing the wrong task in the wrong place.

"Who is your client?" I ask Alice Allen.

"Homeowners, bird-watchers, mountain bicyclists, inner-city youth—we call them user groups."

"It's not the land?"

She shakes her head slowly. "We're in the people business here."

"But you're the park service, not the people service. Somebody has to speak for the land."

"You can. You don't work for the government. You're all alone and unemployed."

AGAIN, SUSAN DROPS ME at a trailhead, but this time there's no trail; the last of the Backbone Trail, a stretch called Dead Horse Trail, has dead-ended at Topanga Canyon Boulevard. From here, I will rely on my intuition and orienteering skills, as well as maps provided by my friend Milt.

I unfurl the topos and trace for Susan the way the park service has planned the Backbone Trail. As planned, the Backbone will pass through native tall grass prairies and savannas, over yucca-covered slopes and through deep barrancas.

Not a bad plan.

Then I point out how I'd improve upon the route, following more of a ridge route to give hikers better ocean views.

Susan laughs. "You'd make a terrible planner. You're soooo *linear.*"

"Trails connect one place to another. Of course they're linear."

"Maybe in the nineteenth century, but not in our late twentieth. By the time the Backbone is built it will never reach all those beautiful places you described. Those places will be gone. I betcha anything the trail will be routed to avoid all the private property that the national park service will never acquire."

"How depressing."

"You've got to understand Cubist thought."

"Huh? You mean like Cubist art?" I try to remember Art History I. Picasso. Braque. Weird geometric shapes. People with isosceles triangles for noses.

"Cubists design things in abstract arrangements rather than attempting a realistic representation of nature."

"You're saying park service planners are Cubists?"

"They have to be. All they have to work with in the Santa Monica Mountains are little squares of land scattered here and there."

Again, Susan leaves me at a border, this one between the end of the old trail and the beginning of a new one. Perhaps I should be thinking of this adventure in more cosmic terms, but all I think about is how heavy my backpack has become. And I packed so light. Except for the water, that is. I'm distrustful of the quantity and quality of water in my home mountains.

I march over Henry Ridge through an oak woodland and across Topanga Meadows. Out of Hondo Canyon I climb up to Saddle Peak—at 2,825 feet hardly one of the great mountains of the world, but about as high as the home mountains get. There's no trail, but Milt's maps and directions are good.

Intersecting Piuma Trail, a short length of the Backbone Trail built by the national park service, I continue west. This on-again-off-again trail, with its gaps, is crazy. Many times I've hiked trails that began promisingly but petered out because of lack of funds or lack of use, but never have I tried to follow a path that starts, stops, and starts again.

A long day's journey brings me to Malibu Creek State Park, where I bivouac. The state park service built part of the campground on a Chumash burial site and the Indians protested in court. No spirits— except the spirit of tranquility—come to me during the night.

Next morning finds me up with the birds and hiking along Malibu Creek. Golden eagles and hawks soar above the rocky points, while ducks and blue herons patrol the waterway.

I take a look at The Gorge, one of the most dramatic sights in the Santa Monicas. Malibu Creek makes a hairpin turn through four hundred-foot volcanic cliffs, and cascades into aptly named Rock Pool. The *Swiss Family Robinson* TV series was filmed here.

Before land for Malibu Creek State Park was acquired, it was divided into three parcels belonging to Bob Hope, Ronald Reagan, and the Twentieth Century Fox ranch. I crest a hill and look down at Reagan's former ranch. Before Ronald Reagan purchased what was to become the most well-known ranch in the world—Rancho del Cielo in the Santa Ynez Mountains above Santa Barbara—he owned another spread in the Santa Monica Mountains. It was here, among the grand old oaks, that the former president's conservative political philosophy began to form.

During the 1950s, when Reagan hosted TV's *Death Valley Days,* he desired a more rural retreat than his home in Pacific Palisades. He bought the 305-acre ranch in the hills of Malibu as a place to raise thoroughbred horses. Land rose greatly in value, and taxes likewise; the tax increases really piqued Reagan and influenced his political philosophy. From this point on, he would be hostile toward government programs that required more and more tax dollars to fund.

Reagan's ranch boosted his political career in another way: it was the locale of many a barbecue and gathering attended by the well-heeled politicos who would support his gubernatorial campaign. When Reagan was elected governor in 1966, he moved to Sacramento, and sold his ranch to a movie company.

Leaving behind Reagan country, I follow the park's trails and fire roads to what was once the location of the exterior sets used by the *M*A*S*H* series. From here I continue on the Backbone Trail, exit the state park, and pass along the spine of the mountains, just below a place called Castro Crest.

Below the crest is a lovely trail descending a hillside spotted with laurel sumac and toyon, and meandering along a sycamore-lined creek to an inviting meadow. Here I camp in a bowl of giant rye. Rockrose frames a lovely panorama of Castro Crest, the tip-tops of the Santa Monicas.

The next day is a rough one, partly on the trail, partly off. My reward for the day's efforts is Zuma Canyon, where I make my camp in a ferny grotto near a little waterfall.

West of Zuma Canyon, Backbone Trail is a mess. The chaparral is so thick that I can't follow the route outlined on my topo maps and have to retreat to fire roads, even paved roads—Mulholland Highway and Yerba Buena Road. It's not difficult, but it is discouraging walking.

To the west beckons Sandstone Peak, highest in the Santa Monicas. It's only 3,111 feet high, but there's no mountain higher than the mountain in your memory. When I was a Boy Scout it seemed like the tallest peak in the world. I spent many a weekend running wild around the peak. The peak was part of the Scout's Circle X Ranch in those days; now it belongs to the national park service.

We scouts and our leaders, in an attempt to honor Circle X Ranch benefactor Herbert Allen, petitioned the U.S. Department of the Interior to rename Sandstone Peak. Our request for "Mt. Allen" was denied because of a long-standing policy that prohibits naming geographical features after living persons.

Not much has changed since I was a scout, I'm relieved to find as I hike up Mishe Mokwa Trail. The soft color of the high chaparral—black sage, golden yarrow, red shank, woolly blue curls—brings back memories as surely as a faded Kodachrome slide.

I note that, botanically speaking, the east side of Sandstone Peak is a strange place. Growing beneath the drought-resistant chaparral plants found along the trail are ferns. The opportunistic ferns take advantage of the shade offered by the chaparral and tap for what in the Santa Monica Mountains is a relatively generous water table located just below the surface. It's a strange sight to see—tough yucca and gentle ferns growing in close proximity on the same slope—a kind of botanical illustration of the Bible story about the lion lying down with the lamb.

My spirits lift as I continue down the trail. Unlike so many coastal scenes from my boyhood memory, this mountain scene is exactly the same as I remember it. Above me is a striking red volcanic formation, well-named Balanced Rock. And the oak-shaded path soon brings me to another aptly named rock formation—Split Rock. We scouts long had a tradition of hiking through the narrow split in the rock. I drop my pack and honor the tradition.

I look up at a pyramidlike volcanic rock we scouts called Egyptian Rock. Even the old outhouse—the historic four-holer—is still at the trail camp, where I bed down for the night. And the creek still flows, music to my ears.

At dawn I climb Sandstone Peak. I watch the sunrise extend its first tentative rays over the Los Angeles Basin, then light the easternmost peaks of the Santa Monicas. I see snow-capped, two-mile-high Mount Baldy towering over the city, Santa Monica Bay, Palos Verdes Peninsula, and Catalina Island.

Descending Sandstone Peak, I bushwhack down the west ridge of Boney Mountain, bound for Point Mugu State Park and the west end of the Santa Monicas. It's rough going, trailless. A remote wilderness it is. Maybe the Backbone Trail, maybe the California Coastal Trail, shouldn't come through here, I muse.

In the Boney Mountain Wilderness I cross trails—spiritually at least since there's no trail on the ground—with Chase, who had a tough time finding his way through this country: "When the trail had climbed to a height of fifteen hundred feet, there opened a still more striking landscape. Near by to the north rose the fine shape of Boney Mountain, its highest crags hidden in dragging mists. . . . More to the west, blue with summer haze, the wide valley stretched away to the Pacific, and between lay the expanse of rough brush hills through which I had to find a way."

Fortunately for Chase, he spotted a small farm belonging to old Jesus Serrano and his son Francisco. The dirt-poor Serranos offered Chase all they had—a bed in their tiny cabin, one of their fine home-made Spanish cheeses, and directions for getting back on the right trail.

In honor of Chase, in honor of the Serranos, I linger a long while in the sweeping grasslands of Serrano Valley. The valley is a beauty, as quiet a place as there is in the Santa Monicas.

Home sweet mountains.

NINE

Black Tide

THE OIL DIDN'T seem so black until the tide carried
it ashore.

From the bluffs above Santa Barbara, I watch in horror
through my Boy Scout field glasses as the oil slick advances
toward the beaches. Onshore, the flow is mixed with sand and
natural gas, which colors it brown. Offshore, it doesn't look so
dark, bathed in the soft south light of Santa Barbara. Every few
hours the slick grows, flowing north, then west, in a longish
hook-shaped streak stretching from Carpinteria to Goleta and
forty miles out to sea.

Five-and-a-half miles offshore, Union Oil Company's Platform A is hemorrhaging oil, a thousand gallons of crude an
hour. Mixed with natural gas, it boils out of the platform like
a cauldron, green and brown and bubbly.

But it's black as tar when it hits Carpinteria State Beach,
Summerland Beach, Biltmore Beach, and Miramar Beach. And
it's thick as tar when it hits East Beach, West Beach, Hendry's
Beach, and Goleta Beach.

I walk these beaches during the Time of the Black Tide,
extricating grebes from the goo and wondering what it all
means. All my life—well, all sixteen years of it that I had spent
near the shores of the sundown sea—I had taken for granted
the roar of the breakers, the soft whoosh of the water covering
the beach, the invigorating tang of the salt-seasoned breeze.
People, older people, people I always figured were lost in the
past, say you don't know what you've got 'til it's gone. And
now the breakers and the beach and the breeze are gone, at
least how I remembered them, along with the cry of the gull,
the mad burrowing of the sand crabs, the tidepools, and all
the creatures that lived at land's end. Gone are the seabirds that
skimmed the tops of the waves, gone are the shorebirds that
advanced and retreated with the waves. Hardly a cormorant,
a pelican or a loon alive, nothing but oil, oil, oil at the whim
of the wind and the tides.

I wander the shore, pulling birds, most dead, some alive, out
of the muck. The oil covers my hands, sticks to my sneakers,
spatters on my shirt and pants. But it isn't so much the feel of
the oil as the sight and smell of it. Especially the smell, the smell
of hell, fumes that catch in my throat, that make me cough and
choke and heave, dry heave because I've eaten nothing, can't eat
anything, not with birds dying screaming in my arms, not with
the black tide bringing ever more corpses to a shore that is itself dying. I gasp for air, every now and then walking away from
the shore to catch my breath, then returning to the bedarkened
beach and the tormented birds, feeling the pain of a world gone
black, the agony of creatures screaming in their death throes.
This is the look of hell before the Devil lit a match.

Lost in thoughts of 1969, I round Rincon Point and enter Santa
Barbara County. I walk the beach, a narrow strand, past the tiny community of Wave and wonder whether Wave was named for its proximity to the ocean or because people "waved" at the train going by.
Maybe they wave at the oil workers on the drilling platforms just offshore.

Between the shore and the Channel Islands are oil wells, lots of them. Although the waters immediately surrounding the islands are a marine sanctuary, the channel is filled with offshore oil wells, busily sucking up the drips and drops of crude that nature has ensconced beneath the sea floor. By day the drilling platforms are an eyesore, by night they appear as garishly lit ships forever at anchor. Day and night they are an omnipresent reminder to me of the 1969 oil spill that contaminated the mainland coast, and a suggestion of future havoc.

I walk over Carpinteria State Beach, what Carpinterians boast is "the safest beach in the world." Although the surf can be large, it breaks far out and there's no undertow. Safe this beach might be for humans, but it doesn't seem so safe from humans. Tar sticks to the bottom of my shoes, accumulating in big black wads. "Natural seepage," say the oil companies and Carpinteria boosters. I look accusingly offshore at the oil derricks and have my doubts.

Way back in '69, 1769 that is, the Portola expedition observed Chumash building their canoes here and dubbed the location Carpinteria, the Spanish name for carpenter shop. Spanish explorers noted that the natives caulked their canoes with asphaltum. The Carpinteria Tar Pits once bubbled up near the state beach. The year after Chase rode past Carpinteria on a dusty road, the tar was scooped up to pave the coast highway in Santa Barbara County. In order to dig the tar, workmen had to heat their shovels in a furnace; the smoking tar would slice like butter with the hot blade. The tar pits had trapped mastodons, saber-toothed tigers, and other prehistoric animals, and may have yielded amazing fossils like L.A.'s La Brea Tar Pits, but it became a municipal dump.

At the end of Carpinteria Beach, I do battle with the bottom of my shoes. I use a stick to scrape off the bigger chunks, then try to loosen the balance with some vegetable oil.

During the Time of the Black Tide, while capturing oiled birds for transport to the emergency bird treatment center at the Santa Barbara Zoo, I relearn the names of the shorebirds. My mother had taught me some of their names when I was seven, instructing me just as she taught her second-grade class

in San Diego. I recall the names as I search for survivors cast
ashore by the black tide. Gulls have curved beaks, terns straight
ones; gulls scavenge food on shore, terns plunge headfirst into
the water after prey. Mother's lessons come back to me as I pull
the blackened birds from the ooze.

"Distressed birds" are what the oil company officials in
charge of the cleanup tell me I'm supposed to be rescuing.
I walk the beach, discovering colonies of western grebes and
some of the smaller shorebirds—tiny sanderlings and plovers—
that are more than distressed; they're dead. I find gulls, godwits,
willits and curlews, ducks, murres, pelicans, and cormorants.
Most of them are dead.

The ideal candidate for rescue, I soon learn, is a bird just
sick, and slick enough from oil to keep it from running away.
The bird with a fighting chance is one that fights. It pecks at
you and you have to put a rubber band around its beak. If the
bird is too exhausted, too oil-soaked to move much, it probably
only has a few hours to live. When I spot a survivor, I try to get
between the bird and the water. If the bird flaps its wings and
can't fly away, that's good; I can usually catch it. If the bird flaps
like crazy and manages to move out of the muck, that's bad; the
bird will flee for what it believes to be the safety of the water,
flopping into the oil-covered sea and dying there from ingesting more oil.

The birds don't help themselves, can't help themselves, can't
stop doing what birds do. Cormorants, their usual white and
brown plumage black with oil, try vainly to clean one another
off with their beaks and succeed only in getting their beaks,
eyes, and the insides of their mouths clogged with oil. Gulls
and grebes too pick at their feathers, ingesting more oil, fatal
amounts of oil. And the ungainly pelicans stay shorebound for
a few days, but get hungry, and take flight, crashing into the
water in their usual clumsy manner, only to get mired in the
ooze, and sink from sight.

On a few beaches, Union Oil has established bird cleaning
sheds, and that's where I deliver the birds. Other birds I wrap in

towels and put in the back seat of my Dodge Dart, then transport them to the zoo.

In the evenings I help out at the zoo. We bathe the oily birds
in the best of modern chemistry, Polycomplex A-11; not a soap,
Union Oil tells us, but a nonsudsing dispersant that will remove
the bad oil but leave the natural oils, the birds' waterproofing,
intact.

We don't believe a word Union Oil tells us.

After we wash the birds, we rinse them, rewash them, rerinse
them, towel them dry, force-feed them vitamins and butter (the
latter to cleanse their insides of oil) and put them in pens under
heat lamps. It's quite a job and it takes two of us a half-hour to
clean up a single bird. At every step along the way, some of the
birds die.

And amidst the squawking screaming waterfowl come the
radio reports. Environmentalists are aghast. This is the ecological
shot heard 'round the world. The secretary of the interior says
he'll stop oil drilling. Then he'll re-start it, then he'll stop it
again. And the president of Union Oil shoots himself in the
foot when it's reported that he said he was amazed at the pub-
licity for the loss of a few birds. And then he shoots himself in
the other foot when he says he was misquoted and what he
meant to say was that relative to all the crime and murder in
Santa Barbara (in Santa Barbara!) the loss of a few birds was
insignificant.

We work into the night, cheering and jeering the radio,
comforting the birds and one another, wondering if the black
tide will ever recede.

I advance up the beach to misnamed Sandyland, where there's not
much sand. I walk atop a seawall next to some expensive houses. The
ocean crashes right against the wall. If there's a sandy beach around
here, I can't find it. As I walk the wall, a woman gets up from the lawn
chair on her deck and yells at me: "This is private property!"

"There's no beach to walk," I explain.

"Then come back at low tide or walk somewhere else."

I shrug and continue my trespass along the sea wall onto her neighbor's property. There's only so much indignation one can work up about the rich and their obsession with property rights. Ironically, in the case of Sandyland, it wasn't Mother Nature or the California Coastal Commission that affected their property rights, it was one of their fellow men of wealth. Elegant homes were built here during the early years of this century. All went well until Santa Barbara millionaire and yeast magnate Max Fleishmann wanted a place to put his yacht and furnished the money to build the Santa Barbara breakwater and harbor. The breakwater acted as a sandtrap, the ocean current south of Santa Barbara was altered, and many homes and much sand washed away from Sandyland and beaches to the south.

From Sandyland I hike to Santa Claus (where a giant Santa stands atop a restaurant), and past what locals hope will become President Bill Clinton's "Western White House"—a beach retreat rented by first-family friends in the movie biz. Then on to Summerland, which was not named for the good weather, but taken from spiritualist literature—something to do with the Second Heaven of Spiritualism. A century ago, spiritualists pitched their tents on the tiny lots in the area.

My thoughts return to the black tide when I spot a historical plaque on the Summerland bluffs telling me that in the waters here, the first offshore oil platform in the Western Hemisphere was erected in 1896. Soon more than three hundred wells were pumping oil from Pleistocene rocks at depths of one hundred to eight hundred feet, an insignificant depth by today's standards.

Oil attracted far more people to Summerland than Spiritualism did, and soon the air was heavy with the smell of gas and oil. It was said that free illumination came easy—one simply pounded a pipe in the ground until reaching natural gas and lit a match. The first night baseball, illuminated by natural gas lights, was played in Summerland. Liberty Hall, the spiritualists' community center, glowed with divine light and for a time Summerland was known as the White City.

Even reading Chase doesn't cheer me up. He seemed a bit bored by the coast and writes only of the little towns, of Summerland, "where a number of black and oily derricks built on wharfs are robbing Neptune of a long unsuspected asset," of Montecito, "a lovely expanse of rolling country sacred to millionaires," of Santa Barbara, "which fulfills her comfortable destiny, dozing among palms and roses beside the bluest of seas."

During the Time of the Black Tide, I watch the deployment of the full arsenal of American industrial might: boats, barges, airplanes, helicopters, miles of plastic and wooden booms, thousand of bales of straw, dozens of vacuum trucks, dump trucks, and bulldozers. A traffic jam of trucks threatens to sink Santa Barbara's Stearns Wharf. I watch men steam-blast the oil off the rocks of the harbor, killing the bacteria that eventually would have decomposed the oil; then the tide comes back in, coating the rocks again, and the men come back to steam-blast them again.

Operation Sea Sweep scouts the spill with submarines, bombs the spill with Corexit, and tries to cap the gushing wells with thousands of tons of drilling mud and cement. Men in uniform gather at command posts and are dispatched into the field by other men in uniform who are in turn ordered about by men in suits. To me, the newspaper pictures of all these men with all this machinery amidst all this desolation are astonishingly similar to the newspaper pictures of Americans struggling in another part of the world, in a place called Vietnam.

The Santa Barbara oil spill of 1969 brought me into the environmentalists' camp. And it radicalized this patriotic Eagle Scout, this all-American boy who confronted the unholy truth that oil was money and money was might and might was right.

I had seen with a boy's eyes the heart of darkness, the impotence of technology, a world out of balance, the callousness of the corporate state. And it radicalized me far more than the propaganda spewed by left and right, the power of the tube, the press, or rock 'n' roll. And when I became a man, the darkness of those Santa Barbara days stayed with me. I had grave doubts that I needed to go to Vietnam to defend the home shores.

Without a doubt, the spill was a hell of a conservation conscious-ness-raiser, yet twenty-five years after the blowout, as I stand and look out into the Santa Barbara Channel, a man now, I see Platform A still out there, a new well next to the old capped one.

The technocrats tell me that Platform A can't possibly blow again because, you see, the old well had a cement casing of only 238 feet deep and the new well has a cement casing of 808 feet deep. So it can't spill, they assure me.

And besides, even if it did spill again, progress in chemistry has given us better chemicals to wash the birds.

And the technocrats assure me that the oil tankers passing through the Santa Barbara Channel on their journey from the Gaviota Termi-nal to San Pedro are state-of-the-art. Not like the infamous single-hulled *Exxon Valdez* that fouled Alaskan shores, Santa Barbara's oil travels only in double-hulled tankers, so they can't spill, you see.

FROM SANTA BARBARA, it's pleasant beach walking to Goleta and Isla Vista and the University of California at Santa Barbara. Some horses gallop over the beach, reminiscent of Peter O'Toole and Omar Sharif's meeting in *Lawrence of Arabia* . . . except there's oil on this beach. I pass Deveraux Slough and march toward Ellwood Beach, scene of one of the more intriguing battles of World War II.

Around 7 P.M. Pacific time, on the evening of February 23, 1942, while most Americans were listening to President Roosevelt's fireside chat on the radio, strange explosions were heard near Goleta. In the first (and only) attack on United States soil since the War of 1812, a Japanese submarine surfaced off the rich oil field on Ellwood Beach, twelve miles north of Santa Barbara, and lobbed sixteen shells into the tidewater field.

Their marksmanship was poor. The unmolested, unhurried Japan-ese gunners were presumably aiming at the oil installations and the coast highway bridge over the Southern Pacific tracks. Tokyo claimed the raid "a great military success" though the incredibly bad marksmen managed to inflict only $500 worth of damage. The submarine disap-peared into the night, leaving behind air-raid sirens, a jumpy popula-tion, and lower real estate values.

Ellwood Oil Field isn't much to look at, or fight over—an old barnacle-covered oil drilling platform on the beach and a couple of wells
on the bluffs—but here the Japanese fired the shot heard 'round the
world . . . and missed. If only the Japanese knew then what they know
now: the way to conquer America is to sell us VCRs, TVs, stereos,
computers, cameras and cars, then lend us money to buy these goods,
and finally lend us more money to service the debt that we've accu-
mulated by spending too much and saving too little.

I beach walk on to Refugio Beach, where I spend the night in the
state park campground. It was at Refugio that Chase left the coast and
rode into the Santa Ynez Mountains that parallel Santa Barbara's east-
west-trending coast. He was bound for Mission Santa Ynez: "I wished
to see all of these relics of California's early days that lay near my
route, so finding here a road that crossed the mountains by way of the
Refugio Pass, I struck inland."

Chase camped at a schoolhouse; fished trout from a stream; and
heard the call of the dove and the moonlight hymn of the coyote.
Refugio Pass isn't so pastoral now, but it's considerably more famous—
home to what was for eight years Ronald Reagan's Western White
House, the most well known ranch in the world—Rancho del Cielo.

Like Chase, I want to get into the mountains, into the glorious
Santa Barbara backcountry, into the hundreds of miles of trail leading
through Los Padres National Forest. But not just yet. I want to first get
to Point Conception, that line marking the end of southern California, the beginning of central California. Climatically, geographically,
and sociologically, it can be argued that southern California ends at
Point Conception. I feel a great need to finish southern California and
walk on to a wilder coast.

In Chumash Indian legend, Point Conception is known as the
"Western Gate." The Indians believed that all land visible from the
point is sacred and disaster will befall anyone who disturbs the land.

No believers here.

Ten miles from Point Conception, just south of Gaviota Beach, is
the huge, futuristic-looking natural gas and oil processing facility.
Gaviota Terminal looks like a gigantic space station. Santa Barbara
Channel oil that's not tankered is shipped through the All American

(yes, that's its name) Pipeline to Texas Refineries. More oil is tankered from here through the turbulent waters of the Santa Barbara Channel to San Pedro.

When I finally reach Point Conception, after being threatened with arrest for trespassing by guards from the two ranches occupying the coast—Hollister Ranch (a residential community) and Bixby Ranch (a cattle ranch)—I want nothing more than to advance inland through the lovely Santa Ynez Mountains back of Santa Barbara.

TEN

Ranchero Country

TEN MINUTES up Tunnel Trail and my spirits soar. I leave behind both the red-tiled roofs of Santa Barbara and the coast. A low fog squats offshore, hiding the islands, the channel, the oil wells. Blasphemy it might be, but it feels good to take my leave of shore.

Tunnel Trail takes me into the Santa Ynez Mountains, part of a series of east-west ranges known as the Transverse Ranges, which encircle southern California from San Diego to Point Conception. The backbone of the Transverse Ranges is made up of the San Bernardino and San Gabriel Mountains back of Los Angeles, while the Santa Ynez Mountains form the uppermost, or most westerly, part of the Transverse spine.

A few million years ago, the Santa Ynez Mountains rose slowly from the sea. The mountains are apparently not secretive about their origin, because one can see their oceanic heritage displayed in a number of ways. Tilted blocks of sedimentary rock provide the first clue to the mountains' former undersea life. Fossils of sea animals give further testimony that the mountains were once many leagues underwater. Even the vegetation betrays the mountains' origin. The mineral-poor sandstone slopes formed in the ocean deep can support little more than dense brush, so it's the chaparral community—buckthorn, mountain lilac, and scrub oak—that predominates.

Tunnel Trail is so named because it passes the mouth of the tunnel leading from Gibraltar Dam Lake on the other side of the Santa Ynez Mountains, which supplies Santa Barbara with water. But I'm no fish so I will have to hike over the mountains rather than through them.

It feels good to follow a trail marked on a Forest Service map. A hot and sweaty journey it is up to Camino Cielo—the Sky Road. Except for my week of walking through the Santa Monica Mountains, I haven't had many steep hills to climb. My pack, laden with seven days of food and warm clothing, is much heavier than the one I carried along the coast. There aren't any burger stands or convenience stores in the Santa Barbara backcountry. Tunnel Trail crests at the top of the mountains, then descends to Matias Potrero, a small north slope meadow camp with a tiny creek. It's the former homesite of Matias Reyes, an old Chumash who used to cut and sell wood in Santa Barbara.

I reach the Santa Ynez River, more of a lazy creek than a river, then begin climbing again into a second range of mountains. Hidden Potrero Camp, Nineteen Oaks Camp, and a half-dozen more campsites, not on the map, beckon me to stay, but I feel energized, invigorated, and push on, along the Santa Cruz Trail and across Oso Creek, where I dip my canteen and have a sudden realization. This is the fist time, after more than four hundred miles of travel, that I've had such water, water free-flowing and sweet—water that's safe to drink! During my southern California coast walk I looked into the mouths of many rivers—the Tijuana, the San Diego, the Santa Ana, the San Gabriel, and the Ventura. And I looked into the mouths of a hundred creeks—Los Penasquitos, San Dieguito, Escondido, Aqua Hedionda, San Onofre, San Mateo, San Juan, Aliso, Muddy, Ballona, Solstice, Malibu, Little Sycamore, Buena Vista, San Ysidro, and many more. But these creeks and rivers, born wild in the mountains, were, alas, thoroughly tamed by the time they reached the ocean. Their waters had been muddied, sullied, and polluted. Their beds had been diverted, perverted, and blanketed with cement. Their mouths had been filled and bridged like bad dental work. No way did I want to drink out of the mouths of such creeks. Cement leaves a bad taste in the mouth.

I cross the face of Little Pine Mountain, through a meadow known locally as Mellow Meadows, so smothered with Indian paintbrush, poppies, and purple lupine that it looks landscaped. From the mountain is a fabulous view of the Santa Ynez Valley and Lake Cachuma, the Channel Islands, and the great blue Pacific. Distance has erased the oil platforms from view.

I stop for the night at Happy Hollow Camp, once a recreation site for Civilian Conservation Corps workmen, who constructed all the roads and trails in these parts. The name Happy Hollow is apt; the camp is indeed in a hollow, and I'm happy after gaining more than three thousand feet in six miles. The hollow traps the cold and I even find patches of snow, which I melt for my drinking water.

The next morning, I slow my pace to a stroll. There's so much to see. I saunter along Santa Cruz Trail through stands of pine, across a sandy, wooded wash, swampy meadowlands, and then two miles on a cliff-hanger trail. I shout at the mountain walls. "Joe!"

Joe! Joe! Joe!

Never could resist an echo. "You should have taken this trail!"

This trail! This trail! This trail!

This trail switchbacks steeply down to Santa Cruz Camp, the major entryway into the San Rafael Wilderness. The camp is situated on a meadow on the banks of Santa Cruz Creek. A little Forest Service station sits at the edge of the meadow, but it is unstaffed. Budget cutbacks, I suppose. After a swim in Santa Cruz Creek, I decide to call it a day.

NEXT MORNING, I head through the backcountry, through more rolling meadows. I march through the Roma Potreros camp at Flores Flat. Joe, the names on the land are all Spanish, just the way you like them. If you had come this way you would have met Leo Flores, who built a cabin here, raised cattle, and grew corn and watermelons. He irrigated his fields by digging an ingenious system of canals, which carried water to his fields from the creek. Flores even fished stray trout from his canals.

Near Flores' meadowland is Coche Creek. *Coche* means pig in Spanish and as the story goes, pigs escaped from ranches along the Santa Ynez River or were turned loose when hog prices were lower than the corn that fed them, and took up feral lives near Coche and Santa Cruz Creeks.

The trail deteriorates as I climb to Mission Pine Basin. A trail maintenance camp was established here in 1924, but I bet the trails around here haven't been maintained since. I relax under pines in Mission Pine Basin Camp and take water from Mission Pine Springs. The word *mission* is prevalent in these parts because legend has it that Jeffrey and sugar pine were logged from the forested slopes to construct the Santa Barbara mission in 1804. Sounds unlikely to me; how did the padres drag the trees down the mountain?

I had planned to exit the backcountry at the Cachuma Saddle Forest Service station, but I'm having such a pleasant stroll and I have two more days of food in my pack, so I duck down to Manzana River Narrows Camp, where I sit in the shade of the alders and laze about in the river. Now, this is the life. A wild life too. When I spot a bear print on the river bank, I string my food from a tree limb, look up at the stars, and give thanks.

Next day I head downriver, spot some deer, visit with some friendly backpackers and fishermen. Pleasant Manzana Trail, shaded by oaks and digger pine, descends to NIRA (National Industrial Recovery Act) Camp, named for the federal government program launched during the Depression. Part of NIRA was the creation of the CCC (Civilian Conservation Corps), the group that built most of the trails and camps in Los Padres National Forest and in other forests around America. I give silent thanks to the CCC boys and push on.

It's a long day going downriver. At nightfall I reach Manzana School House Camp. The camp and the turn-of-the-century schoolhouse are situated at the junction of Manzana Creek and the Sisquoc River. It might be a dramatic meeting of the waters after a winter storm, but the confluence by my camp, during this dry springtime, is more like a trickle meeting a mudhole—and the trickle and the mudhole have been fouled by livestock. The water is really grim and I wonder how much filtering and boiling will be required to render it fit for human consumption.

Next morning, feeling no ill effects from the awful water, I hike a few miles to a junction with Horse Gulch Trail. And here I'm at an impasse. One way out of the wilderness is by trespassing along the Sisquoc River through the Sisquoc Ranch. The other way out, through Horse Gulch, and via another thirty miles of trail, is impassable because of brush. These trails are on my Forest Service map, but my map is of 1968 vintage. Almost out of food and safe water, I decide to trespass.

I hike down a dirt road, past the remains of an old cabin, to the locked gate of the Sisquoc Ranch. I'm happy to see that the sign posted on the gate reads NO THOROUGHFARE rather than NO TRESPASSING. I figure NO THOROUGHFARE refers to vehicles, so I climb over the gate. Lovely old oaks shade the ranch road, which fords the Sisquoc River a dozen times. Not much life is evident along the river, just sand and rock in the riverbed, cattle standing motionless on the brown hills, plus clouds of flies and mosquitoes to plague me.

I have been warned by three experienced Santa Barbara hikers that the ranch foreman, popularly known as Banana Nose behind his back, will probably arrest me if he catches me. Still, as I hike along I pass plenty of cows but no cowboys. Not a living soul anywhere.

Seven or eight miles along, I ascend a small rise and get a pastoral view of the lower Sisquoc, checkerboarded with patches of green, irrigated oases on this dry land. I hike a few more miles, past houses and vineyards and reach the Sisquoc Winery. To my deep regret the tasting room is closed. I know I must be nearing this journey's end at Foxen Canyon Road and am silently celebrating when a pickup truck rolls up.

Uh-oh. I know by the proboscis who has stopped for a chat.

"This is private property," says the foreman. "I could have you arrested."

Jeez, what a schnoz.

"I said, this is private property," he announces a little louder.

"And beautiful property it is," I reply. "You must be very proud to be foreman of such a nice spread."

"Well, it's a good job, but . . . how did you know I was foreman?" My mind goes blank. Sun, dehydration, the long hike. All I can think about is this man's nose. It's not really banana-like; it's squashed and red, more like a bell pepper. Maybe I should offer him some of my No. 30 sunblock.

"Do I know you?" he inquires.

"Oh, they probably wrote to you about me," I fumble, dropping my pack and fishing out one of my California Coastal Trails Foundation cards.

"You're a long way from the coast," he says, squinting at the card.

"We had to go inland. Our coastal trail had a little trouble getting around the Hollister Ranch and the Bixby Ranch," I admit.

"Well, you're gonna have a helluva time getting around this ranch too, because you sure aren't going through it. Didn't you see the sign back there twelve miles? It said NO THOROUGHFARE. What did that mean to you?"

"I thought that just referred to vehicles."

"I oughta make you walk back the way you came, 'cept that would mean you'd trespass twice and you'd probably die on our land and we'd get sued by this . . ."—he looks at my business card—". . . this California Coastal Trails Foundation."

"Nice meeting you," I smile, shouldering my backpack. "I've got somebody to meet down Foxen Road."

"Hope it's somebody with more sense than you."

Another few minutes of walking brings me to a cemetery (probably filled with trespassers) and the junction with Foxen Canyon Road. Foxen Road is rich in history, I learn as I walk along it, extending my thumb to the few passing cars for a ride to Mission San Ynez. I spot a roadside plaque honoring Benjamin Foxen. When General John C. Fremont and the American Army invaded California and marched on Santa Barbara, the Californios (Spanish Californians) lay in wait for the Americans near the coast at Gaviota Pass. American sympathizer Benjamin Foxen led the general inland, through the Santa Barbara backcountry, thus avoiding annihilation and saving Santa Barbara from the Californios.

So there you have it. Improvise a trail at the right time in history and you're honored as a hero and get a plaque. Improvise a trail at the wrong time in history and you're threatened with arrest.

CHASE STAYED three days with hospitable Father Alexander Buckle at Mission Santa Ynez. In exchange for his keep, he took some photographs for the padre. He found the mission to be a warehouse of Spanish days gone by: candlesticks and ritual vessels, creaky corridors, parchment scores of church music with old square notes, records of births, deaths, christenings, and conversions in rawhide-bound books. His favorite discovery was a vast umbrella of yellow silk with which the padres shielded their shaven pates from the hot sun on their long marches. Quite the walkers, those Franciscans.

I find quite a different scene at Mission Santa Ynez, located on the outskirts of Solvang, an ersatz Scandinavian town that caters to tourists. Riding out of Danish Disneyland is a long procession of horsemen.

"Ride, Rancheros, ride!" shouts the crowd of a thousand gathered at the mission.

The riders, six hundred strong, belong to Los Rancheros Visitadores (The Visiting Ranchers), the largest private riding club in America, whose membership includes some of the wealthiest and most powerful men in California, indeed in America. I don't recognize any faces as the men ride by, but I do recognize some expensive horse-flesh when I see it. Some of the horses prancing by are worth more than a Mercedes.

Each May, when lupine and poppies blanket the Santa Ynez Valley, the Rancheros begin their weeklong ride through the gentle back-country of the Santa Ynez Valley, what locals in the 1980s dubbed Reagan Country, for the former president whose Western White House put this land on the map. The alfresco social season extends throughout the long California summer with a ride in Santa Barbara's Old Spanish Days Fiesta Parade. Sometimes fellow Ranchero Ronald Reagan invites some of the boys up to the ranch for a barbecue.

One of the few public appearances of the publicity-shy Rancheros is their gathering at Mission Santa Ynez on Day 1 of their ride. It's a spectacle that would bring tears to the eyes of any right-thinking American.

Placing their cowboy hats over their hearts, the corporados sing "God Bless America," then listen with bowed heads as the padres bless them.

The solemnity over, the Rancheros dismount and split gleefully for Solvang's nearby bars. I follow them into town, but as a would-be member of the paparazzi I feel at a distinct disadvantage. I don't watch much television, read *People* or *BusinessWeek.* How will I know a celebrity or Fortune 500 face when I see one? Wish these Rancheros wore nametags.

I barhop until I find a face I know. At least, I think I know it. It looks like—can it be?—a former secretary of the interior. Drinking beer with him at the booth are two clean-cut guys in western wear.

Slowly, I approach his table. "Having a good time?" I inquire.

"Six hundred of the finest guys in the world," answers the man-who-looks-like-the-former-secretary-of-the-interior. "A great outfit."

My mind races as I stare at him. Damned if he doesn't look different from the guy I remember in the newspaper photos and TV sound bites. He was always wearing a suit and tie for the photo opportunities and now he's clad in plaid shirt, jeans and cowboy boots. This man was in charge of our national lands?

"Is the whole California coast going to be leased by the oil companies?" I blurt out.

He looks at me quizzically.

Uh-oh. Maybe I got the wrong guy.

He smiles at his companions, who look like they'd like to invite me, as the guest of honor, to a necktie party, then turns to me. "I don't know. Find some of our boys in the oil business and ask them."

I'm still wondering who the hell I'm talking to when he and his buddies walk out the door. I slink over to the bar, order a beer. John, you yo-yo, why didn't you ask him if he was ever secretary of the interior?

As the beer cools my parched throat, I review what I know about this outfit of the greatest guys in the world. I've read up on this group, tracked them, made some discreet calls.

Los Rancheros Visitadores take their name from pre-Yankee California, when the Spanish dons held a celebration each spring about round-up time. The *vaqueros* rode with their neighbors from rancho to rancho and helped one another with the round-up and branding. Fiestas and barbecues were intermingled with the more serious side of California's first industry.

During the 1930s, this mixture of party and industry was reincarnated by wealthy Chicagoan John J. Mitchell, who married Lolita Armour of the meat-packing family and moved west to the Santa Ynez Valley where he bought a huge cattle ranch. "Rancho Juan y Lolita," as he called it, became home base for the southern California version of the Bohemian Club, whose idea of a party of powerful men in a beautiful setting seemed worthy of imitation. Instead of the solemn redwoods of the Bohemians, the Rancheros would camp in the Santa Barbara backcountry and use the horse as motif.

On the first ride in 1930, the men simply picketed their horses, gathered in a circle to sing songs, and enjoyed a nightcap. But the idea of becoming a "visiting rancher" for a week appealed to many a Captain of Industry and membership soared to a thousand. Celebrities such as Roy Rogers, Gene Autry, Bob Hope, Clark Gable, Leo Carrillo, and Tom Mix often joined the trek.

Ronald Reagan, who played many a western role in his pre-political days, sometimes rode with the Rancheros when he was governor of California. Today's Rancheros include judges, partners in the country's leading law firms, as well as very influential financiers and industrialists. Although Ranchero officials deny accusations that Rancheros are all men of wealth, their secret membership list is said to read like a "Who's Who" of the Fortune 500.

The Rancheros' week together is a busy one and is centered around a horseback ride from one private ranch to another in the Santa Ynez Valley. Some of the older Rancheros ride in a buckboard. Perhaps as a concession to the membership's age (RV's are an older group), the ride has been shortened in recent years and the stays in camp made longer. When the Rancheros do ride, it is through a Santa Ynez Valley that is rapidly changing. Great cattle ranches are being subdivided into suburban ranchettes. Under the influence of Ranchero

Brooks Firestone, tire magnate-turned-vintner-turned-California leg-
islator, much of the valley is planted with grapes, a pastoral counter-
point to the many oil wells working the land.

The men are divided into camps, sporting such Spanish names as
Los Vigilantes, Los Tontos (Bums), Los Bustardos, and Los Machos.
These Spanish names are as cherished as the Greek letters of a frater-
nity and many members brand their equipment with their camp
names: Los Chingadores use the raunchy "4Q" and Los Flojos (The
Lazy Ones) use "2N2P"—2 Lazy 2P. Eastern dudes gather in Los
Gringos, while teetotalers reside in Campo Seco (Dry Camp), and
L.A. Rancheros gather as Los Borrachos (The Drunks).

As I finish my beer, I wonder what influence the Rancheros have
on the vast environment of Rancho *Norteamericano,* on our California
coast. I decide that I too want to be, at least for a short time, a visiting
rancher. I purchase a cowboy hat in Solvang and make plans to crash
the party.

Just after sunset, I make my move. I know the roads and trails of the
Santa Ynez Valley pretty well and it's no problem getting to within a
quarter-mile of the Rancheros' campsite without detection. As I dip
into a creekbed, then slip from oak to oak, I get closer to the campsite
and am somewhat surprised at its size: there's not one camp, but a lot
of smaller ones—all the better to infiltrate, I figure. So far no land
mines, guards, or spiked trenches.

Plan A is to pretend I'm a Ranchero; Plan B is to pretend I'm one
of the many wranglers or hired help. But as I close to within seventy-
five yards of the camp and spot a man pissing in the bushes, a Plan C
comes to me: I'll piss my way in. If there's one thing a man will never
do to another man, it's bother him when he's pissing. Looks like the
Rancheros have restrooms nearby, but who wants to bother? We men
love to pee outdoors. Slowly, I move from tree to tree, closer and closer
to camp, pretending to drain my bladder.

I've picked a great time to visit. The boys seem to be returning
from dinner. Lots of movement, laughter. I pick up an empty beer can,
hold it like I'm part of the party.

Out of the corner of my eye, I see another one of the boys pissing.
I try to imitate him, one hand on my beer, one hand at my fly. Like

him, I draw out the process of elimination in the most manly way. First the fumbling at the fly and the tugging at the shorts, as though letting a bull out of a paddock, then the call-of-the-wild "ahhhhhhh," and the shaking of the organ as though it weighed several pounds instead of a few ounces. Then another, quieter yet more profound "ahhhhhh," and the gun is returned slowly to its holster.

My fellow pisser acknowledges me with a wave of his beer can. I walk the gap between us in my best bow-legged, just-got-off-my-horse strut.

"One thing about beer—you don't buy it, you rent it."

It's getting rather dark, but he seems to be a rather good-looking, close-cropped guy of about sixty. Like just about all the Rancheros, he's wearing a hat, plaid shirt, blue jeans, and cowboy boots.

I politely guffaw at his joke and add, "Sure goes through you, doesn't it?"

"Worse in the old days," he replies. "We did more ridin' and less sittin' around in camp. Drinkin' and ridin' isn't easy. You have to keep gettin' offa the horse. Then you say the hell with it, and try to piss from the saddle."

This guy's had a lot to drink, I figure, but he can hold his liquor.

"Who you hooked up with?"

"Bankin'. Not that I'm thinkin' business this week. What's your line?"

My mind spins. I can't tell him my line is writing lines. Too lowly for a Ranchero. "Publishing. *Forecast Magazine.* Not that I'm thinkin' about business this week."

"Met Malcolm at a dinner once. He was an optimist. Like me."

Oops, he thinks I'm connected with the late Malcolm Forbes' magazine. Well, no need to correct him.

"Know what I'd tell *Forbes* magazine? We're gonna win!"

"What?" He's getting louder and I look anxiously about.

"The damned media are so negative. They say we can't compete, that we make shitty stuff, that we're gettin' our asses kicked by the Taiwanese, the Ko-reans, and the Japanese. Bullshit! All the Japanese can do is imitate us. They're never gonna be leaders like us. Know why?"

"Why is that?"

"Because we've got balls. We've got *cojones,* balls, man. We got 'em; the Japanese don't." His arms sweep the camp. "And we've got this."

"This?"

"This land! The camp, the ride, the boys!"

"Six hundred of the best guys in the world!" I add enthusiastically.

"No shit." He staggers off toward the lights of the camp. "How can we lose?" he shouts at the stars.

As night rolls in like a black tide, and I hike back to my camp, I wonder how to answer that question.

ELEVEN

Homage to Chaparral

THE SUN IS STRONG, the trail faint, and we are up to our hats in chaparral. "I think," Bob McDermott says hesitantly, swinging his machete at the six-foot-high ceanothus in the middle of our path, "we're still on the trail."

We are bushwhacking north up Horse Gulch in what seems at the moment to be a futile attempt to locate a thirty-mile-long missing link in the California Coastal Trail. The link we're seeking is not a new trail, but a very old one, now desperately overgrown with chamise, ceanothus, fremontia, manzanita, scrub oak, and yucca—the shirt-sleeve-shredding community of life called chaparral. Beneath our boots faint traces of Horse Gulch Trail can be discerned, but chaparral has grown over the trail in a three-foot-high canopy, compelling us to alternately crash through the brush or crawl on all fours through it, in either case taking an awful beating from the horns, the thorns, and thick, leathery leaves.

Actually, my friend McDermott (trail coordinator of the California Coastal Trails Foundation) and I came to this remote section of the

Santa Barbara backcountry for flagging; not flogging. Equipped with lengths of blue ribbons, we are supposed to be flagging the trail—that is, tying the plastic strips onto bushes for the purpose of enabling hikers with fewer pathfinding skills than us to stay on the trail. As the brush gets thicker, however, our flagging becomes motivated not so much by the *noblesse oblige de hiker* as another reason: The flags will prove invaluable if we're forced to abandon this expedition and find our way out of this godforsaken place.

Jim Blakley is the party responsible for our immersion in Horse Gulch. He's a contentious, square-jawed Scoutmaster of a man, who has spent many of his sixty-five years gaining an encyclopedic knowledge of Los Padres National Forest trails. Blakley is chairman of a Santa Barbara organization called CRAHTAC (County Riding and Hiking Trails Advisory Council) and a man obsessed with walking and talking trail.

In the "war room" of his home, an 8 by 10 den chock-full of trail dispatches, maps, and aerial reconnaissance photos, he outlines our expedition: McDermott and I are to depart the Sisquoc River at the mouth of Horse Gulch at 0600 hours, proceed up-gulch, ascend the south fork of Roque Canyon, bushwhack up this canyon to its junction with Kerry Canyon, follow the Indian Trail then the Willow Spring Trail to Highway 166 where, hopefully, three days later, a cold beer and a car will be waiting for us.

Blakley stresses the importance of our mission. "This is a vital link in the Trans–Santa Barbara County Trail."

"And a crucial link in the California Coastal Trail," McDermott adds.

My job is to describe this stretch of trail and the harsh land through which it passes. Judging from the grim expression on Blakley's face, it is harsh country indeed.

"We're not the first ones to recognize the importance of this trail," Blakley lectures. "From the turn of the century, foresters were aware of the need for this route and in 1909 construction began. The trails were maintained and used until the war."

"Vietnam?" I ask.

Blakley grimaces. "World War II."

"Has anyone used the trails in the last fifty years?"

"Bears," declares Blakley. "They're the only ones who can stand pushing through the brush. I've done about 80 percent of the route. The chaparral is brutal. Impassable."

"I like chaparral."

Blakley's big square jaw drops and he stares at me as if I were poison oak. A silence fills the room and it becomes apparent I have committed a trailblazer faux pas of mountainous proportion.

"You'll hate it after this trip," he replies.

Now that my vegetal preference is out of the closet, I feel obligated to defend myself. "The yucca blossoms. . . ," I fumble. "The clouds of blue and white ceanothus, the beautiful manzanita . . ."

I'm given a map and handshake and shown the door.

"Good luck, brush lover," Blakley says, shaking his head in warning. "People go crazy out there."

People do go crazy out here. As we beat through the brush, we spy Wheat Peak, named for Hiram Preservid Wheat, an 1890s homesteader from Wisconsin who, it was said, had the power to heal with his hands. Hostile natives were so impressed by the spiritual theatrics of this white man that they inscribed his wagon with a sign indicating he was to be granted protection.

We, too, are feeling like a couple of wild and crazy guys as we buck the brush in Horse Gulch. Black sage is the most powerful of antihistamines, and after sneezing our brains out, we have become thoroughly intoxicated with the smells of chaparral and spring. Crush a sprig of sage between thumb and forefinger and you release that characteristic odor meaning chaparral country: tortured sandstone formation, warm, dry winds tickling the skin, a coyote in the bush, a condor in the heavens.

We fight our way through those thickets daring to stand in our line of march. We scorn to admit any brush is too thick for us to get through. On occasion, we lie down on our bellies and worm under the thickest clumps. Sometimes one of us smashes through and the other follows on his heels, tying ribbons on the vanquished brush to mark our progress. The brush is awarded the ribbons of honor, but we feel deserving too.

We practice different bushwhacking techniques. Although a gentle man by nature, McDermott's Army training reasserts itself and he marches through rather than around the brush. He punches out the bushes with a one-two combination of macho and machete. My technique is more evasive and skin-saving. Emulating a tailback, I straight-arm the opposition, and with legs pumping, let my forward momentum carry me through. If I'm about to be ensnared, I spin, pirouetting through the limbs of would-be tacklers. This technique works splendidly with chamise, ceanothus, and sage, but I meet my match with scrub oak. Dancing along, I'm stopped in my tracks by what seems to be the entire defensive line of the Los Angeles Raiders; suddenly the ground disappears from under my boots. A branch grabs my backpack and I'm suspended in midair. I struggle to free myself but am caught fast, like a side of beef on a meat hook. Bob frees me with his machete.

We struggle out of Horse Gulch with increased respect for the hardy heather. Crossing over to the south side of La Brea Canyon on washed-out trail, we meet my old nemesis, a plant repelling any bushwhacking technique, poison oak. I cringe, thinking of how often these glossy, three-lobed leaves have blistered my skin. Alas, the body builds up no immunity to poison oak; in fact, dermatologists believe the more you get poison oak—or poison oak gets you—the less resistance you have to future encounters with the plant's toxic oil, urushiol. I agree with the dermatologists. After a dozen doses in as many years, my skin has become a magnanimous host.

While McDermott charges through the poison oak, I decide discretion is indeed the better part of valor and attempt to sweep the nasty bushes aside with a stick and crab sideways down the trail. The sap is most toxic in spring, I remember. If I wasn't so allergic, I'd consider this member of the sumac family a pretty plant. Poison oak is particularly conspicuous in fall when its leaves turn a flaming crimson or orange. However, color is more a response to heat and dryness than season; its "fall color" can occur anytime in California. Here in La Brea Canyon the leaves on some plants are turning yellow and red while the majority are putting out green leaves.

Mind over matter. I will not get poison oak. I will not get poison oak.

McDermott watches my gyrations. "You're not allergic are you?"

"Sadist!"

It's hopeless, the poison oak is unavoidable. I feel like a condemned man. Forty-eight hours until the itching begins. How shall I treat it this time? Lukewarm baths with baking soda? Dips in the ocean? Oatmeal skin-packs? A mugwort poultice? Cortisone injections?

Hiawatha Camp brings an escape from the poison oak, an end to a long day. Brush has all but overgrown this abandoned campsite on La Brea Creek and we work hard to clear the fire ring and flatten out a tent site.

Longfellow's poem *The Song of Hiawatha* inspired our camp's name, though I really don't know why. The banks of anemic La Brea Creek are hardly the legendary shores of Gitche Gumee. If chaparral grew in the great North-Land, Longfellow did not sing its praises.

And beyond them stood the forest,
Stood the groves of singing pine trees,
Green in Summer, white in Winter,
Ever sighing, ever singing.

No singing pine trees around here, only smoky, blue twilight settling over a 360-degree panorama of chaparral. Sarcasm, homesickness, or perhaps a lack of perception prompted an anonymous Forest Service–camp namer to immortalize this site as "Hiawatha."

Much of the chaparral problem (yes, there's a problem and it's serious) is one of perception. California is a state of immigrants, who often bring their provincial floral biases to the Chaparral Belt. Transplanted Easterners are particularly unappreciative of chaparral. Every time they venture into nature they expect Hiawathaland: lush meadows, singing pine trees, bubbling brooks. They are forever comparing chaparral to a "real forest" with chaparral inevitably getting the short end of the botanical stick.

On the surface of things, it must be conceded that chaparral lacks the aesthetic appeal of an eastern hardwood forest. California's sun is a thirsty one and for more than half the year, chaparral at close range appears to be a pale brown mass of shriveled herbage. But look closer at this brown, for it's a very special and beautiful brown, unique to California. The brown of California's backcountry and the brown of the East's backwoods are completely different. Here little snow or rain rots the herbage or drains away its vitality. Chaparral grows ripe and aromatic, bursting with a life that has not been diluted, blanketing slopes and canyons with the effect of bear fur, so that it seems this sun-kissed country has the yielding surface of a living creature. The brown of California is the brown of regeneration; not decay.

It's going to be a cold night. In chaparral country, the temperature often drops fifty degrees from high noon to dawn and sometimes plummets from 100 degrees at midday to the 20s at night. We spread a tarp on the ground and sit next to our small brushfire. We won't unroll our sleeping bags until bedtime; we want to save the day's warmth inside them. Our tuna surprise bubbles over the low flame. (Bob will not tell me what he added to the tuna, noodles, and powdered cheddar cheese substitute. "It's a surprise," he says.)

The night fills with stars. The brush that hides the earth does not obstruct our view of the heavens. Orion's Belt arcs over the San Rafael Wilderness. The Milky Way pours down upon Hurricane Deck.

I throw a manzanita branch onto the fire. Even chaparral's critics have to admit it burns well. One need not be a pyromaniac, merely a chaparral admirer, to enjoy a burning bush. I observed a recent brushfire in these mountains, a few miles above Santa Barbara. Truly an inspiring sight! Fire doesn't race across chaparral: it moves steadily, making a clean sweep. The thick leaves distill their oil in hissing sheets of white flame. Sometimes the flames leap from bush to bush like a forest fire, but more often as one bush burns, the flame dies down as the fire creeps through the ground litter. The heat of the burning litter ignites the lower branches of the next bush and it too flares up.

Many chaparral plants choke out the growth of other vegetation, even their own kind. The arid climate slows the recycling of dead material into the soil, so nature must find another method to clean house: fire. Dead buckwheat, fallen yuccas, and tinder-dry chaff of all kinds accumulates and is cleaned out by fast-moving brushfires. Contrary to what television reporters say while standing near smoldering hillsides, fire is actually a beneficial pruning process. After a fire, there's prompt revival. Brushfires move rapidly and seldom damage root systems. Within a few weeks, using stored ground water, plants send green shoots above ground. Some chaparral seeds, like those of ceanothus, require the heat of fire to crack their coating, thus allowing them to germinate after the next rain.

Winter showers bring spring flowers to fire-cleared areas. Owl's clover blossoms early in spring and later in the season, yellow, orange, and red monkey-flowers dot the hills. (The petals viewed head-on resemble a monkey's face. Each flower, like each primate, has a different expression.) Mountain lilac covers the slopes with a veil of white and blue. Golden California poppies and yellow Mariposa tulips add to the riot of color.

I stir the dying embers of our own little fire and, with the help of a little firelight and a lot of starlight, find my sleeping bag. Far away, a coyote howls at the sliver of moon suspended low on the horizon. My Polargard cocoon radiates its stored warmth. My belly gurgles contentedly at the half-digested tuna surprise (the "surprise" was that it was edible—McDermott's cooking usually is not).

A no-nonsense sunrise. A low yellow flare in a cloudless sky. I struggle into cold boots and shuffle up the hillside into dawn's light. As it warms the land, I'll follow the sun back downslope to camp and breakfast. I take charge of the morning meal; McDermott's the only one I know who can burn instant coffee.

I can never tell direction by the sun in these mountains. The sun always seems to come up the wrong way. The mountains extend east-west, meaning as I hike up-state along this stretch of the California Coastal Trail, the sun sneaks up behind me. "Up the coast" in other parts of the world is taken to mean north, but it's not north in the Santa Barbara backcountry; it's west toward the sundown sea.

Time to inspect the forest. I refer to the elfin forest all around me, a million acres protected by the Los Padres National Forest, and including the San Rafael Wilderness, the first wilderness area in America set aside under the Federal Wilderness Act of 1964. "San Rafael is rocky, rugged, wooded, and lonely," remarked former president Lyndon Johnson when he signed the San Rafael Wilderness Bill on March 21, 1968. He was right on three of four counts: rocky, rugged, and lonely. Not very wooded though. Ninety percent of the wilderness, in fact ninety percent of the Los Padres, is chaparral. Did the president, did Congress, did anyone know the homage they were paying to chaparral?

"I believe that it will enrich the spirit of America," declared Johnson. Enriching my spirit is a helluva lot of chamise. This gray-green bush is the most prolific member of the chaparral belt and probably the most common plant in California. Eight percent of California vegetation is chaparral, and 75 percent of chaparral is chamise. It's not thorny, but has stiff, leathery leaves that lash the trespasser. From the summits of the coastal mountains, it sweeps down to the sea, an impassable three- to eight-foot-high barrier.

Chamise may also be the most dangerous plant in California. It doesn't burn, it explodes. A curse to firefighters, it lives up to its common name, greasewood. Chamise thickets burn with intense heat, like a grease fire, sending up huge clouds of black smoke.

One would think that a plant as common as chamise would be ignored, but Native Americans, a practical people, used it for medicine. Oil from the leaves was rubbed on skin infections. Chamise tea by the gallon was supposed to cure syphilis, as well as tetanus and rabies.

Chamise may be the most populous, but ceanothus, with its blue spikes, is the showiest chaparral shrub, at least in spring. Often called California lilac, this three- to twelve-foot-high evergreen blossoms with clouds of blue, white, or lavender flowers. About twenty different species of ceanothus grow in California, with the Bigpod and Wartleaf varieties predominating here in the Santa Barbara backcountry. You have to be a good botanist to tell one species from another.

Toyon can also be a showy plant, but not in spring. Also called Christmas berry, it features large clusters of bright, red berries and dark green leaves. The berries, which look like miniature apples, appear about Christmastime. Toyon is also called California holly. This last name was given to a certain southern California city where movies are made.

Like chaparral flora, chaparral fauna is not, at first glance, particularly noble. It's doubtful any of the TV nature shows will ever stalk the beechey ground squirrel, brush rabbit, or California Pocket mouse. Chaparral reptiles such as the Coast horned lizard and Western fence lizard engender little human interest, nor do typical invertebrates like the ceanothus silk moth and hedgerow hairstreak.

Contributing to chaparral's anonymity are its characteristic birds, the scrub jay and rufous-sided Towhee, which are neither the most brilliantly colored, nor the most majestic denizens of the air. And the wrentit, whose distinctive call—an increasingly rapid cadence of notes on a single pitch—has given it the appellation, "voice of the chaparral," cannot be said to be the most musical songster.

Me, I prefer the call of the California gray quail, another familiar voice of the chaparral. The East Coast quail, usually known as the bobwhite, calls "bobwhite, bobwhite." Here in the West, the quail speak Spanish: "*Cuidado, cuidado.*" Take care, take care.

Though often as dull-colored and unassuming as their habitat, chaparral animals earn grudging admiration for their ability to survive in this land of little water or shade. It's a shame no filmmaker is rushing forward to film a chaparral cinema verité documentary, for animals of the brush have hunting, burrowing, and mating habits as fascinating as the residents of any other wild kingdom.

Descending sandstone slopes back to camp, I pass a plant whose armaments make other chaparral plants seem almost weaponless in comparison. This hostile native presents a formation of fixed bayonets, thrust upward and outward, each yellow-green blade narrowing to a deadly, needle-sharp point. The stalk rises high above the neighboring bush and blossoms with clusters of creamy white, delicately scented flowers. The plant, more often associated with desert rather than chaparral environments, is a member of the lily family. Whipple Yucca and Our Lord's Candle are two of its common names. Like a trained soldier, the yucca always seems to occupy a strategic position atop a ridgeline or rocky outcropping. This strategy accents its steadfast beauty.

Despite its self-possessed and uncompromising appearance, the yucca is dependent on a tiny moth for the survival of its species. The Pronuba, or Yucca Moth, and the yucca have evolved over the ages a remarkable mutual aid society, vital to the survival of each. The female moth pays a nocturnal visit to the yucca flower when the flower's ready to be fertilized, gathers pollen in her mouth, then, using her ovipositor, pricks the ovary of the flower. The moth's larvae, as they grow, feed upon the developing seeds, eating only enough of them to grow to maturity and leaving the rest, allowing the yucca, aided by chaparral winds, to scatter its kind. In exchange for this prenatal care, the moth does a favor for the yucca. While entering and exiting the yucca flower, the moth—by cosmic accident or divine intent?—deposits the gathered pollen in the plant's pistil, thus achieving pollination.

Also within sight are several stunted versions of the oak tree called scrub oak. On the southern, or warmer, slopes these squat trees rarely grow taller than man-sized, but often exceed ten feet on the northern, or cooler, hillsides. It's one of the most water-conserving members of the community. During the heat of summer, scrub oak leaves discharge a waxy substance to prevent evaporation. The leaves also curl downward like upside-down spoons to offer less leaf surface to the sun.

To Spanish settlers, scrub oak looked like a plant from back home and that gave it the name *chaparro*. The territory where *chaparro* grows we now call chaparral, and that is why cowboys wear chaps.

No chaparral inventory would be complete without mentioning woolly blue curls, a bush with elaborate clusters of two-lipped, blue-purple flowers covered with a dense purple wool; Fremontia, ornamenting the brushland with its dark evergreen leaves, yellow flowers, and bristly thistles; aromatic lemonade berry, which guided early California farmers to plant citrus, because where lemonade berry survives the winter, so will lemons and oranges; California buckwheat, host to a zillion bees; and mountain mahogany, king of the mountain, its short hardwood trunk, leathery leaves, and dense profile helping it survive on windswept slopes where nothing else will grow.

So much for the morning inspection. Except for the yucca, which stands head and shoulders above the rest, chaparral plants are a communal lot, life crowded upon life in the humus-poor soil. I have described chaparral as a forest, and it is a forest; despite its Lilliputian appearance, it functions like any other, catching and conserving water, stabilizing slopes, sustaining wildlife. Still, the Los Padres is considered one of America's most worthless national forests. Those areas not smothered in chaparral consist of barren sedimentary rock, testifying to this land's former undersea life. The elfin forest defies all human endeavor. We can't log it, farm it or ski down it. Chaparral country boasts no boatable lakes, few fishable streams, and virtually no extractable minerals. It is a Tom Thumb forest, unharnessed by the titans of industry. It is undoubtedly a harsh land, wild and worthless, a frontier that can be pushed back but not conquered.

The diversity of life around me this morning prompts me to make a silent vow. Never again will I write another sentence in a trail guide like, "The trail ascends through thick brush." I shall, in the best tradition of green prose, be descriptive, celebratory, maybe even poetic.

I think that I shall never see a
Poem as lovely as manzanita.

Well, maybe not poetic. It's tough rhyming lines when branches are tangling the legs. This morning we meet lots of manzanita, varying in size from low, prostrate shrubs to woody trees. Its branches are a handsome maroon and now, in spring, flowers hang from them in clusters of tiny pink-and-white bells. This bush is so prevalent in the Santa Barbara backcountry that we really ought to name at least one mountain range the Manzanita Mountains.

The manzanita envelops our trail in jungle-like growth, but there's nothing lush or yielding about this jungle. The stiff branches part unwillingly as we press through, then snap back, their broken points flicking like switchblades. McDermott and I agree that it would be easier cutting through the Amazon.

There are said to be sixty-eight paths to Heaven, but one is the true way. As we bushwhack along the bottom of Roque Canyon, we often mistake a gap between bushes for the trail, or a narrow gully where rainwater has scarred the land for the true path. We tack back and forth through the bush, marveling at how ingeniously this trail utilizes

little ravines, sandstone ledges, hogback ridges, and dim vestiges left by
the lower animals.

Tying blue ribbons to the bushes is the only way we can sign this
path. "Monumenting" or "ducking"—that is, piling rocks atop each
other (the favored technique in the High Sierra)—is impractical here
in the bush; rarely can a hiker see more than twenty feet ahead. Blaz-
ing trees with an ax is out of the question: there are no trees worthy of
the name to blaze. So we continue beating around through the brush,
leaving a thin blue line over God's gray earth.

Bless the brown bears. If the Forest Service has abandoned Trail
30W04, the bears have not. Tufts of fur clinging to the bushes show
where they have forced themselves through. Since the rangers stopped
ranging here, a few dozen bears have inherited all responsibility for
keeping this trail open.

Few Californians realize the contribution bears have made to our
civilization. Old bruin designed many of the best trails, speeding ex-
ploration and settlement of the state. One reason bears are such good
trailmakers is because they're somewhat lazy and hate to expend un-
necessary energy in traveling to places. And they hate to go down
steep hills, I suppose because their forelegs are so short. They are,
therefore, skilled in choosing the best route through the mountains,
and once having made the choice, sticking to it, until they've worn a
smooth path. The old prospectors used bear trails to get over passes,
and many of today's best recreation trails are superimposed over the
prospectors' trails, picked out by bears long ago.

I wish more bears used this trail. I'm no scatologist, but the bear
scat around here doesn't look very fresh. Do you bears bother with a
winter hibernation in the chaparral zone? Well, it's springtime now.
No excuses. No lollygagging around the cave. Get out here and walk
the trails. Don't you know federal trail maintenance funds have been
drastically reduced?

As I bushwhack along, I worry that without good trails, few people
will take the trouble to visit California's great brushland and prejudice
against brush will continue unabated. This prejudice is long-standing.
Even John Muir, who usually had a good word for every scenic Cali-

fornia vista, complained about hiking through chaparral: "The slopes are exceptionally steep and insecure to the foot and they are covered with horny bushes from five to ten feet high."

Californians don't wait until they are in the backcountry to express their prejudice, they do so in the city. Consider how many California motels, coffee shops, and boulevards are named "Redwood" or "Palm." Now try to recall anything named Scrub Oak. Barberry? Bladderpod? Fremontia? Hundreds of shops and restaurants are named "Lake" or "Forest" or "Seashore," but with the exception of the Chaparral Lounge in Ventura, I've never encountered a business honoring the stuff. The very name chaparral is a no-no. Nursery workers, gardeners, and landscape architects substitute the terms "drought-tolerant land-scaping," "native flora," and "Mediterranean shrubbery."

Enough kvetching about chaparral; it's quite able to take care of it-self. The plants thrive on abuse. Phylum Masochistum. When California's out-of-state water supply is cut off, only chaparral will survive. When exotic pests like the gypsy moth and Mediterranean fruit fly attack the green world, only chaparral will survive. Probably after a nuclear war, only chaparral would survive, though I suppose no one would be around to confirm my hunch.

Thoughts of cold beer put a spring in our step and we forget our torn shirts, our indecently split seams. "We haven't seen a human in three days!" I shout.

McDermott laughs. "The Forest Service bureaucrats call this 'dis-persed recreation.' I think that means nobody's crazy enough to come here."

We journey on over the crumbling sandstone, through a prism of tertiary colors—the violet, olive, and amber hues of the arid heartland. Our nostrils embrace the hot, dry perfumes. Our eyes contemplate the desiccated beauties, our ears fill with the hum of bees and the chirrup of locusts. And the warm California sun embalms it all in a peaceful forgetfulness.

A hiker's mind is most selective and mine is no exception. Already memory is washing away the more unhappy landscapes full of plants only a botanist could love, retaining a single idyllic image—a vision of brush-covered slopes bathed in amethyst during that magical time at day's end the poets call "owl's light." I will forget, until my next journey to this land, that chaparral is one of the most formidable obstacles on the planet: too thick to crawl through, too low to crawl under, too high to climb, too short to provide any shade.

Memories, however imperfect, are all you can take from this frugal land. Chaparral even defeats your best efforts at photography. You can frame a High Sierra peak in your camera's viewfinder, but these mountains of brush sprawl to the horizon, row upon row extending into an azure infinity, overflowing the widest of wide angle lenses. Your eye can't hold it all. Only your heart can.

TWELVE

Brave New Forest

Pathfinding is essentially an aesthetic, intuitive process.
—Thomas J. Peters and Robert H. Waterman, *In Search of Excellence*

THE OUT-OF-SHAPE Forest Service mules sweat and snort as the trail switchbacks up and out of American Canyon and enters Machesna Mountain Wilderness. Halting his train of six mules, Ranger Bob Stone savors a wondrous panorama, one like those that greeted Spanish *vaqueros* during the days of the great ranchos. Oaks dot rich rolling grassland, a landscape painted in soft greens, golds, and browns. A solitary bull keeps watch over a dozen cows. Above the trail is a ridgeline where Coulter pine touch the sky. Below rise the headwaters of that famous "upside-down" river, the Salinas, of which American Canyon Creek is a tributary.

"Now this," Stone declares, gesturing to the magnificent view of pastoral California, "is excellence."

Excellence is something very much on Stone's mind. Los Padres National Forest management is on "a search for excellence," which means employees are strongly urged to participate in seminars adapted from the bestselling book some years back, *In Search of Excellence,* by Thomas J. Peters and Robert H. Waterman. The Forest Service is attempting to take on a new image, one more like a dynamic corporation than a sluggish bureaucracy. Motivational seminars are only part of its new look. In the Forest Service's search for excellence, the traditional managers of public land—the old-time rangers such as Bob Stone—are giving way to computer experts and planners schooled in the latest corporate techniques. The from-the-saddle surveys preferred by Stone are rarely made anymore; a ranger's seat-of-the-pants judgment is being replaced by a Forest Service computer program called Forplan, which calculates how public lands are to be used and allocates resources according to mathematical formulas. Cattle-grazing, for example, is figured in AUMs (animal unit months) and trees in terms of MBF (million board feet).

Even the language of the modern ranger is changing: today it is sprinkled with acronyms, computer jargon, and catchwords. *Values clarification* is a phrase currently in vogue. A recent Toward Excellence session revealed that many Forest Service employees were uncertain about the exact nature and purpose of the jobs—so a Values and Norms Workshop has been scheduled. The trouble is, Stone, after three decades with the Forest Service, figures he has his values straight and is less than thrilled about cutting short his Pine Spring Camp clean-up expedition and California Coastal Trail research in order to rush back to Goleta to watch videotapes titled *Looking at Barriers* and *What You Are Is Where You See,* or to participate in an exercise called "Values I Seek in an Organization." "If the Forest Service doesn't know its values after ninety years, God help us," he grouses.

The pursuit of values clarification and the search for excellence are of more than academic interest. As the Forest Service seeks to change its image, it is also planning for its future. Hanging like a low cloud over Machesna Mountain and American Canyon—and over all 1.8 million acres of Los Padres National Forest—is the "Land and Resource Management Plan." This massive document—accompanied by an equally massive environmental-impact report and enough maps and charts to fill a saddlebag—establishes the management direction for Los Padres for the next half century. Every national forest is undergoing the same process. The Los Padres plan lists seven detailed scenarios for how the land could be used. Whether the Forest Service chooses to fill the ridge tops with oil wells or set aside great tracts for wilderness depends a great deal on the kinds of values it chooses to embrace—those of fast-track young planners or off-the-beaten-track old rangers.

Bob Stone, a thirty-six-year veteran of the Forest Service, is one of the last of the old-timers. A beard, growing gray, half covers a face weathered from a lifetime spent outdoors. He's the kind of guy who sits tall in the saddle, cusses mules, and tips his hat to ladies. He knows a couple hundred people and an equal number of horses on a first-name basis. He's fought fires, treed and tagged mountains lions, and may be one of the last rangers who can tie a diamond hitch.

When I told Stone about my walk, the California Coastal Trail, he offered to show me the country, his country, the San Luis Obispo County backcountry. And when I complained about the difficulty of crossing all that private property along the coast, he offered an alternative journey through the coast ranges, which are in the public domain. His domain. He's patrolled these ranges for many years, and enthusiastically offered to guide me through part of this land he loves.

Stone patrols by horseback, sometimes by muleback, and offers to lend me a mount for our trip. It would be nice, I tell him, to let a mule carry my pack for awhile. "I'm not much of a rider," I warned him. "I'll probably walk most of the way."

"The mules are a hard ride," he admits. "Might do some walking myself."

As the mules catch their breath, Stone dismounts and tries to figure out where he'll post the ENTERING MACHESNA MOUNTAIN WILDERNESS sign he's ordered from headquarters. It strikes him that official Forest Service boundary sign 027-6A, as bear- and vandalproof as modern technology allows, might be a bit ponderous for such an isolated land.

The trail rises sharply out of the canyon. (Doesn't every Zane Grey novel begin like that?) We pause often to let the mules cool. Foxy, Mandy, Honey, Shelly, Disney, and Gilroy practice their own kind of animal socialism—none want to lead, all want to follow. Most cantankerous of all is old Disney, a few hundred pounds overweight. For many years, she patiently took tourists around Tom Sawyer Island at Disneyland. When rising insurance rates canceled the mule ride, Disney was shipped from Frontierland to the auction block, with the Forest Service narrowly outbidding a dog food company. So Disney left the Magic Kingdom for what is often lyrically referred to as the "Middle Kingdom," those majestic, fog-touched coast ranges that stretch from Ojai to Monterey. Except for the occasional fat ranger and the annual indignity of marching in Santa Barbara's Fiesta Parade, life as a Forest Service mule isn't particularly taxing. Helicopter and computer surveys have eliminated many ranger patrols—and the need for beasts of burden. Ironically, nowadays it is the mules who see the most beautiful parts of the forest; their services are most often used in wilderness areas, where motor vehicles are prohibited.

As the mules plod up the eroded old trail that leads into the heart of the wilderness, Stone points out some peculiar trees. The now-rare Valley oak, once common in California cow country, is having reproduction problems and researchers have fenced off a stand in order to determine whether browsing by animals is affecting the trees' ability to propagate. The Coulter pine growing in the Machesna Wilderness are also a bit odd. Botanists believe that these pines—unlike Coulters in other parts of California—may need fire to burst their large pine cones and thus help scatter their seeds.

But it's strange plans, not strange pines that perplex Bob Stone. If time has forgotten this land, Forest Service planners have not; their new plan will affect every creek Streamside Management Zone, every trout harvest species, and every panoramic viewshed from Matilija Canyon to Uncle Sam Mountain. Stone worries that when planners give a VD (visitor day) a value of $11.50, they are shortchanging the recreational needs of wilderness lovers. Stone fears that when the Department of Agriculture's giant Univac computer multiplies a small number of visitors by $11.50, a place like the Machesna Wilderness will be adjudged practically worthless.

Pine Spring Camp offers two tables, two stoves, and a wooden pit toilet. Stone soon has a fire started and a huge hunk of steak sizzling on the grill.

As we unpack the mules and turn them loose in a nearby meadow, we witness a most bizarre sunset. The purple and gold rays of day's end strike the huge ARCO solar mirrors stationed down on the Carrizo Plain. Colored light prisms off the mirrors and throws eerie beams at Machesna Mountain. We stand in the shadows of the nineteenth century and look down at the weird glow of the future. We have entered the twilight zone. And so has the Forest Service.

If there is one striking feature of the excellent companies,
it is this ability to manage ambiguity and paradox.
—from *In Search of Excellence*

L O C A T E D   F A R   from the wilderness but close to the freeway, the Los Padres National Forest Service headquarters in Goleta is a thoroughly modern building sandwiched between a shopping center and the suburbs of Santa Barbara's little Silicon Valley. Next to the handsome, expensive-looking building, the forest-green pickups and horse trailers look a bit incongruous. Interior decor is nouveau corporate, with plenty of cubicles, computers, and potted plants. Everyone wears civilian attire; the only uniformed ranger in evidence is the mannequin standing in a glass case in the lobby. Garbed in full fire-fighting gear, it stares pensively through thick goggles at all who enter.

Here in these immaculate second-floor offices, forest planners drafted the new management plan. It's a plan that incorporates a lot of other plans: the Oil and Gas Application Assessment, the Santa Ynez Recreation Plan, Smith's Blue Butterfly Recovery Plan, the Threatened and Unique Wildlife Plan, and the Forest Off-Road Vehicle Plan. Plans are offered for those critters with "local viability concerns," including the Mount Pinos lodgepole chipmunk, prairie falcon, rubber boa, and giant kangaroo rat.

The recreation needs of humans are also factored into the plan. The Forest Service foresees a gradual aging of the population; consequently, the population is predicted to become more interested in picnicking than backpacking, more inclined to sightsee than ski.

Plans abound for ocean beaches, subalpine forests, redwoods, chaparral, desert badlands, and oak woodland. The plan divides the Los Padres into thirty-six management areas and offers seven options for each area, ranging from Alternative I, the "maximum amenity" option, which would set aside great tracts of land in wilderness areas, to Alternative VII, the "maximum commodity" option, which in the eyes of some conservationists would open the forest to pillage and plunder by oil and mining interests.

"But the Forest Service's preferred alternative is what we're doing now," explains Gerry Little, chief planner for the forest and the man responsible for gathering data for the new plan. "We tried to head for where we think the middle is, where the bulk of the people are. But that's just our perspective until that's either agreed with or disagreed with. We think the plan meets the needs of most user groups."

A sober civil servant, Little displays a sincere dedication to the craft of planning and rarely breaks out of the vocabulary peculiar to his profession, a jargon of teams and targets, major scoping and minor scoping, management methods and mitigation measures. "The plan is our contract with the public on how the forest is to be managed. What we're really doing is documenting what management is. It's never really been written down before."

Forest management has changed of late, explains Little, because forest managers have had a change, in part, because of the "Toward Excellence" training and other business courses and self-improvement seminars given forest personnel.

"First we started out by training our people in meeting management," explains Little. "Then each team member scoped out critical areas and set bottom-line standards. After that, we started looking for solution spaces that didn't violate the bottom line."

Little says the seminars really helped the planning process. "We were able to stay out of the confrontational mode and work on consensus building—reaching what we call a win-win situation."

The Forest Service will always need fire chiefs, wildlife managers, and even rangers, but the managers of the future will be a different sort, Little predicts. "The new Forest Service manager has to be a person who can communicate. More than ever before, he or she has to be very much a social scientist. As we consider the kinds of characteristics we look for in tomorrow's managers, we give increasing weight to the social science skills—communication, listening, that sort of thing."

Kim Rivard, Forest Service computer scientist, is just the kind of person Gerry Little has in mind as a manager of tomorrow. She's a brisk, thoroughly professional young woman who says the major agent of change in the Forest Service occurs right in her "shop," a nearly Arctic-temperature room full of computers. "Management information technology is changing the way we do business," Rivard declares over the noise of two high-speed printers spewing out data. "Old Gifford [Pinchot, the father of modern forestry] never had any idea about computers. Even the good old boys here in the Los Padres realize we have to do business differently now," she adds, proudly displaying a lapel button that reads BAU with a slash through it (No Business as Usual).

Contrary to popular belief, she says, she and her fellow programmers don't count trees, but do run a program called Forplan, a linear programming model used for developing and analyzing forest planning alternatives. Forplan is a mathematical method used to determine the most effective allocation of resources between competing demands. Objectives, costs, and environmental restrictions are all expressed as mathematical equations. It's as simple as $y = a + bx$.

Besides championing the new technology, Rivard is also a big booster of the Toward Excellence programs. She's a graduate of Learning to Lead Tomorrow, Toward Excellence, and courses in lateral thinking. Recently she underwent training to become a facilitator for the Forest Service's Values and Norms Workshop.

A values workshop is necessary, she says, because times are changing and people's values are changing. For example, the Forest Service has always expected employees to work more than forty hours a week, but this conflicts with personal needs and family concerns.

Conflicting land ethics are also discussed in the workshops. "We compare Gifford Pinchot's values with ours and see how Forest Service values can be updated. People realize that values are a matter of interpretation and there's room for a lot of difference in opinion."

So far, the workshops have been a bigger hit in California national forests—such as Los Padres and the Mendocino—than in more conservative regions of the country, admits Rivard. "I tried to start some of this values stuff in Utah, and wow, did I run into a lot of resistance! But here in California, folks are a lot more open to it, a lot more adaptable. You won't find a lot of new management techniques in Utah. But here in Goleta, we're on the leading edge of the new Forest Service.

"These values workshops are great for the people participating, great for the Forest Service. Everyone gets something out of them. It's a win-win situation."

" I F   I   H E A R   the phrase *win-win situation* one more time, I'll go berserk," Bob Stone declares, looking up at the stars as if for divine guidance. "This search-for-excellence stuff is getting out of control. The motorpool gave me a truck with no gas and bad brakes. I told them, 'Guys, this is not excellence.'"

The Milky Way spills over Machesna Mountain. A sliver of a moon perches over the pines. Brandy is passed around the campfire. "I'll tell you what I mean by values. Keeping my pulaski [a fire tool] sharp is part of my job. But the new guys in the district say, 'Stone, why don't you let some maintenance guy sharpen that?' No way. You keep your tools sharp because they're your tools and you may have to use them someday in a critical situation."

"C'mon Stone, get with it," I needle. "Doesn't the future belong to somebody who can push a pencil rather than sharpen a pulaski?"

Stone shakes his head slowly and throws another log on the fire. He's silent for a few moments, then begins to talk with feeling about the places in the Middle Kingdom he's come to know—of Horse Canyon and Queen Bee, Buckeye and Sulphur Pot, Pozo, La Panza, Paradise Spring and Hi Mountain Potrero. He speaks affectionately about the people he's met on patrol—miners, ranchers, cowboys, hikers, horsemen, fishermen.

Few rangers have ranged as far and wide, but then Stone isn't really a ranger; he is classified by the Forest Service as a "multidisciplinary technician, capable of cross-functionalization." Translation: He's a guy who can fight a fire, build a trail, check on a grazing permit. But this is the age of specialization and the Forest Service has specialists for everything: wildlife management, watershed management, range management. Stone is a generalist in an age of specialists, though he insists he's not worried about being replaced: "Overspecialization leads to extinction; look what happened to the dinosaurs."

A large owl flaps by. "Who's our client?" Stone asks the campfire. "The people? The Department of Agriculture in Washington? I think the land, but I probably have a minority viewpoint. Fundamentally, we have to answer why we exist. I mean, for the Forest Service, this isn't some abstract philosophical question. Are we custodians taking care of public land? Or are we servants of the people, trying to please all user groups?"

It's when the managerial mind focuses on wilderness areas that the need for values clarification becomes most apparent, we decide. Some Forest Service employees look upon wilderness as a kind of library—a place for research, learning, and relaxation. Others with a Department of Agriculture bent regard national forests as corporate farms and are uncomfortable with the whole concept of wilderness. A wilderness, by definition, should be left alone, but planners want to plan and managers want to manage.

"How Should Wilderness Be Managed?" is Issue 12 in the new Los Padres plan. Some observers, both in and out of the Forest Service, feel that a better question to ask would be: Should wilderness be managed? This is, of course, heresy. Plans and projects are what put employees on the fast track, and the thought of a planner declaring, "I did nothing in the Santa Lucia Wilderness," or "I did nothing in the San Rafael Wilderness," is almost too ridiculous to consider.

If some of the more gung-ho planners have their way, Stone relates, ugly fuel breaks will be bulldozed atop all the ridges to protect the wilderness from fire, all the vegetation and wildlife will have a management plan, and each year portions of the wilderness will be set on fire in an attempt to stave off a potentially more serious (and more costly to fight) conflagration. "Planners plan with the best of intentions, with no malicious feeling whatsoever, but often their plans take the wildness out of wilderness," Stone says. "There's a spirit out here that doesn't show up on the computer."

"Maybe," I suggest to Stone, "you could bring up the subject of wilderness at the next Forest Service Values and Norms Workshop?"

"Pass the brandy," Stone answers.

The rational model causes us to denigrate the importance of values. We have observed few, if any, bold new company directions that have come from goal precision or rational analysis.

—from *In Search of Excellence*

IS THE FOREST SERVICE asking us about its plan or telling us about its plan? This is the question confusing about five dozen of us citizens gathered at the Santa Barbara Museum of Natural History to air our views on the future of the land called Los Padres. The meeting is one of a dozen road shows scheduled around the state designed to give the public a chance to comment. Forest Service "facilitators," cheerful and clean-cut as flight attendants, promise to take the assembled on "a walk through the document."

On comes the slide show. Pretty pictures of Los Padres National Forest. "Why is such a plan needed?" intones the voice-of-God narrator.

The plan is needed, explain facilitators, because of the National Forest Management Act, which calls upon Forest Service supervisors to spell out detailed prescriptions for their forests for the next fifty years. Timber, grazing, minerals, recreation, wilderness, wildlife, roads, trails, and every other facet of national forest operation must be examined and projected.

Los Padres, the only forest in California easily accessible to both southern California and the Bay Area, gets about 4,293 MRVD (thousands of visitor days per year) and ranks fifteenth in total recreational use among the nation's national forests. Each year, thirty-three watersheds provide 715,000 acre feet of water; 400 miles of streams produce 13,000 pounds of trout; and 1,175 miles of trail cross the forest, 50 percent of which is highly sensitive to slope failure and 68 percent of which is blanketed by chaparral.

Gerry Little gets a big laugh when he jokes that "reading the plan is a sure cure for insomnia."

Citizens are not bored, however, but bewildered—mostly by the language of the plan. Once upon a time that old forest spokesman Smokey the Bear warned: "Remember, only you can prevent forest fires." Today, the Forest Service declares: "Use preventability indices, initial attack objectives and burned acreage targets to hold unplanned ignitions within tolerable numbers or loss limits."

The plan's jargon sends citizens scurrying to the glossary. A favorite piece of land may be CAS (capable, available, suitable) and ready for BMPs (best management practices). The astute student of forest planning must learn to distinguish between "naturalness" and "apparent naturalness," and between a "minor disturbance" and a "major disturbance," which is not to be confused, of course, with an "irretrievable effect" or an "irreversible effect." Squirrels are "cavity dwellers," and lizards, toads, and other animals not killed or eaten are "nonconsumptive species." The language is so obscure that a reader can't tell the forest from the TS (timber stand).

Some terms seem mildy salacious until the glossary explains otherwise: *decadence* is really decaying brush; *breast height* is a measurement of a tree's diameter at four feet, six inches from the ground; *VD* is a visitor day; *horizontal diversity* refers to plant distribution; and *T & E* is a threatened and endangered species.

The plan does not ignore people. The number of humans packed into an area is expressed as PAOT (Persons At One Time). Public sentiment generates ICOs—Issues, Concerns, and Opportunities. Humans seem to be a management problem for the Forest Service, perhaps because the agency has assigned them to "common interest groups," then given an uncommon definition to common interest group: "People with a common interest, but who do not necessarily recognize that common interest or cooperate to pursue common interests or mutual goals."

Ironically, the Forest Service's *Values and Norms Workshop Handbook* suggests: "We are contributing to the public's misunderstanding of what conservation and wise use is by the development of the language we are using in planning. We need to eliminate acronyms in dealing with the public."

A dozen people step forward to make comments on the places that mean something special to them. Forest Service facilitators write down all comments and promise that all responses will be entered into and considered by the computer.

"Nothing is written in stone; the document is just a draft," Gerry Little assures the citizens. "In the end it all comes down to implementation."

> If we want change, we fiddle with the strategy or we change
> the structure. Perhaps the time has come to change our ways.
> —from *In Search of Excellence*

The detritus from generations of camping trips lies half-buried a hundred feet from Pine Spring. We stuff cans, bottles, a rusted lantern, and an old camp stove into giant plastic garbage bags. Even the most amateur garbologist can divine that many campers rolled their own; Prince Albert appears on a hundred cans.

The mules prove difficult to round up, even though Stone tells them that if they haul out the trash for him, he'll provide some extra feed for them. "It's a win-win situation," he shouts, but the recalcitrant animals have found mule heaven and pay no heed. After finally capturing them, Stone is faced with another problem: there appears to be no tidy way to load 150 pounds of trash onto each mule. He tightly secures the cargo, but the lumpy loads offend his muleteering ethic.

Back on the trail, it's Gilroy who slows progress. She shows her love of the wilderness by trying to eat most of it. To Gilroy, nature is a well-stocked delicatessen full of black and white sage, manzanita and chamise, and that most unusual gastronomic delight, poison oak.

Slow the mules may be, but slow is the only way to see this quiet country of tumbled-up hills, ancient oaks, and infinite blue distances. Machesna Mountain, by the numbers, is only twenty thousand acres, 1 percent of the national forest, two-tenths of 1 percent of California; however, its importance lies not in terms of gross acreage locked up, but in the amount of wildness preserved. It is a commitment to wildness that seems missing from the Los Padres master plan. To the few who seek out these places, to the many who care how public lands are managed, it's less than reassuring to know that Forest Service plans call for Machesna Mountain Wilderness to be "managed to preserve wilderness values," when the agency must hold workshops in order to discover what these values really are. Perhaps when Forest Service planners state that Management Area 64 will offer "maximum solitude, self-reliance and challenge while traveling on primitive trails," what they are really saying is that they plan to leave Machesna Mountain Wilderness alone.

"I guess I'll keep patrolling out here until they teach the computer how to pick up trash," Stone says, pulling on old Disney's lead rope.

Quail scurry for cover under the chaparral, a faint ocean breeze carries the fragrance of salt and pine, and the oak-studded potreros glow golden in the sunlight of late afternoon. God and Forplan willing, this land will remain forever wild.

Thirteen

A Canyon Called Diablo

A HUMAN BLOCKADE, that's what we are. Two thousand of us, maybe more, at the front gate of the Pacific Gas & Electric Company's Diablo Canyon Nuclear Power Plant.

"No Diablo . . . no Diablo over me," sing the protesters, led in the sing-along by a woman wearing a *Who Killed Karen Silkwood?* T-shirt.

The blockade, organized by the Abalone Alliance, has two goals: to prevent low-energy testing of the plant and to bring this ill-built plant, situated on an active earthquake fault, to the nation's attention.

The second goal seems far closer to realization than the first. Judging by the radio, TV, and newspaper coverage, the power plant—or this protest against it, anyway—will certainly be brought to the nation's attention this September day in 1981.

I'm blockading because my letters, petitions, phone calls, testimony at hearings, letters to editors, and editorials in local newspapers, as well as the communications of thousands of other citizens, failed to stop Diablo's start-up. All legal options have been exhausted.

It is time now to put my body on the line—or I should say over the line because the blue line painted on the entrance road to the power plant is the border between peaceful assembly and criminal trespass. On the Diablo side of the line is massed law enforcement—San Luis Obispo County sheriffs and sheriffs from neighboring counties, California Highway Patrolmen, and National Guard troops. On the other side of the line assemble the protesters.

Every so often a half-dozen, a dozen, sometimes two dozen protesters cross the blue line, then sit on the power plant entry road. After the sheriff asks them to disburse and they refuse, they are placed under arrest. Some blockaders go limp and are carried to waiting buses. One smiling county sheriff links arms with a pretty young woman in a flowing white dress; she too is smiling. From a distance, she looks like a bride being escorted by her proud father.

Most arrests are mellow procedures; too many cameras are trained upon the local constabulary for them to be on anything but their best behavior, though the CHP does pinch protesters' ears with wooden dowels to hurry them along.

I'm reluctant to step over the blue line for a variety of reasons. First, I've never been arrested before. Will an arrest forever blacken my record? Henceforth, I shall be a man with a rap sheet. True, I can't imagine how miscellaneous misdemeanor trespass charges could affect my career goals or credit rating.

Second, I fear I might lose my temper, though I matriculated from six hours of Nonviolent Protest Training and remained calm, even when pummeled with rolled-up magazines wielded by Abalone Alliance trainers playing cops. With all due respect to model protesters—from Mahatma Gandhi to Martin Luther King, Jr., to the woman with the *Whistleblowers Make Better Lovers* protest sign who just got arrested—going-limp-pacifism is just not my style.

Given my strong feelings, crossing to the other side of a blue line is insufficient protest for me. I want my arrest—and I'm morally committed to being arrested—to count for more. I've roamed this coast, these Irish Hills, from Montana de Oro south to Diablo Canyon, Coon Creek Canyon, Irish Canyon, Rattlesnake Canyon and See Canyon, and grown fond of this land, a slice of California almost no one—except us trespassers— has seen since the mid-1960s, when PG&E acquired it. I want my arrest to be visible, in part because what I'm fighting for and against is all so invisible—the coast, the canyons, the money, the power plant itself (many miles from the front gate in Avila Beach), the radiation and radioactive waste that could so easily kill us.

I want to violate the Nuke's security the way Diablo has violated mine. Amidst the noise and confusion of the protest swirling around me that nineteenth-century crank from Concord, whose writing has challenged me so many times, speaks to me once more: "As for adopting the ways which the state has provided for remedying evil, I know not of such ways. They take too much time, and a man's life will be gone."

Henry David Thoreau's essays "Walking" and "Civil Disobedience" merge as one, and where and how I shall protest become as clear to me as the reason why.

Twelve years later, I am part of another gathering at Diablo's front gate. We have come not to demonstrate but to celebrate—to dedicate the newly constructed Pecho Coast Trail, which opens up a few miles of coastline south of the nuclear plant to walkers escorted by tour guides.

I am in the company of PG&E publicists, coastal commissioners, and local politicos. Half of our party rides in PG&E-provided vans over the back roads to the trail dedication site, while the more hearty of us hike the new trail.

Hiking here is a rare treat. The land between Avila Beach and Montana de Oro State Park is ten miles of coast that nobody knows, where nobody goes. The reason for this obscurity is that this land has been privately held since Spanish mission days. For the last thirty years, public access has been strictly forbidden because of a very security-conscious landowner—Pacific Gas & Electric, whose nuclear power plant is located in the middle of this pristine stretch of coast, at the mouth of a canyon called Diablo.

Never have I walked a more expensive trail. Pecho Coast Trail was built by the California Conservation Corps, at a cost to PG&E of $300,000, or exactly $100,000 a mile for the three-mile trail.

The numbers make me dizzy, as if I'm beginning a trail at ten thousand feet in the High Sierra rather than ten feet above sea level in Avila Beach. As absurdly expensive as a 100K-per-mile trail might sound, by this standard a Mexico-to-Oregon 1,500-mile California Coastal Trail could be built for $150 million, or for less than 2 percent of Diablo Nuclear Power Plant's construction cost.

How could Pecho Coast Trail have cost PG&E so much money? Perhaps there was a cost overrun, similar to the one the utility experienced with the nuclear plant, which was projected to cost $200 million, but came in at $8 billion, or 3,900 percent over budget. Maybe the trail cost was initially budgeted at only $5,000 a mile, but there was another 3,900 percent construction cost overrun. Perhaps mere mortals are not supposed to comprehend the accounting practices of utility companies.

At first, Pecho Coast Trail appears to be entering a minimum security prison but soon leaves Diablo's gates and barbed wire behind and begins ascending the dramatic bluffs above San Luis Bay. We're treated to great over-the-shoulder views of Avila Beach and the Bay. Pacific currents carry sand past mostly rocky San Luis Bay, but deposit sand en masse at Pismo Beach and its southern neighbors—Grover Beach and Oceano. Forming a dramatic backdrop to these beaches are the sparkling Nipomo Dunes.

"Great view of my hometown," enthuses the hiker behind me, who introduces himself as Peter Keith, city councilman of Grover Beach, emphasis on the *Beach*. He's a good-looking guy, jauntily clad in fashionable outdoor wear.

"We used to be Grover *City*, you know, until the last election. But we convinced voters to change the name."

"They need much convincing?" I ask.

"Some of the old-timers did. But the rest realized we had an identity problem. All the other towns around San Luis Bay—Oceano, Pismo Beach, Shell Beach—have names linking them to the California coast, but not Grover City. Identity-wise, we might as well have been located by Bakersfield, or a hundred miles inland."

"Now that you're Grover *Beach*—how will that help your town?"

"There's magic to the California coast, even these days," Keith replies. "The coast brings more tourist dollars, higher property values. You have better community spirit in a coastal town than one inland."

Keith focuses his binoculars on the Nipomo Dunes. "I love walking this coast. Do you know you can walk all the way up the coast from the county line to Avila Beach?"

AFTER MY LENGTHY Los Padres National Forest sojourn, I resume my coast walk at the Santa Barbara–San Luis Obispo county line, the line being the Santa Maria River. At the river's mouth is a wetland area where several endangered species reside, including the California least tern and brown pelican. Across the river is the highest sand dune on the West Coast, 450-foot-tall Mussel Rock. It's not really all sand; most of it is actually a rock formation, though there's an ancient dune deposited atop it. Still, it's an impressive landmark.

Brightening the dunes on my way north are yellow and magenta sand verbena, daisies, and white-fringed asters. It would be easier walking on the broad, hard-packed sand by the ocean, but I like wandering this Sahara-by-the-sea, even if progress is of the two-steps-forward-one-step-back variety.

The Oceano Dunes, Guadalupe Dunes, Pismo Dunes, and Callender Dunes are known collectively as the Nipomo Dunes, the highest and whitest sand dunes in California. These dunes evolved many thousands of years ago, between ice ages, through deposition by the Santa Maria River, and the sculpting of land and sea. The cliffs of Point Sal acted as a sand trap to keep the dunes from straying south.

The dunes, one to three miles wide, are a dynamic ecosystem: they've been building up and shifting in response to northwest winds, for the last 18,000 years or so. Flowers, plants, and grasses keep some of the dunes in place while others are periodically assembled and disassembled by the prevailing northwest wind. The active, moving dunes are those with little or no vegetation.

In the Nipomo Dunes, humans have had to learn repeatedly that old lesson about building castles of sand—or building castles on sand. In 1904, the duneside community of Oceano boasted beach cottages, a wharf, and mammoth La Grande Beach Pavilion. Developers' grandiose plans of turning Oceano into a tourist mecca did not materialize and pavilion, wharf, and cottages were buried beneath advancing dunes.

During the Great Depression, the dunes were home to the "Dunites," a motley collection of writers, artists, hermits, nudists, and astrologers who lived in driftwood shacks and published their own magazine, called *Dune Forum*. Eventually the Dunites' driftwood shacks and enterprises too were covered by the relentless sands.

Pismo Beach presents a weird contrast. Part of the Nipomo Dunes have been given special governmental protection in Pismo Dunes Natural Preserve, an aeolian landscape of swales and hollows. The dunes, like their desert cousins, offer a special solitude and quietude; only the tang of the salt air and the seashell fragments sparkling on the surface of the sand tell the traveler that these dunes are sculpted by ocean winds.

The drama of the dunes, the haunting patterns of light and shadow, inspired the great photographer Ansel Adams, who did some of his best work here. If ever one photo is worth a thousand words, or could be said to represent a thousand miles of coast, it is his 1963 photo of these dunes. Rippled foredunes and a dark ridgetop frame an infinity of sand. In the center of the photo your eye may be drawn to either a soft bosom of sand or a heart of darkness. Considering all the glorious color photographs of the California coast available (a veritable industry in and of itself) Adams's emotionally complex, black-and-white photo is certainly a surprising selection for the cover of the California Coastal Commission's *California Coastal Resource Guide*.

I hike from the hillocks and foredunes down to the beach and find an altogether different picture: Pismo Dunes State Vehicular Recreation Area. It's not a pretty picture. California's answer to Daytona Beach is famed as one of only two state beaches where the public can drive on the sand. The beach is a traffic jam of cars, trucks, and off-road vehicles filled with families, low-riders, and what seems to be half the population of Bakersfield. Mixed with the roar of the breakers and the cry of the gulls is the roar of traffic and the sound of FM 89.5, the state park radio station, broadcasting rules and regulations.

Side-by-side concordant and discordant uses of the land such as I find at Pismo Beach never cease to astonish me. My astonishment at such cross-purposeful land use should, by all rights, have diminished over the years. But it hasn't, even though I've witnessed so much of it: in the California desert, where mere signs divide massive, off-road vehicle use from a tortoise reserve; at lakes, where only passive placards separate ski boats and jet skis from a bird sanctuary; and now Pismo Beach, where flags separate the solitude of the dunes from the car crowd at the beach.

As if possession of the highest dunes and busiest beach were not sufficient notoriety for any coastal town, Pismo Beach has yet another claim to fame: the Clam Capital of the World. Pismo has been famous for its succulent clams since before the turn of the century. From 1916 to 1947, an estimated 100,000 pounds of clams were commercially harvested yearly; sport clammers took even more.

These days the Pismo Beach Chamber of Commerce won't provide a clam count, but even the most optimistic beach boosters admit the catch has been drastically reduced. Locals blame sea otters for the decline. Otters float on their backs and use rocks to break open the clams. A single otter can consume twenty to twenty-five pounds of shellfish a day. Marine ecologists suspect that human clam diggers, who've been visting Pismo for decades, have taken a greater toll on the species.

Pity the poor Pismo clam. If *Tivel stultorum* is to survive *Motoris californicus* it will jolly well have to evolve a harder shell, or learn to dig deeper into the sand.

Leaving Pismo's clams and cars behind, I walk along San Luis Bay to Shell Beach and Avila Beach. While many obstacles on the coastal trail will challenge me in the days ahead, at least I won't have to worry about autos on the beach for another five hundred miles.

P E C H O   C O A S T   T R A I L   ascends to an oak grove, which shades a memorial plaque dedicated to Pat Stebbins (1940–1990), an access director for the California Coastal Commission. She is fondly remembered by colleagues and by conservationists for her tireless advocacy of public access, and for her encyclopedic knowledge of coastal politics.

I remember her fondly, too. She had the most cluttered office I've ever seen. Though computers and clerical staff were ready to file and store her voluminous coastal data, she kept head-high stacks of paper in her office. So high were the piles of paper that it was impossible to see if she was at her desk. Fortunately she was not at her desk whenever earthquakes shook San Francisco. Whenever I asked her about access to an obscure stretch of coast, she usually had the answer in her head; if not, she could fish the relevant file out of a tall stack in minutes, if not seconds. She left her desk, and this life, too soon, with much undone that only she could do. All of us who love the coast mourn her passing.

Pecho Coast Trail was one of her pet projects. I would love to have walked this trail with her and asked her what she thought of it, as well as of the decade-long struggle to build it.

Enjoying the view of the Nipomo Dunes from the new trail is eighty-six-year-old Kathleen Goddard Jones. The "Lady of the Dunes" is a living legend of coastal preservation, a nationally recognized environmentalist, a tireless champion of the dunes.

With her walking stick and big sun hat, she seems just another octogenarian out for her morning constitutional. But this frail-looking demeanor is deceptive; for four decades she has battled—is still battling—to save one of the most endangered environments in the state. She lists the many threats to her beloved dunes: off-road vehicles, oil company dumping of dangerous waste, encroaching development.

But from Pecho Coast Trail, such threats seem far away and the dunes seem as pristine as those of the most remote desert. "Tranquility—that's the word I most associate with the Nipomo Dunes," she tells me.

"And this trail? What's the word you associate with it?" I ask.

"It's not as tranquil as walking in the dunes," she dodges with a diplomatic smile.

Diablo Canyon was to be built in the Nipomo Dunes. During the mid-1960s, when nuclear energy was on the governmental fast track, permissions and permits were coming rapidly and construction seemed imminent. Chief among the dune preservationists was the Sierra Club, and it negotiated with PG&E. The utility agreed not to construct the plant in the dunes if it could build in nearby Diablo Canyon. Club leaders agreed with PG&E that Diablo Canyon was a practical alternative site to the beloved dunes.

During a time of epic conservation battles, such as those trying to prevent dams being built in the Grand Canyon and Glen Canyon, and the attempt to establish Redwood National Park, Diablo Nuclear Power Plant became one of most contentious and divisive issues in Sierra Club history.

Some Sierra Club leaders argued that the tactic of trading off one area in hopes of ransoming another was likely to backfire. These leaders wrote: "We believe the Club attained national prominence and gained at least half its current members because it projected an image of resolute adherence to principle; if we now adopt the posture of an opportunistic trader, we must expect not only to lose support, but to lose respect also." Among those complaining about this abandonment of principle was David Brower.

Other Sierra Club leaders argued that America needed power plants, that intransigence on the subject made the club appear unreasonable, and the club must learn to negotiate. "The impairment of [Diablo] Canyon, we believe, must be balanced against the greater values in the Nipomo Dunes. Are we to dissipate ourselves in endless and largely fruitless battles, or can more be achieved by ad hoc agreements on what is to be preserved and what may be developed?" Among those insisting it was an either-or situation was Ansel Adams, Kathleen Goddard Jones's good friend.

Club directors put the matter before the membership for a vote in 1967 and in 1969. Both times a majority of members supported the trade-off.

The trail dedication set-up looks like an outdoor wedding ceremony. Under a large canopy, rows of folding chairs face a podium and the Pacific. The caterer has put out a fine spread. In front of a Victorian-era lighthouse, resembling many of those East Coast beacons, we nosh hors d'oeuvres and sip mineral water.

Before celebrating the new trail, a Coast Guard captain and assorted local officials commemorate the Old Point San Luis Lighthouse, built in 1890. The "Victorian Lady," as it's known, warned ships of the rocky coast until 1975, when the facility was deactivated and replaced by an automated beacon.

As speakers wax nostalgic about the hundred-year-old light and soot problems from the not-very-clean-burning kerosene that kept keepers busy polishing glass and worrying about surprise visits from supervisors who conducted "white glove" inspections, I wonder if a century from now visitors will marvel at the grossly primitive technology of Diablo Canyon Nuclear Power Plant. Will such visitors be amused at this quaint artifact from the late industrial age? Or will they be a little horrified, the way we modern museumgoers regard the Civil War surgeon's medical bag with its knives and saws?

Of course, a far worse prospect than a moth-balled nuclear plant turned museum is possible. A sudden convulsion of the Hosgri Fault beneath Diablo Canyon, a temblor that's too much for the power plant, could cause a Chernobyl-like accident. The coast could become a radioactive dead zone with human entry forbidden for ten thousand years.

I recall a wicked cartoon, drawn during the days of dissent at Diablo Canyon by master political cartoonist Paul Conrad. He pictured the nuclear power plant as a lighthouse, glowing ominously in the darkness of the central coast. "Diablo Light House," read the caption.

Thomas Gwynn, Coastal Commission chairman, takes the podium and returns us to the business of dedicating the Pecho Coast Trail. He praises the efforts of the Nature Conservancy, PG&E and, of course, the Coastal Commission. "This is a fitting way to celebrate the twentieth anniversary of the beginning of the Coastal Commission and its work to protect and open access to the California Coast," he says.

"We are providing an excellent opportunity to allow managed access to a previously inaccessible section of the California coastline," affirms Ken Wiley, director of the Central Coast chapter of the Nature Conservancy. "Views from the trail will be spectacular and hikers will be able to see a big wild stretch of the Central Coast in a sort of private way."

Wiley's eyes wander from his prepared speech—first down the coast, then north toward Diablo Canyon. "This land is almost heartbreakingly beautiful," he says.

Apparently, I lack the requisite patience to be a blockader. We've been encamped for days on the outskirts of San Luis Obispo awaiting the decision to begin the blockade and I am going stark, raving, mad. Important decisions—not to mention many less consequential ones—are hard to come by in a camp, in an organization, without leaders.

In keeping with our communal goals, we protesters are not supposed to take any action without the full consensus of all members. Such consensus is, to say the least, time-consuming because Abalone Alliance rules forbid groups to pick leaders. We group members are supposed to take turns stimulating decision making by assuming ad hoc roles as group facilitators. (I thought the revolutionary rallying cry was "Kill all the lawyers!" not "Kill all the leaders!")

Within each affinity group are blockaders, who intend to get arrested, and blockade supporters, who don't. AGs, as they're called, include a spokesperson, a contact person, a legal spoke, peacekeepers, and vibe-watchers.

Affinity groups include the Mutant Sponges; the Radioactivists; the Whales, from Mendocino; and the Oaks and Acorns, from San Luis Obispo. My group is Solardarity and numbers five backcountry blockaders—two carpenters, a graphic designer, a grad student, and a nature writer—as well as a half-dozen Santa Barbara supporters, recently reinforced by three USC coeds.

Affinity groups, I learn during one of our interminable discussions about the politically correct process of protest, go back
to the anarchist movement in Spain in the early part of this
century. Whatever did the *groupos de affinidad* accomplish anyway? I ask in one particularly impatient moment and am not
surprised when no one can tell me a thing. At the speed at
which the consensus process works, I imagine the *groupos* are
still plotting their revolution.

I'm so bored I even read the 60-page *Diablo Canyon Blockade/
Encampment Handbook,* complete with "Declaration of Nuclear
Resistance," and chapters entitled "Dogs, Mace and Tear Gas,"
"Dynamics of Non-Violence," and "Feminist Process: Over-
coming Masculine Oppression."

If there's anything harder for me than sitting, it's sitting and
talking. Endless discussion about "the action," which for all but
a few of the affinity groups will take place at the main gate,
seems irrelevant for those few of us planning to protest afield.

In recognition of (or punishment for) my being an un-
happy-without-anything-to-do camper, Solardarity "consenses"
that I be sent to represent them at the spokes council. (Under
the rules, several affinity groups can operate together under the
auspices of a spokes council made up of representatives called
spokes.) At the council meeting, I'm asked to describe our
group's feelings about nuclear power, empowerment, and non-
violence. ("In a word, *impatience,*" I tell the council.) We spokes
are serenaded by a lesbian affinity group from Berkeley, who
sing a very long song with a refrain blaming most, if not all,
of the world's evils on "rapist men and their machines."

In discussions with the four or five affinity groups intending
to trespass into the Diablo backcountry, I make several attempts
to steer the discussion away from internal feelings about our
action to the more external obstacles to our success. To get to
the plant, we blockaders will have to traverse miles of rugged,
isolated, rattlesnake-infested wilderness and dodge several hundred lawmen, I remind the group. If we manage to penetrate

these barriers, we'll find a plant ringed by two barbed-wire-topped cyclone fences and protected by attack dogs and armed guards. I stress that our action is much more complex than crossing the blue line at the front gate.

When I bring up the question of route, I am told not to worry because a guide will be provided by the Abalone Alliance. When I unfurl my topographic map and start describing the steep terrain of the Irish Hills, I am told that ours is not a military operation. One wild-eyed guy of about forty tells me not to believe anything on my map. "There are trails and places the government doesn't want you to know about," he declares. He further hints that government mapmakers may very well be on PG&E's payroll. Just when I'm about to call him paranoid, he reminds me that PG&E managed a corporate cover-up of a geology map that showed the Hosgri Earthquake Fault extending just offshore from Diablo Canyon, a fault that might have scuttled the whole project if discovered during the early phases of plant construction.

As we struggle for consensus, the *Los Angeles Times* sneers at us with its lead editorial: "We doubt that pictures of and stories about protesters being dragged off to jail for crowding onto public roads leading to and from the plant will add much to the world's understanding of nuclear power.

"Under the circumstances, the risk of generating power at Diablo Canyon seems far smaller than the risk that the demonstrators plan to take to spend a few seconds on the television screen."

Four affinity groups, about thirty blockaders, wearing boots and backpacks, assemble at eight in the morning alongside See Canyon Road. With a wave to the supporters who transported us here, we traipse into the woods. Our backcountry blockade seems to be the worst-kept secret in San Luis Obispo County. As we walk along a dirt road, a police helicopter hovers over us. A radio reporter, clad in a long skirt and fasionable boots, dogs us with inane questions.

We are led over the Irish Hills by a leather-headbanded, blonde Indian—a tall, silent fellow introduced to us as a local San Luis Obispo resident who grew up in the area and knows the hills.

A half-mile along, the high-heel-booted reporter, complaining about erupting blisters, turns around. A mile or so into our journey the helicopter dips low, hovers over us for some minutes to intimidate us, then flies away. Our guide leads us slowly along dirt roads, delivering us, after a few hours' tramp, to an apple orchard.

The blonde Indian announces that he can take us no farther. He cannot get arrested with us, he explains, because there may be other parties to guide into the backcountry. Such parties will need his skill to keep from getting lost, he says. He points the way to the main plant road, a half-hour's walk away. Whenever we're ready we can easily descend to the entry road and get arrested. Before he melts into the woods, he suggests we kick back, relax, pick some apples, have lunch, and enjoy this beautiful spot.

Much to my surprise, my fellow blockaders actually follow his advice. Packs are removed and blankets spread upon the ground, as if readying for a picnic.

By my calculations, we remain several miles from the power plant. If we descend to the Diablo entry road and are arrested, we would be about four as-the-crow-flies miles from the front gate at Avila Beach. A credible effort, to be sure, but not good enough for me. Map, compass and heart tell me to continue north.

"We need to have a meeting and get some consensus on our action," one blockader suggests.

"Let's form a circle and talk about things," others agree.

Perhaps it is four days of Socialist Summer Camp and the madness of consensus building, perhaps it is these Irish Hills, that make my Irish temper surface. "We're here to protest," I tell the circling blockaders, who interrupt their apple picking and picnic preparations to glare at me. "We're here to get arrested in the most effective way possible, not to have another pointless round of discussion, and not to pick fruit."

"I'm hearing hostile vibes, brother," a sister counsels me.

"Sit down and mellow out," calls out another sister.

"I know the way to Diablo Canyon Nuclear Power Plant," I reply, my voice rising. "Anyone who wants to come with me is welcome. I'm leaving now."

Furious, I hike north. Some minutes later, as I thrash up a grassy slope, I hear shouting behind me. It's my affinity group. "It's our consensus we've had enough consensus," Mike tells me when they catch up with me.

"Thanks, guys."

"What are affinity groups for?" Debbie grins.

Solardarity is in solidarity about our mission: We want to get as close to Diablo as we can. As one, we follow the spine of the Irish Hills.

We ascend Green Peak, no doubt green in winter, but gold now at summer's end. We continue along a ridge to another, unnamed promontory, where we stop for a late lunch and gaze down at the power plant. There's something quite voyeuristic about looking down at the enemy.

Briefly, we consider camping up here at Diablo Lookout, but we all know we're here to get arrested and the sooner we get arrested the better; the police who were so mellow in Avila Beach in broad daylight could very well be nasty if we're busted right next to the power plant at nightfall.

No conception whatever of the plant's size can be had from photos, and as we plunge down the south wall of Diablo Canyon we are silenced by the sheer enormity of the Nuke. We walk in the shadow of the twin reactor buildings, feeling ever smaller as we descend to the entrance road on the coast.

We congratulate one another for accomplishing our mission—getting so close to the plant—just as a National Guard truck pulls up alongside us. A half-dozen Guardsmen come out with their rifles, but no weapons are pointed at us, and their jolly commander seems not angry, but impressed. "How'd you get over those hills?" he greets us. "We don't have to march over anything this steep in training. You guys ought to sign up with us."

"You should sign up with us," I return.

The commander laughs good-naturedly. "We've got to keep you here until the county sheriff comes by to, uh, arrest you. You mind sitting down over there?"

We sit, surrounded by the troops—as cheerful a platoon as we lawbreakers could ever hope to meet, such cheer broken only when a county sheriff's car screeches to a halt alongside us. Out step four baton-brandishing deputies, in possession of enough plastic handcuffs to subdue fifty subversives. They look pissed.

"How the hell did they get way up here?" bellows the sheriff.

"They hiked through the mountains, right up to the plant," replies the National Guard commander.

"Holy shit!"

His three deputies move in with the cuffs.

"You're under arrest," he tells us.

Master of ceremonies, former *Sunset Magazine* publisher Melvin Lane, who sits on the board of the Nature Conservancy, on the board of directors of PG&E, and is a former chairman of the California Coastal Commission, is surely the most qualified individual to speak about this section of the central coast. Lane praises the beauties of this land, the wondrous views, and the new hiking trail, but is most enthusiastic about what he calls the "path of cooperation" taken by the partners in the project—state government, PG&E, and the Nature Conservancy.

As Lane speaks of PG&E and its commitment to coastal preservation, I experience a profound cognitive dissonance, his words clashing against my experience. My eyes wander past Lane to the tantalizing, publicly inaccessible coastline behind him. My ears—which had been hearing Melvin Lane with the surf in the background—now hear the surf with Melvin Lane in the background.

Unlike in the old days, government/private industry/environmentalist cooperation is common now. This tripartite system is not too difficult to understand. What baffles me is how one man like Melvin Lane can represent three such different interests at once. It's as if one simultaneously pursued careers as an Army general, a defense contractor, and a peace activist.

This triplicity of purpose must lead to a conflict-of-interest, not in the illegal sense of an officeholder acquiring shares in a company seeking government contracts, but in the internal sense of a single conscience with three directors. Does one choose a direction at daybreak and stick with it all day? ("Good morning, honey. I'm in a corporate kind of mood today. I'm gonna kick some Sierra Club butt.")

On second thought, it's not a conflict-of-interest that's bothersome, but a conflict of interests. I want to see more of a conflict between competing interests. The private sector, government, and public interest groups are *supposed* to mistrust one another; this inability to get along ensures the durability of our democratic process and is what keeps America great.

Melvin Lane is not a man conflicted about anything as he continues to praise PG&E's commitment to coastal conservation. Practically the whole length of the coast, Lane reminds us, has been subjected to housing developments, but not this part of the central coast. "Thanks to the construction of the Diablo Canyon power plant, this coast wasn't developed," he concludes to polite applause.

The building of a nuclear power plant *saved* this coast from development? I ponder this deducto absurdum as I leave the party and hike the last mile of Pecho Coast Trail, which dips down to a coastal terrace from the old lighthouse.

This then is the New Conservation: utility company execs, government policy wonks, and environmentalists all wearing the same expensive suits, talking the same talk, walking the same walk, building three miles of outrageously expensive coastal trail over the course of a quarter-century, and believing a nuclear power plant saved the coastline from development.

Is this an example of end-of-the-twentieth-century environmental ethics? We're all working together now. But for whom? And for what? Unlike me, reasonable people all work together, reason together, and make reasonable compromises. Who am I to critique pure reason and how it can conflict with rational morality? Immanuel Kant said it best two hundred years ago, when he warned us of compromising our values in situations like Diablo Canyon: "Woe to him who creeps through the serpent windings of utilitarianism."

Pecho Coast Trail dead-ends in an oak grove. I look longingly up-coast, my mind sketching a continuation of the trail over the bluffs and ridges. As I gaze into the blue distance, I wonder exactly what Nature Conservancy director Ken Wiley meant when he called this coast "heartbreakingly beautiful."

Beauty itself is not heartbreaking. Beauty that's unobtainable, beauty that's defaced, will break your heart every time.

Back at the trail dedication, the celebrants are climbing into PG&E's vans for the ride back to town. I collar Ken Wiley. "Pecho Trail is a good start," I tell him. "When will it be extended?"

"Maybe in our children's lifetime," Wiley replies.

In fact, there's even trouble with the public using the three miles of trail we just dedicated, Wiley confesses. Before the Nature Conservancy can begin its program of docent-led hikes, it must comply with PG&E's demand that it carry an enormous amount of insurance indemnifying PG&E from all liability for anything that might happen to a walker on its property. Insurance is always a part of Nature Conservancy operations when the group manages a property or a trail for a private landowner; it's the amount of insurance that's a problem, Wiley explains. As a condition for using the trail, PG&E is insisting on a huge and—in the Nature Conservancy's view—budget-busting amount of insurance, an amount far greater than the Nature Conservancy carries on any other property in its care.

"Why would PG&E require so much insurance just for your nature walks?" I ask.

Wiley looks up-coast in the direction of the nuclear power plant. "You tell me."

THE PEOPLE OF THE STATE OF CALIFORNIA
v. JOHN CHARLES MCKINNEY, DEFENDANT

The San Luis Obispo County District Attorney complains and
accuses the above-named Defendant on information and belief
of the following specified crimes:

Count I

Defendant is accused of a misdemeanor crime in violation of
Section 602N 409 of the Penal Code of the State of California
committed as follows:

That said John Charles McKinney on or about September 15,
1981 did willfully and unlawfully refuse and fail to leave land,
real property and structures belonging to and lawfully occupied
by another and not open to the general public, upon being requested to leave by the owner.

Count II

That said John Charles McKinney did willfully and unlawfully
remain present at the place of a riot, rout, and unlawful assembly, after the same had been lawfully warned to disperse.

All of which is contrary to the Statute in such cases made and
provided, and against the peace and dignity of the People of the
State of California.

Apparently it's not the Diablo Canyon Nuclear Plant, but
me that has violated the peace and dignity of the people of
California. Two thousand of us are jailed on trespass charges,
the greatest number of people arrested in an antinuclear
demonstration in the nation's history.

The San Luis Obispo county jails are full, so I'm locked
up in the Cuesta College gymnasium with two hundred other
men. Except for the overpowering fragrance de locker room of
unwashed bodies, and the twice-a-day meals of baloney sand-
wiches, it's easy time. After three days' imprisonment, I'm bused

to the county courthouse for my preliminary hearing, and to
answer for two counts of 602N 409 of the Penal Code.

"How do you plead?" the judge asks me.

"Not guilty," I reply.

During the last day of summer 1981, a couple of days after
my release from jail, on the same day that the few remaining
protesters abandon their two-week-old blockade of Diablo,
PG&E discreetly discloses an error at its plant. A junior pipe
analyst discovers that the wrong blueprints have been used
when building the bracing that supports safety equipment at
the Unit 1 reactor. Somehow, PG&E engineers had mistakenly
used a mirror-image diagram for Unit 2 when they built Unit 1
and vice versa. Further inspections reveal that the safety equipment itself had been drastically underweighed, invalidating the
calculations used to design support beams. If the floor holding
the equipment 141 feet above the reactor failed during a plant
accident or earthquake, more than one hundred tons of safety
apparatus would cascade to the ground, disrupting the emergency core-cooling system. This could cause the ultimate horror, a Class 9 accident. A meltdown.

Hours before fuel-loading is to take place and Diablo Canyon brought on-line, the Nuclear Regulatory Commission
halts the firing-up of the plant. Although PG&E insists that all
problems can be solved in a matter of weeks, the case of the
switched blueprints creates an uproar. Over the following
weeks, one frightening and publicly embarrassing miscue after
another is exposed, finally culminating in a decision by the
NRC to revoke PG&E's low-power testing license for Diablo,
pending a thorough review of the plant's safety engineering.

For some who sat-in and were arrested at the gates of Diablo, the presence of so many engineering flaws is vindication
enough for their illegal behavior. Others feel complete vindication cannot come until their case is proven in court; until
a judge, a jury, and the American public agree that nuclear
power is not safe, not clean, and not cheap; until their actions

are viewed not as civil disobedience but civil obedience to a
higher law.

Rather than hold two thousand separate trials, the prosecu-
tion and defense agree to hold a showcase trial called *The People*
v. *MacMillan*. In the trial, which began in May 1982, fifteen of
the protesters, chosen to represent the others, base their defense
on an old California "choice of evils" statute that allows the
intentional commission of an illegal act when the purpose of
such an act is to prevent a greater harm or greater crime.

During the trial, we defendants admit we broke trespass
laws, but argue we were "compelled by necessity" to protect
our community from the greater harm posed by the start-up
of the nuclear plant. We are not so much defending ourselves
as prosecuting the adversary—putting on trial the Diablo plant
and by implication Pacific Gas & Electric Company, the Nuclear Regulatory Commission, and what we feel is the nuclear
nightmare that industrialists, technologists, and politicians have
laid upon our lives and the lives of our descendants for thousands of years to come.

A man may break the words of the law and yet not break the
law itself . . .
    —*Reninger* v. *Fagossa* (1551)

Thus did an English court centuries ago express a concept
today familiar to lawyer and layperson alike—that the spirit
of the law may sometimes be at variance with the letter of the
law. On occasion, the just and law-abiding citizen will feel
compelled to "break the words of the law" in order to preserve
not only his or her own life and the lives of family and friends
as well, but those of society and generations unborn.

The defense of necessity is simple enough: if a house is
burning down and you break in to rescue a child, you won't
be charged with trespass or breaking and entering—society
recognizes your actions are for the greater good.

Thus, it's justifiable for a ship's crew to revolt and return to port if their vessel is unseaworthy; for a person to kill a bear in violation of game laws to protect his property; for a person to violate traffic laws in order to apprehend a speeding felon.

Given the facts of American corporate life, there was little likelihood of PG&E voluntarily abandoning its project at Diablo Canyon. Therefore, we defendants felt compelled to act to prevent the operation of the reactors because a greater harm would immediately occur—the contamination and death of an unknown number of people and genetic damage to infants in utero or as yet unconceived. Further, all legal avenues had been exhausted and proven futile; fuel-loading was imminent, and no other recourse was available but physical intervention.

One of the elements of our defense of necessity was the requirement that we prove we had a "reasonable belief" that nuclear power posed an imminent danger to our lives and property. It's up to the judge to decide whether this belief was reasonable.

The defense calls expert witnesses—among them a pipe-fitter, a nuclear physicist, a geophysicist, a geneticist, a public health officer, a reactor safety expert, a quality assurance inspector, and a structural design engineer—who illuminate topics such as the nuclear fuel cycle, accidents at nuclear plants, atmospheric emissions, and human response to radiation. Also, that the Nuclear Regulatory Commission has become the advocate of the evil it is mandated to police and that nuclear power is little more than a front for nuclear weaponry. Further, that even the "normal" cost of nuclear technology is more than our society can bear. A dominant and repeated element of the testimony in the trial is the unresponsiveness of the Nuclear Regulatory Commission to the concerns of the people of San Luis Obispo, the state, and the nation in regard to the horrendous dangers posed by any nuclear plant and particularly Diablo—built by inept and indifferent workers, built backward in many important respects.

Putting nuclear power on trial is a reasonable way to justify the defense of necessity, but not nearly as compelling to me as

bringing into the courtroom a discussion of moral values and
the role of individual conscience. It is for these rare discussions
of values sprinkled amongst the nuclear tech talk that I sit
through the three-week trial, scribbling notes and rereading
Thoreau. "Can there not be a government in which majorities
do not virtually decide right and wrong, but conscience?"
Thoreau asks in his essay "Civil Disobedience."

ROBERT FOSTER (*prosecutor*):
   You broke the law. Didn't you consider your actions con-
   trary to the democratic principles of this country?
BILL EVANS (*defendant*):
   I considered it my patriotic duty to blockade. I never felt
   more American in my life.
FOSTER:
   Our federal government is for nuclear power. Wasn't Ronald
   Reagan elected in part because he advocated nuclear power?
EVANS:
   I didn't vote for him.
RICHARD FRISHMAN (*defense attorney*):
   Objection! Move to strike. Ronald Reagan is not on trial
   here.
JUDGE CHOTNER:
   Objection sustained. Question and answer stricken.
FOSTER:
   Mr. Evans, everyone who disagrees with the government
   does not feel 'compelled by necessity' to break the law.
EVANS:
   There was no legal recourse. I only had two options. One of
   them was to blockade. People are responsible for the actions
   of their government. I thought that was the lesson we
   learned from Nuremberg.
FOSTER:
   You said there were two options open to you. What was the
   second one?
EVANS:
   Intense prayer.

On this Diablo foray, I begin hiking from See Canyon Road. Jake See raised apples in the canyon, and his wife, Clara, made chocolate. Her chocolate got better reception than his apples, and they eventually relocated to Santa Barbara to launch a chain of chocolate shops—See's Candies.

Although the coastal canyons are lovely, with some truly enormous live oaks, the hiker's way to go is via the grassy ridges of the Irish Hills. If I were to design an extension of Pecho Coast Trail, I would use the high coastal ridge.

The ridge route was the one I boosted to Pat Stebbins of the Coastal Commission. My suggestion for the alignment of a coastal path came from field reconnaissance—read trespassing—a way of gathering information officially frowned upon by the Coastal Commission, unofficially encouraged by its best employees, such as Pat Stebbins. In appreciation of the delicacy of her position (wanting the information, not wanting to know how it was gained), I would always preface my trail reports with "From what I've read . . ." or "Historic use patterns suggest . . ." Coming from me, this bureaucratic double-talk always made her laugh.

In Diablo Canyon, Chase came upon the devil himself—in the form of a rattlesnake. He was disappointed when the snake disappeared into a cranny and neither shot, stick, nor stone could reach it. When I reach the ridge overlooking Diablo Canyon, I too see the devil—in the form of the last nuclear power plant built in the West.

In all the environmental impact reports prepared for, during, or after the nuclear plant project, no planner ever attempted to quantify what bad vibes could fall upon the land, or how such bad vibes might be mitigated. Reports quantified the numbers of octopuses parboiled, birdies electrocuted, and plant life lost, but never addressed any possible contamination of the spirit that might result from a power plant sited dead center on the California coast.

In retrospect, the 1980s here on the California coast, or elsewhere in America, were a poor time to discuss values and ethics. At least that seemed to be the case in the San Luis Obispo County courthouse where our defense of necessity pleas was heard.

Dr. Ernest Partridge, a university philosophy professor who specializes in the effects of technocracy on mankind, testified about the ethics of nuclear power. Unfortunately for the necessity defense, Judge Chotner ruled that a philosophical discussion of nuclear power is not admissible as evidence.

We tried hard to sell the concept of self-defense. In the past, threats to humans were often more tangible and it was easier to understand the concept of self-defense. The world is more complex today. Technology and chemistry, thought to be unalloyed boons only a generation ago, now present dangers as fearsome as any fire, flood, or armed robber. If the right of necessary self-defense is to be upheld, we have to take an expanded philosophical view toward our times and technology, Diablo defendants argued. Are we to be mere automatons existing for the purposes of corporate and governmental power, or are we to be human beings whose dignity demands of us moral patterns of behavior?

The doctrine of necessity is founded on the policy that the law ought to promote the achievement of higher values at the expense of lesser values. Consequently, not only must the defendant who is successful in a necessity plea be acquitted, it is often also appropriate that he or she be praised.

We Diablo protesters were not praised for our trespasses. We weren't exactly convicted or acquitted either. The defense of necessity was allowed, but narrowed and hamstrung so severely that it became nearly useless as a moral justification for civil disobedience or to contest Diablo in a higher court, the cost of such contesting far beyond the means of we protesters. Years later the slow-moving judicial system gave the blockaders credit for time served and dismissed criminal trespassing charges.

I linger, looking down at Diablo Canyon for only a moment, before pressing on toward Montana de Oro State Park. The time for protest has passed, and I am left only to contemplate the morality of what has transpired here. I walk past Diablo Canyon, trapped in this land's history, its history trapped in me.

FOURTEEN

Big Sur

I SEE HIM in the mist, a lone horseman on this Big Sur trail. Bedroll and saddlebags are tied to a sturdy chestnut mare, the warm breath of which is visible in the chilly morning air. A campaign hat tops his weathered face. A walrus mustache covers the trace of a smile. Again, for an instant, I glimpse the ghost of Joseph Smeaton Chase.

He acknowledges me with an almost imperceptible nod, and then he is lost around the next switchback, lost in the mist.

So many times on the coastal trail our paths have crossed. The ghost rider haunts me; I was compelled to take a little time off from my walk to read all his writing, journey around the southland and research what I could about his life.

While I hadn't expected to conjure him in Big Sur, I did mean to ponder him; that is to say, to try to gain the measure of the man behind the mannered writing, to consider the bon homme behind the bon mots.

Now, nearing the halfway point of my journey, seems a fitting time to ponder the life and letters of this fellow nature scribe. And what better place to contemplate Chase than the middle of this wondrous coast range called the Santa Lucia Mountains? In the Ventana Wilderness, in Big Sur country, in the heart of California.

It is not a gentle heart. A mile-high coastal ridge plunges abruptly to a rocky, wave-lashed shore. Steep redwood-shaded canyons, accompanied by rain-swollen streams, slice deeply into the western ridge. Exposed upper ridges are smothered in impenetrable chaparral. Many trails crossing the wilderness are washed-out or burned out, overgrown or abandoned.

My trail this morning is Salmon Creek Trail. Digger pine and Santa Lucia fir bristle atop the nearby peaks. Files of oaks follow the mountains' folds.

I'm guessing this Trans–Big Sur route will be the most difficult stretch of my coast walk—with the possible exception of that considerable bit of bushwhacking through the chaparral in the Santa Barbara backcountry.

Residents of San Simeon and Morro Bay warned Chase not to enter the Big Sur country: "Several people told me that I should get lost in the rough and little-traveled country I was entering; but my saddlebags held provisions for a week and I knew that water would be plentiful, so felt sure I could get through."

I too have plenty of food, fuel, and water. I'm as ready as I'll ever be for a week in the wilderness, a hundred miles alone.

Chase left the coast a few miles south of where I now walk, and rode into the Santa Lucia Mountains up San Carpoforo Creek. The mouth of this creek is private property these days, which is why I entered the mountains from the mouth of the next canyon north—Salmon Creek.

Salmon Creek Trail climbs through lush streamside vegetation, then heads out across an exposed slope dotted with lupine. Lingering summer fog must protect the wildflowers here; unlike their southern cousins, they survive into early summer.

"Flowers grow best where broad ocean leans against the land," I intone pompously to a rabbit.

The black-tailed hare wiggles its nose at me, apparently unimpressed with my recitation of British poet Oliver Goldsmith's immortal words.

Thought you'd like that, Mr. Chase.

No doubt JSC's love of nature was colored by the fact that he was British-born. He dedicates *California Coast Trails* "To my Brothers, whose lot it has been to remain in the Old Home Land."

California's Central Coast reminds him of the rocky shores of Guernsey and Jersey. Purple foxgloves growing along the coastal trail recall the flowers decorating the lanes of Surrey and Devon. The cypress at Point Lobos are "Lear-like fellows." He looks down at the Big Sur coast and spouts Keats:

. . . magic casements opening in the foam
Of perilous seas in faery lands forlorn.

"I often wished I were some fraction of Keats myself," he sighed, "to put the beauty of such incidents into felicitous phrase."

Some of Chase's English imagery is less clear. How could he get excited over gorse, that prickly shrub of the British Isle wastelands, a menace to California ranchers, an unwelcome alien growth to ecologists? And how could he compare the tinder-dry, fire-ravaged Santa Monica Mountains with the lush downs of England?

Dartmoor and Exmoor, the Lake District and the Peak District, and everywhere else I hiked in Britain, reminded me not a whit of California. Well, there was this one time, after walking the Cotswolds for a week in incessant rain, that the sun came out for an hour on the last day of the trek, and I thought to myself: My God, England really is part of the same solar system as California.

Truly, it could not have been the similarity of British and California ecology that compelled Chase to strain for comparisons. These comparisons, from an accurate botanist and keen wordsmith, are most un-Chaselike. But who can blame a man when on occasion he stops being the dispassionate observer and speaks from his heart? Joseph Smeaton Chase, twenty years removed from the Old Home Land, was homesick.

A thousand feet above sea level, my trail crosses a stream and ascends into a forest of Douglas fir, often called spruce, which accounts for the names Spruce Creek and Spruce Camp on the Los Padres National Forest map.

I reach a junction with a trail leading south toward Dutra Spring and Carpojo Creek. Carpojo Creek is the same Carpoforo Creek Chase followed, but appears to have lost a few letters over the years. Chase camped for a full two weeks along San Carpoforo Creek, by far the longest he lingered in one spot during his whole coastal ride. It must have held considerable attraction for him. I wonder why.

Pausing for a moment in the deep shade of Douglas firs, I decide to retrace part of Chase's route, even if it means turning south for a short time. Spruce Creek Trail climbs steadily through woods, soon rewarding my decision to strike south with a fine display of wild iris.

From a distance, a big cone spruce could be adjudged similar to a Douglas fir; both have distinct pyramid shapes. Botanists call both *pseudotsuga,* "false hemlocks."

Up close, their differences show. The spruce has the bigger cones—four to eight inches long, about twice as big as the fir's. But the fir stands quite a bit taller (150 to 300 feet) than its 40- to 60-foot-high cousin. However, the Douglas fir here in the southern part of Big Sur, and in drier climes to the south, stand considerably shorter than those dream trees of Pacific Northwest loggers.

Big cone spruce range through California as far north as northern Santa Barbara County, in effect heralding the end of southern California, the beginning of central California.

Is the end of big cone spruce the end of southern California?

It's the kind of question Chase, the consummate tree lover, would ponder. In fact, the first reason Chase gives for stopping for two whole weeks in San Carpoforo Canyon is his intent to study the rare Santa Lucia fir. Only after he sets up camp does he admit that poor Chino's withers were too inflamed to proceed further and that he was stuck there until his horse recovered. (And he was probably pretty tired himself, though he doesn't admit as much.)

With me are Los Padres National Forest maps from 1938, 1971, and 1984. San Carpoforo stayed on the map from Chase's day until 1984, when the Forest Service succumbed to popular usage and shortened it to San Carpojo.

My most modern map also shows me I'm not really in the wilder-

ness, at least not the official capital *W* Wilderness delineated in a special green shade by the cartographer. The most *sur* part of Big Sur was
geographically gerrymandered out of the Ventana Wilderness by the
governmental powers that be when the Wilderness was established in
1984.

Wilderness activists have been trying to put the left-out crests and
canyons back in the Ventana ever since.

Exactly where he camped, Chase doesn't say. He might have liked
Dutra Flat, with its small creek and spacious meadow. Near the camp
are signs of an old homestead: four tall cypress trees and some fruit
trees. I wonder if the settlers who planted them were in residence
when Chase rode by in 1912.

San Carpojo Trail continues down a gently-sloping grassy valley to
another trail camp, Turkey Springs Camp, then to a wagon road. I follow the old road, as Chase-like a byway as I can imagine. The trail
turns south across a meadow and comes to San Capojo Creek, crosses
and recrosses the creek and soon leads to San Carpojo Camp. It's level,
grassy, well-shaded—an ideal camp. Across the creek is a fence marking the boundary of the Hearst property.

I look longingly beyond the fence and a delicious idea comes to
me: I bet nobody has ever walked the length of the Hearst Ranch.
Yeah, San Carpoforo to San Simeon. A Hearst Castle Hike, from the
Ventana Wilderness to La Casa Grande.

At twilight, when dusk chases the color from San Carpoforo
Canyon, I see two black and white horses, tinted a rose color by the
setting sun. Wild horses? I approach the creatures slowly, trying not to
spook them. I squint harder into the twilight.

They're not horses at all.

Zebras!

From the Hearst Ranch, no doubt.

As the zebras gambol across the grassland, I reconsider my notion
of walking across Hearstland. With my luck, lions and tigers prowl the
ranch, ready to feast on trespassers.

I put on a jacket and throw a log on the fire. Early summer days are
long: the red sunset comes at 8:00, darkness by 8:30. I'll try coaxing the

campfire into staying up with me until 10:30 or 11:00. It is uncomfortable to spend ten-plus hours balled up in a sleeping bag; the body will
rebel.

I see Joseph Smeaton Chase in my campfire. In my mind I shuffle
through the old black-and-white photographs, trying to get some
sense of the man, for he reveals little that is personal in his books.

He worked twenty years in Los Angeles, first as a social worker,
later in a camera store, before he hit the trail around 1909. Los Angeles
was hardly a busy metropolis in the first decade of the twentieth century, but Chase no doubt felt confined by city life and his isolation
from the green world. "The human palate is, in fact, strangely dead to
the majestic ingredient," he wrote in *Yosemite Trails*.

After Chase left his home in El Monte and began journeying
around the state, good things happened to him: He saw California at
its most beautiful, got book contracts, moved out of L.A., met and
married a fine woman.

It all appears to be working out the same way for me too I think as
I fall into a deep and peaceful sleep.

NEXT DAY I double-back to Salmon Creek Trail and hike up
hot, brushy slopes to Coast Ridge Road, a fire and military road
marking the boundary between Fort Hunter Liggett Military Reser-
vation and the National Forest. I see the ocean to the west, the Salinas
Valley to the east.

If I wanted to cover a lot of miles, relatively quickly, I could follow
this road north for twenty miles, but I don't want to walk a road, not
when trails beckon; no point skirting the wilderness when I can walk
right through it.

I follow Coast Ridge Road for only a mile, then drop off the crest
to a waterless camp called Lion Den. I then follow a footpath along
Villa Creek, and soon encounter the last of the year's wild strawberries
and California's southernmost stands of redwoods. It's nice to meet the
redwoods; I expect to spend a lot of time in their company on the way
to Oregon.

In the middle of a meadow near Buckeye Camp, I view what appears to be the world's slowest ballet—performed by a troupe on Tho-

razine. On closer inspection, it's a dozen men and women practicing t'ai chi chuan.

They're a New Age outfit out of Berkeley, they tell me during their break between t'ai chi and *za-zen*. They are here in Big Sur for a week of Hatha yoga, Zen meditation, breathing exercises, deep massage, and Sufi dancing, as well as a cleansing, macrobiotic diet.

They serve me some fine sun tea and are curious about my journey. I explain my walk up the coast, my mission to create a California Coastal Trail.

The only one with gray in his beard, whom I take to be the leader, teases me. How is it possible to find my way through the woods when I haven't yet found my true path? "Perhaps a little meditation, a little *za-zen* would help," he suggests.

"I don't know about *za-zen,* but I could use a couple z's," I reply. There's some good-natured laughter.

When pressed, I explain, as delicately as possible, that an overly caffeinated hiker like me is never going to find unification with myself, with the universe, or with myself and the universe, through formal sitting meditation.

A half-hour, an hour passes. We sip more sun tea. Coffeehouse discussion without the coffeehouse. Or the coffee. I feel a bit mentally dull, frankly, not doing well at all in our debate about the subjective nature of reality and whether there's a sound if a tree falls in a forest and no one is around to hear it. My belief system obviously includes too much God and too little human transformation for the group. Gray Beard calls, "What I detect is a certain resistance on your part to self-discovery."

I try to tell them I turn on with just trails, but they will have none of it. Gray Beard pushes me to acknowledge that the trail is really myself. As one, they believe that nature is a stage for plays they are writing, a dance floor for the human dance.

Maybe it's my imagination, but the circle around me grows tighter. I begin to feel a native among missionaries. But we run out of arguments. Gray Beard reaches back to consult a higher authority. "As the great Sasaki Roshi said: 'Everyone has the desire to climb high mountains. Why? Because the mountain is yourself.' "

No-no, the mountain is not myself. I can't let this go unanswered but Gray Beard has left me, if not speechless, quoteless. There's a satisfied murmur among the za-zenners, a smile as wide as the cosmos on Gray Beard's face. My memory banks on this Big Sur trek hold only the words of Joseph Smeaton Chase. Ah-ha!

"As the great J. Smeaton Chase said," I offer, " 'Physiology and psychology meet in the borderland of dreams and the onion is a potent and treacherous vegetable.' "

Bidding my baffled friends adieu, I hike toward Alder Creek Camp.

I've always been more than a little uncomfortable with contemplating inner nature when there's so much outer nature around me. My ways have never been as interesting a study to me as nature's. True, I am part of nature. But a small part. And I find a bit odd this notion that nature is but a backdrop for human potential. Does a bear shiatsu in the woods?

Motorists can jounce up a not-for-timid-drivers dirt road to reach Alder Creek Camp, but none have braved the road today. I have the large pleasant campground to myself.

As I set up camp I wonder if Chase ever considered what his true path was. He must have had some reflection in his mid-forties, a time of life that finds many men examining the miles covered and the trail ahead. He was sick of city life, and city people whom he observed to be easily bored prisoners of fashion, out of touch with the natural world, and ever in pursuit of the almighty dollar, or in what he reports as the Spanglish slang, pursuing "Don Dinero."

Like Chase, I too find that the voices that speak to me are the voices of the wilderness.

Next morning I double-back to Coast Ridge Road, follow it for a few miles, descend to Prewitt Ridge Camp, navigate through a confusion of dirt roads, and descend sharply with Prewitt Ridge Road through mixed oak and pine forest. A few clearings offer sweeping vistas of the coast. The lovely road drops down through madrone, yerba buena, and scads of gooseberries to road's end at Alms Ridge. Or what used to be called Alms Ridge. The recreation site on the 1971 forest map is not on the most recent map.

In hiking for Alms Ridge I'm committing myself to a shortcut. I really don't want to take any more fire roads, or double-back yet again to Coast Ridge Road. If the old maps are right, a primitive trail connects Alms Ridge with Mill Creek.

My decision followed consultation with that prized possession, a 1971 Los Padres National Forest map. To most modern travelers, an out-of-date map might not sound like much of a prize, but to a trailblazer a map showing old trails can be very valuable. We veteran bureaucracy watchers know that trails often disappear from modern maps because the Forest Service has neither the interest nor the funds to maintain them; the Forest Service figures that the best way to "maintain" trails under these circumstances is to take them off the map.

We sly hikers know that just because a trail vanishes from the map doesn't mean it vanishes from the face of the earth.

In theory, according to my 1971 map, an "infrequently maintained" black-dashed trail (as distinct from a red-dashed "maintained" trail) leaves Alms Ridge, heading first east and then north for a mile to Mill Creek Trail. In practice, on the ground, what appears to be the correct trail contours along a cool redwood slope for a few hundred yards, then promptly dead-ends in an abandoned stock enclosure. Other trails appear to be ancient cattle or deer trails.

Uh-oh. Maybe in this instance the Forest Service removed the trail from its map after it was removed from the ground.

I give up on trails, mapped or not, consult a compass, and strike cross-country on a steep northerly descent to Mill Creek. An hour of pathfinding brings me to Mill Creek, which is paralleled by Mill Creek Trail.

A mill located on the creek shaped the canyon's felled redwoods. A hundred years later the detritus of this enterprise—stray posts, shakes and beams, along with odds and ends of machinery—are still strewn about the forest floor. The cool, moist, fern-covered canyon must boast more banana slugs crawling along the trail than any other Big Sur footpath. I climb the chaparral slopes to Naciemiento-Fergusson Road, then walk a mile down to Coast Highway.

I PUT IN FOR REPAIRS at Esalen Institute, where my longtime friend Anya Kucharev is temporarily in residence. An expert Russian linguist, she is a pioneer of the Soviet-Esalen Exchange Program. The idea, she explains, is to help speed the new world order by raising the consciousness of newly liberated Russian and Eastern-bloc opinion leaders. With some hot-tubbing and heavy talking, perhaps Old World ways will dissolve into New Age consciousness.

Chase visited the majestic blufftop where Esalen now stands, although it wasn't a metaphysical fat farm then but a primitive hot springs resort called Slate's. He enjoyed a hot bath in a tub perched on a cliff, with the gulls screeching above him and the breakers roaring below. "Here some hot sulphur springs issue from the face of the cliff, and a couple bathtubs have been hauled up and the water led into them. This makes a decided novelty in the hydropathic line, and would be worth money to the enterprising owner if the place were more accessible."

An enterprising owner, Esalen Institute founder Michael Murphy, made the place more accessible in the mid-1960s, and created a center for movement and massage classes, group therapy sessions, and New Age classes that put Esalen—and Big Sur—on the map.

Standing in Esalen's coed showers (a de rigueur ritual cleansing before hot tub immersion), I am suddenly very conscious of how my well-tanned arms and legs contrast with my lily-white buns and torso. Further bodily inventory reveals a wide array of bites, punctures, and abrasions on my legs—the inevitable result of this hiker's disdain for long pants. A gut-check reveals that my love handles, that extra flab around the middle that mysteriously appears on we over-thirty guys, have all but vanished during the walk.

Emerging from the mist at the far end of the showers are two enormous women. Together, hip to hip, they fill the doorway, where they pause for a moment to contemplate the Pacific. Six feet tall, broad-shouldered, muscular—such were the women who populated the 1510 Spanish novel *The Deeds of Esplandian* by Garci Rodriguez Ordóñez de Montalvo. The novel's setting was "an island called California, very close to the Terrestrial Paradise."

The two women in animated conversation seem to fill a tub by themselves, so I plop into another nearby, followed by the graceful Anya whose entry reflects daily practice.

The voices in the next tub are not Californian but Russian. The ruddy-faced Russians talk excitedly; one of them notices me smiling at her and smiles back.

I wonder what's being discussed in the 105-degree water. Could they be two former Communist Party *apparatchiks* struggling with the concept of democracy? Two would-be entrepreneurs? How exciting to ponder the human and societal transformation emerging from these healing waters! "We live in exciting times, Anya. Those Russian women, what are they saying?"

"You really want to know?"

"Of course."

"You're kind of small, but you have a very cute butt."

AFTER TWO DAYS of ease at Esalen, I head back into the hills via Vincente Flat Trail, which zigzags up the steep coastal slopes of the Santa Lucia Mountains. It has about everything a Big Sur trail should have, including solemn redwood canyons, oak-studded potreros, meadows smothered with pink owl's clover and California poppies, and—when the foggy curtain parts—a view of the tempestuous Pacific.

Big Sur has some beautiful canyons, all right, carved into the east flank of the Santa Lucia Range. What this means to a hiker is that Big Sur is far more easily explored west to east, that is to say up one canyon and down the other, rather than south to north, the course of my journey.

Big Sur's resistance to south-north travel was the very same problem that faced Captain Gaspar de Portola's expedition of 1769 as he and his fellow Spaniards attempted to march through the Santa Lucia Mountains to Monterey. Without much difficulty, the soldiers and missionaries had marched close by the shore from San Diego to San Luis Obispo. The coastline, rather accurately described by Spanish navigators, was walkable until some fifty miles north of San Luis Obispo. And then . . . *Ay, caramba!* Greeting Portola and his men were huge mountains rising right out of the surf and precipitous muddy slopes cloaked in impenetrable chaparral, worse even than the mountains of Spain. And every dark spooky canyon filled with ferns and redwood trees. God knows what heathens hid in such places. Neither beach nor bluffs nor mountains looked passable. Portola ordered an about-face and the party headed inland to California's Great Central Valley. The way to Monterey through the valley was easy.

In short order, the Spanish called the road between missions *El Camino Real,* the King's Highway. And what was more or less a coastal trail from San Diego to San Luis Obispo now went inland for well over a hundred miles. But that is the great difference between the journeys of Chase and McKinney and the journeys of the Spanish. Portola and Father Serra intended to link one mission to another by road.

Chase also visited every mission, behavior that seems curious, unless you know he was researching his next book—on California missions. He rides to Jolon, then down to Mission San Antonio. After the climb from Carpoforo Canyon to the San Antonio River, Chino's withers inflamed again so in Jolon, Chase exchanged Chino for a sturdy Forest Service steed he named Anton, after the nearby Mission San Antonio. Like a good freelance writer, Chase had multiple projects: while researching *California Coast Trails,* he was also taking notes for a later book about the California missions.

Monterey became the capital of Alta California. North and east of the capital was plenty of flat land for the ranchos, so the Spaniards probably figured, why bother with that godforsaken country to the south?

Early on, the coast south of Monterey was known as *la costa del Sur,* the coast to the south; a wild, little-known land, with two rivers; and these two rivers were known as *sur chico* and *sur grande,* the little river to the south and the big river to the south.

Then came the gringos who Spanglished it to Big Sur.

When the townsfolk asked those unfortunate settlers on the rancherias in Big Sur backcountry where they were from they reportedly answered: *"Allá de la costa del Sur, allá lojos al diablo"* (From the coast to the south, from down there to the devil).

When Chase visited the Big Sur country, he reveled in its wildness, and the hospitable mountain people captured his heart. "I was glad to find . . . that it was yet possible to live where mail comes once a week and telegraph or telephone messages are impossible, and still be comfortable and contented."

In some ways, Chase's journey through Big Sur was easier than mine, in some ways more difficult. Why it was easier was the existence of a true coast trail that extended along much of the Big Sur coast. As Chase described it: "A long bridle trail wanders up the coast, threading its way through deep gorges of redwood, madrone and tanbark oak,

and along league on league of bold cliff and breezy mountain slope—
ever in sight or sound of the gleam and boom of the Pacific."

That coastal trail is now, for the most part, Highway 1, hardly a
good walk.

Chase's passage through the Santa Lucia Mountains was made more
difficult by the lack of reliable maps. Although much of Big Sur had
been set aside as Monterey National Forest in 1908, no good forest
map had been produced. I have a pretty good map of Big Sur imprinted on a cheap souvenir bandanna.

Even if he got lost a couple times, good reviews for his first book,
Yosemite Trails, must have put a spring in his step, like this rave from the
magazine *Out West:* "If you have wanted all your life to make a trip to
Yosemite and cannot go, the next best thing is to read *Yosemite Trails* by
Joseph Smeaton Chase. You will forget while reading it that you are
not there, and when you have finished you will find a way to go. Each
paragraph is a picture, each page a poem, there is not an uninteresting
line in its entire 340 pages. . . ."

Yosemite Trails, an account of three rides through the High Sierra, nature notes, and a little practical advice for the traveler, appeared in 1911,
when Chase was forty-seven years old. In my opinion anyway, it's second only to John Muir's books as a description of the Sierra Nevada.

That same year Chase also wrote *Conebearing Trees of the California
Mountains,* "prepared not by a botanist for botanists, nor by a botanist
for students, but by a tree-lover for tree-lovers." Trees don't change
very much over the years, and this handbook is as useful today as it was
in 1911.

I stumble toward the faint murmur of Hare Creek, pop into my
sleeping bag and marvel at a million crystals in the sky. Just before I
fall asleep, I hear Chase whispering to me: "Is that the wind or the
river booming softly ten thousand miles away? Or can it be truth, cosmic sound, the very sound of the earth? It might be. It might be."

I'M FILLING my Sierra cup with coffee when I hear another
voice in the wilderness. This one belongs not to the old ghost rider
but to a woman with long, black braids and Birkenstock sandals. "Am
I still on the trail?"

"It depends on where you're going."

"Esalen."

As she walks closer, I see the Indian blanket and rolled-up yoga mat, the bag of soy nuts tied to her belt, the beatific smile." Go back to the trail junction and head downhill on the Vincente Flat Trail. It will take you to Highway 1."

"Was I on the right path?" Her intense eyes sparkle. "I mean in the narrow sense of the word."

"In the narrow sense, no."

I enjoyed my stay with the Esalenites, who always proved to be interesting conversationalists, and am anxious to talk. "Coffee?" I offer.

"Poison," she replies, heading for the trail." Besides, I'm just into soy nuts this trip. At Esalen they fed me a little too well."

Chase whispers to me once again: "One meets out-of-the-way characters, naturally, in out-of-the-way places."

My route today takes me over the shoulder of Cone Peak, which has been a geographical landmark to coast travelers for one hundred years and is the most abrupt pitch of country on the Pacific Coast. It rises to just under a mile high in a mere three-and-a-half miles from sea level. On a clear winter day, I've stood on warm Sand Dollar Beach and looked up at snow-covered Cone Peak—a stirring sight, indeed.

Botanically, it's a very important mountain. On its steep slopes, botanists Thomas Coulter and David Douglas discovered the Santa Lucia fir, considered the rarest fir in America. (Tree lovers know that when names were attached to western cone-bearing trees, Coulter's went to a pine, Douglas's to a fir.) The spire-like Santa Lucia fir is found only in scattered stands in the Santa Lucia Mountains. It grows above the highest coast redwoods, about two thousand feet in elevation, concentrated in steep, rocky, fire-resistant spots.

Another unusual tree, the tanbark oak, which Chase called "that curious link between oak and chestnut," grows on the slopes of Cone Peak. Before synthetic chemicals were manufactured to tan leather, an astringent tannic acid made from oak bark was used. At the turn of the century, the gathering and shipping of the bark was a considerable industry in these parts. On old maps are a couple of Tan Bark camps. Occasionally I've spotted blazed trees, used by the tanbark gatherers to find their way through the woods.

NEXT MORNING'S TRAIL is nearly the same as the one used more than eighty years ago by Chase. I ascend into Lime Kiln Canyon, where, late in the last century, lime was quarried, burned, packed into barrels, and shipped from a cable landing at the mouth of the canyon. By the time Chase explored the fern-lined canyon, he found only moss-covered buildings and rusty machinery.

As I hike into the upper reaches of Lime Kiln Canyon, the trail becomes difficult to follow because range cows have trampled the main trail into oblivion and added a few paths of their own. Chase and his loyal horse, Anton, got lost here. "The complication of cattlepaths among which we now wandered was quite beyond my trailcraft. About midafternoon I found myself entirely at fault, high up on a steep and slippery slope that was cut by frequent gullies choked with sharp rocks and stubborn brush."

I catch my breath at Goat Camp, then switchback up through chaparral and grassland to the Gamboa Trail. The name of this trail honors the Gamboa family, who had a ranch on these slopes. They treated Chase to a supper of venison, frijoles, and tortillas. "The house is a quaint little place, clinging precariously to the hillside and commanding a view that millionaires might envy. The good Spanish woman made me welcome, and I slept in the orchard on a mattress slung among the boughs of an apple tree."

High atop the coast ridge, I break for lunch. As I dip into a bag of figs, I wonder what kept Chase on the trail day after day, night after lonely night. Incessant rain, lip-cracking heat, poison oak, sand fleas, no-trespassing signs, rattlesnakes, quicksand—nothing discouraged him.

Would Chase enjoy a repeat of his 1911 to 1912 ride in the late twentieth century?

Gone are those equine versions of Motel 6, the livery stables. Gone are some of the names on the land, and gone is much of the land itself—covered in concrete and condominiums. Gone are most of Chase's coastal trails; roads now make the coast easier to reach, but harder to know.

Along most of the coast, Chase would be allowed to camp only in a numbered site and make his evening fire only in an official state park stove (designed for charcoal briquettes, not wood). At day's end, in order to view the sunsets he so loved, he would be required to reach the beach via a regulation coastal accessway. Sleeping on the beach could be hazardous to his health; he might easily be pulverized by one of those huge mechanical sand rakes manned by beach maintenance crews.

Would Chase blink uncomprehendingly at the amount of land razed, or marvel at the great tracts of land placed under government protection? Would he find the proverbial glass half-empty or half-full?

Of all the coast trails he explored, those that have changed the least during this century wind through the Big Sur backcountry. He would still like it here.

Ahead lies Madrone Camp and Arroyo Seco, Higgins Creek and Lost Valley, and the second half of a perfect day. As I hit the trail, Chase speaks to me: "Why does complete beauty, in which there is innocence, make us sigh? Is it that we are conscious of separation and sigh, perhaps less for the innocence that must be than for that which has been lost?"

The beauty of Big Sur does make me sigh. And laugh. And rejoice. For five more days I walk the heart of the Middle Kingdom, first over the flanks of Cone Peak, a geographical landmark to travelers since Spanish days, the mountain spiked with the spire-like Santa Lucia fir, that grows high above the highest redwoods, and only in the steepest, rockiest, most fire-resistant parts of Big Sur. Greeting me from atop Cone Peak is a panorama of peaks: Pinyon, Ventana Double Cone, Junipero Serra, and Uncle Sam. Then down through madrone and oak and knob cone pine, down to the Arroyo Seco River, not *seco* at all, still flowing, swelling as I walk its banks, and a hard rain beginning to fall. I find myself in lovely Lost Valley, crossing and recrossing Higgins Creek, walking in the shadow of Marble Peak, pushing north into a wet world of Zig-Zag Creek, Tan Oak Creek, and Pick Creek. The rain soaks into the dry slopes, waters the wildflowers, flows, as do I, down to the banks of that most famous of rivers, the Big Sur.

And then more water, hot water this time, along the Big Sur River—Sykes Hot Springs—rock-rimmed pools surrounded by redwoods. Here in the no-cost, natural hot tubs I soak away what few cares remain, then hit the trail again. Up and over Ventana Double

Cone, one of Big Sur's loneliest summits, over Church Creek Divide, down to Pine Valley Camp, surrounded by towering ponderosa pines, survivors of numerous fires, and then along that other big Big Sur River, the Carmel, and onto the broad shoulder of Uncle Sam Mountain. Pat Spring, Spaghetti Camp, Devils Peak, and Botchers Gap— I'm running out of food now and really should hike for the highway, but I want more and more and keep walking to the great white mountain Pico Blanco and then along the Little Sur River.

Granola, that's all I have left to eat, but I don't care; I can live on inspiration in Big Sur, in this land that has me craving only more of its beauty. I dally in the redwood-shaded grottos, in the tanbark woodlands, atop a ridgeline a mile above the sea. I inhale great draughts of the rain-soaked chaparral, a faintly astringent perfume, the smell of spring fading away and summer born.

FIFTEEN

The Boutiquing of California's Coast

MAYBE MONTEREY'S Cannery Row, formerly the site of a flourishing sardine canning industry, isn't the most intensively boutiqued stretch of California coastline, but it seems that way to me.

Certainly Carmel, a whole town boutiqued, which I had visited earlier in the day, could compete for this dubious honor. If there is anything to do in Carmel except shop, I did not find it.

Cannery Row, the rough, brawling, lusty street of corrugated warehouses, fleabag hotels, and whorehouses immortalized by John Steinbeck, has become, depending on your point of view, either a unique array of specialty shops or a tourist trap. The old cannery buildings have been gutted, prettied, and stuffed chock-full of knick-knack shops, restaurants, and art galleries. Visitors with a historical interest find few clues to the rise and fall of the sardine. In fact, so extensive is the boutiquing that visitors are unable to reach the waterfront, unable to see the shores, for the stores. In a particularly ironic juxtaposition, a bust of Steinbeck mounted on a pedestal faces a row of cutesy shops. Steinbeck's words, taken from his novel *Cannery Row,* were imprinted on his pedestal:

Cannery Row is a stink, a grating sound . . .

Dog-tired, I check into the least expensive waterfront hotel I can find, leave my pack, and return to the Row. I take a seat near Steinbeck, watch the tourists stream into the Monterey Bay Aquarium, and try to figure why this particular mockery of history, literature, and the coastal environment has me so upset.

It's not the aquarium, which is a stunning, state-of-the-art display of underwater life; an altogether fabulous submarine view of Monterey Bay.

It's not the shops, the wax museum, or the carousel.

It's the idea that nature itself can be boutiqued.

After months of walking along land's end, the evidence is clear to me, in the form of plans and planning commissions, stucco and steel, that our citizenry either has not learned or has chosen to forget that the California coastline is a natural ecosystem—as vital, as dynamic, as special as a redwood forest or a Sierra lake. And we continue to treat the coast as a commodity to be auctioned off to the highest bidder. All along the coast, but particularly in southern California, rivers no longer run to the sea to deposit sand for beaches; estuaries, the tidelands' genetic reserves, are drained for development; longshore currents are disrupted by groins and jetties; cliff erosion is thwarted by blankets of cement. The utilitarian function of shoreline, its ability to carry out nature's chores, is being grossly altered. The coast is also losing it utilitarian value to most Californians as the coastal industries of fishing, dairy farming, and agriculture disappear and the last affordable seaside cottages are razed and replaced by high-priced townhouses.

This real-estate sale affects both public and private lands and is having profound influences on California culture. A unique coastal history is cheapened when the marketable is substituted for the memorable. Coastal architecture suffers when the frivolous is substituted for the functional. Coastal ecosystems are degraded when the expensive replaces the priceless. In short, economically and ecologically, what we are witnessing is the boutiquing of California's coast.

The boutiquing of a coastal town does not end with the building of a few dozen or even a few hundred expensive homes. Theme parks—

collections of shops and homes done in a nostalgic nineteenth-century style—complete the boutiquing. Three dominant themes prevail along the California coast: the New England seacoast village, the Victorian, and the mission.

The New England seacoast look is favored by Ye Olde Shopping Mall developers, though the illusion of authenticity suffers when palm trees are included in the landscaping. Whaler village–style condominiums, complete with plank boardwalks and braided rope handrails, electric gaslights, and fake lighthouses, have proved attractive to consumers. The Cape Cod bungalow is also a popular condo style imported from the East Coast.

Of Queen Anne tract houses, fake cupolas and gables, and other manifestations of ersatz Victorian architecture along the coast, the less said the better. This congested sort of architecture appears ill at ease along the coastline, though perhaps in a million years or so, when the next ice age arrives, the steep-pitched Victorian roof will prove invaluable in shedding snow.

Dominating the new architecture along the coast, however, is the mission style—Mission Savings and Loan, Mission Auto Body, Mission Inn, Mission Cemetery. On a hot day, all that white-washed stucco strains the eye. The characteristic black iron grillwork adds a vaguely sinister flavor, giving even a luxury apartment house the profile of a Mexican penitentiary. It is said that mission-style architecture is "natural" for California, but when I gaze out at all those red-tile roofs crowning Santa Barbara, I have to disagree. I know of no shade of red in nature like those tiles, save that of boiled crustaceans.

So widespread is the mission-look that visitors often jump to the conclusion that coastal towns like Carlsbad, Oxnard, and Palos Verdes, given their presiding architectural bias, are mission towns, founded by the Spanish padres. Their mission motif, however, is an afterthought facade; in fact, these towns were born of boosterism, not Catholicism. Local chambers of commerce downplay the circumstances of their towns' birthrights, for fear of being considered illegitimate perhaps.

Only a few angry Western historians have suggested Californians regard the mission era with less romance and more realism. They claim the missions were little more than Chumash Indian concentration camps, and portray Father Junipero Serra as a kind of marketing expert, franchising missions like so many Subway sandwich shops. Despite these revisionist historians, advocacy of the missionary position continues unchallenged. Junipero Serra is honored by Serra Plaza in San Juan Capistrano. The padre's life is depicted on large tile murals installed near the Bank of America building and other offices.

Much of what passes as homage to the past is really a hustle of the present: witness the condominiums built on the historic San Diego ferry landing site on Coronado Island. From 1886 to 1969, the San Diego & Coronado Ferry shuttled a quarter of a billion passengers back and forth from the mainland to Coronado. Generations of visitors flocked to the "Del," that queen of Victorian-era hotels, the Hotel del Coronado. In 1970, the Coronado Bay Bridge opened, considerably altering Coronado's charm and retiring the ferry. At the old ferry landing site, Watts Industries built The Landing, an enormously expensive condominium project on the last major undeveloped piece of private property on San Diego Bay. Construction of The Landing was approved by various planning commissions in large measure because the condos architecturally ape the old Hotel del Coronado, with pitched-roof design, dormers, and awnings. Of course the ersatz Del was constructed of stucco, not wood.

On Catalina Island, not far from Avalon, five hundred condos with prices as high as $1.5 million were built recently. Avalon's mayor declared that the condos "will bring a nice type of person to the island." In homage to the nearby historic Casino building and ballroom, the developers have adopted a 1940s Big Band theme to promote their project, chauffeuring prospective buyers to the condos in a 1941 limousine.

Countless more examples of boutiquing could be given, but it's sufficient to note that nothing is sacred. No, not even a national park. The National Park Service is considering building extensive tourist facilities on the Channel Islands. A park service report contemplates an "early twentieth-century island resort" on Santa Cruz Island and mentions the possibility of inns, airports, and all-terrain shuttle buses, all designed for a "high-quality leisurely experience."

Richard Henry Dana's legacy is a marina and a bluff full of expensive homes. Father Serra's life is inspirational decor for a Bank of

America. Those historical figures lacking ornamental value are over-looked. Homesteaders Pfeiffer, Gamboa, Wheat, and Flores have left their names on coastal slopes, but the importance of their lives has been allowed to fade away. Trailblazers De Anza, Portola, Smith, and Brewer are forgotten and so are their expeditions up the coast. Uniquely Californian events such as the world's first water-to-water airplane flight, from Balboa to Catalina, have sunk into oblivion.

When history is boutiqued, past genius, past labors, past lives, and even life itself are nullified, as if obliterating them from the pages of history. The boutiquing of history and historical landmarks trivial-izes our civilization and what our civilization is entitled to—namely, the accumulation of the best products and visions of preceding gen-erations.

If merely coastal architecture was suffering the pox of boutiquing, one might have a good laugh and carry on, but a more sobering prospect is on the horizon, the boutiquing of the natural world. All along the coastline, whole ecosystems are being replaced with, in the future-world jargon of planners, "pocket beaches," "pocket parks," "SEAs" (Significant Environmental Areas), "scenic turnouts," "vista points," and "view corridors."

The Battle for Bolsa Chica, one of Orange County's most valued and undeveloped coastal properties, epitomizes oceanfront boutiquing. Signal Oil Company, the owner of the oil drilling–degraded Bolsa Chica marshland, envisions a residential development of 5,700 homes and apartments, a shopping center, and a marina with 1,800 boat slips. Conservationists wish to rehabilitate the wetlands for fish and fowl. So far, two hundred acres of the once-extensive wetlands have been re-stored by the U.S. Department of Fish and Wildlife, but the future of the remaining one thousand acres is in serious jeopardy. Wildlife biolo-gists argue that encircling a "duck pond" with homes, boat slips, and commercial development is not the same as preserving a sizable, un-stressed ecological reserve.

Ninety percent of southern California's wetlands have been drained for exclusive residential and marina developments. Habitat for native and migratory waterfowl has disappeared. Commercial and sport fish-ing has suffered. Still, even the last tideland remnants are threatened.

Summa Corporation has offered to preserve a duck pond–sized portion of Ballona Wetlands near Marina del Rey in exchange for permission to drain much of the rest and build a community called Playa Vista, consisting of 8,837 housing units, 2,400 hotel rooms, 4.5 million square feet of commercial space, and a marina.

Coastal bluff ecosystems are also subject to boutiquing. Depending on how you look at More Mesa in Goleta, it's either one of the last untouched natural habitats on Santa Barbara's south coast or an ideal site for two hundred high-priced homes and townhouses. A University of California, Santa Barbara, research team has determined that the mesa, with its wide variety of habitats—including a creek, oak woodlands, wetlands, and grassland—is "environmentally sensitive." The mesa is home to creatures such as frogs, lizards, turtles, and several bird species including the marsh hawk, the white-tailed kite, and the short-eared owl.

"The short-eared owl doesn't pay taxes," scoffs developer Bill Simonsen of Simonsen Group. "We're going to use the land for something that will be producing income, taxes, the things that make society work. We're developing an outstanding development."

Though his development will obliterate a natural environment, Simonsen suggests that the public should be content with the sixty-acre park he has offered to put in.

What passes for ecology along the coast often consists of identifying a few rare species, such as the California least tern or peregrine falcon, and giving them just enough habitat between housing developments to permit their survival. Often, this results in a temporary increase in the population of an endangered creature and it's proclaimed "saved." However, in terms of the long-term success of a species, it's a serious error to believe an increase in population can substitute for the elimination of habitat.

Time will tell if many endangered plants and animals can survive in the ever-smaller niches allowed them. Surely a time will come when a smaller representative environment can no longer substitute for a larger habitat. As quiet is more than an absence of sound, and peace more than an absence of war, an ecosystem is more than an absence of building. Boutiquing the shoreline tampers with the collective gene pool, nullifies species, decimates habitats, and makes it impossible for many life-forms to survive.

As I hike along the coast, I have a recurring fantasy: When the millennium arrives, when navy battleships return to San Diego for conversion into floating universities, their guns, as a last act before being spiked, will be allowed to blow to sand the hideous, continuous, and disfiguring chain of hotels, haciendas, and shopping malls that by then will have completely smothered the coastline.

Other than subversive dreams, what alternatives to boutiquing can I offer the Captains of Industry that will absorb the unemployment problem, the housing shortage, and so on, so well? It will be useless for me to point to the billowing brome grass, the cry of the gull, the crescents of white sand. No, the Master Planners conjure seaside condos facing a concrete promenade. It will be useless for me to point out that we have no right to destroy what's left of our rural citizenry by taking their land and employing them for our own money-making purposes, negating their identity and merging them into Metropolis. No, the Joint Chiefs of Shaft insist on extending the benefits of boutiquing to every coastal nook and cranny.

Combating boutiquing is tough because of the difficulty in recognizing the enemy. The conflict is often oversimplified by the media into ecology versus economy or rich versus poor. Of the first false division, let it be noted that ecology and economy share a common Greek word, *oikos,* meaning "household," and a common ground: the degradation of one leads to the degradation of the other. As for the rich versus poor division, I think there's only so much indignation one can raise at the affluent and their conspicuous consumption of the coastline.

Some boutiquers befouling the coast for private gain, such as the well-organized and well-financed Signal Oil Company or Summa Corporation, are easy to spot. Other boutiquers are ordinary working folk who've simply cut their ties to the coastline on which they live. And still other boutiquers are all the rest of us—all of us who look but don't see or who look the other way.

Rarely questioned is the board of realtor's rationale for boutiquing: An owner has the right to do with his land as he pleases. If he wants to bulldoze his coastal bluffs and put up Moorish castle condos, well, that's his business and this is a free country and what right does anyone have to stop him?

Nearly all Californians agree that some regulation of coastal development is necessary. It's acknowledged that to go as you please is not always to arrive at what is pleasant. But those who would regulate boutiquing are faced with a dilemma: We know a man's home is his castle, but we recognize the dangers of building castles on sand.

The answer to boutiquing in this age of deregulation cannot come from lawmakers. The new taste must grow from within the populace; it cannot be decreed from above, as the California Coastal Commission has found out. It is beyond the commission's mandate to encourage a new coastal ethic. No Harry Truman–like commissioner has a sign on his desk reading THE BOUTIQUE STOPS HERE.

Perhaps Californians can take the approach of consumer advocate David Horwitz: Become educated consumers and fight back. Sunsets and tidepools are not products to be consumed, of course, but they are vital processes to be appreciated, and the difference between a boutiqued environment and a real one is obvious. The consumer has become a fair judge of computers, cars, and chardonnays and is keenly interested in their looks and quality. If consumers can rate products, can they not evaluate living processes? Citizens should be encouraged to judge both built and unbuilt environments by what they are, not by what they pretend to be.

The coast's condition reveals California's culture and tradition as directly as does a newspaper, because the coastline, even its most natural parts, are shaped by this culture. The coastline, either boutiqued or wild, is a historical document. Whether future historians report a path of preservation or the track of a bulldozer is up to us. Today's choice is tomorrow's reality. A bulldozer biting into a coastal terrace can perform the equivalent of a thousand years of erosion in one hour. The choice to not boutique involves a conscious exercise of human will.

Those battling the boutiquers must try not to effect a retreat to the real past, wherever that may be, but to plead for an honesty in the treatment of the built and unbuilt environment. Coastal conservation is more than saying, "Look how wonderful the past is, let's keep it that way." There's no modeling the future solely on the past. The coast's future depends to a large extent on citizens adopting a new visualization, another way of looking at land and sea, a vision of the coastline not as a sandbox for play but as a living thing placed in our trust. Until a new visualization is generally accepted, the problems of zoning, population density, housing, erosion, and cliff collapse will be extremely difficult to solve, and boutiquing will continue unabated. Until a new visualization is accepted, the forces of Cut and Fill and Grade and Pave will continue their assault against landmark and landscape.

While searching for a style, Californians will have to put up with the ongoing orgy of revivalism along the coast. Nineteenth-century-style condos are nothing but surface fashions, the architectural tranquilizers of a dazed age, but they indicate that the flow of tradition is lost and not yet found. As the hideousness created by these revivals brings a reaction, perhaps we'll realize that tradition is not a wave breaking and retreating but a wide, slow current flowing on from the past to the future. If this current is so feeble and so negligible along the coast, architects are hardly to blame.

Like it or not, we have a generation of Californians uncomfortable at the very mention of the word *beauty*, valuing this spurious boutiqueyness over a genuine suitability and harmony with the coastline. Among this generation are coastal commissioners, developers, and other planners of the built and unbuilt environment, the men and women in whose hands the whole coastline is passing. Unless some means can be found of sharing with them not an unblinking reverence for the good old days, not a superficial knowledge of the way we were, but a live, dynamic sense of history, beauty, and natural proportion, the present path of vulgarization and defilement of California's coast will continue.

It's too late to save Dana Point and San Juan Capistrano. Once a pleasant mixture of the urban and rural, they are fated to become, in the parlance of developers, "destination resorts." But it's not too late for Leucadia, North Malibu, Carpinteria, Davenport, Jenner, and Gualala.

"In the hands of an enterprising people, what a country this might be," Richard Henry Dana wrote of California.

The future is in the hands of our enterprising people. If boutiquing comes to dominate the California coast, we shall look coastward and receive no inspiration from the earth. Dune and cliff and wave and beach will be only spectacle, and the binding force they once exerted on the character of Californians will have to be entrusted to planning commissions. May planning commissions be equal to the task.

SIXTEEN

San Francisco, Here I Come

THE WALK from Monterey to San Francisco is a seven-day work week. It's not difficult work—no insurmountable obstacles, no bad weather—but there's plenty of it, miles and miles of beaches and bluffs to walk and walk and walk. Just an hour's walk up-coast from the maddening side of Monterey is all that it takes to calm me.

My first stop along Monterey Bay is Sand City, which is not a city at all, or even a hamlet, but a beachfront mining operation. Enormous mechanized buckets scoop sand from the beach. The sand is then heaped onto conveyor belts, which carry it inland to be washed and sorted by crystal size. Railroad cars carry the sand to industries around the country. A young Sand City employee informs me that various grains of sand have various kinds of uses—in pool filters, glass manufacturing, and graffiti removal. Graffiti removal is fast becoming a boon industry of the 1990s, he tells me. Special sand-blasting techniques have been developed to remove the spray-painted messages left by the cretins vandalizing California's cities. Such sand-blasting is particularly useful on rocks and other surfaces not appropriate for covering by a fresh coat of paint.

Musing that two years of hard labor at the Sand City Sand Mine might be an appropriate sentence for convicted graffiti vandals, I walk north onto Fort Ord Beach. Walking the fort's five miles of beach has long been forbidden, but Fort Ord, once a staging area for troops sent to the Pacific during World War II, and to Vietnam, is one of many military bases around the country about to be closed by military budget cutbacks. Wisely, troops still stationed at the soon-to-be-decommissioned fort have better things to do these days than patrol the beach for walkers, and I cross the fort's beach without anyone in uniform challenging my right to pass.

I pause near the mouth of the Salinas River and reflect on the course taken by this river, one of the state's longest. I last glimpsed this river at its headwaters deep in the Machesna Wilderness of Los Padres National Forest. The Salinas is an upside-down river (flowing south to north) and for many of its 170 miles flows underground. A walk along the Salinas River, through the California heartland, over some of the most fertile land in America, would certainly be an intriguing undertaking, I think, one considerably different from a walk along the coast. I wonder what my impressions would be if I had been raised a Central Valley farm lad in the 1950s and 1960s, and then returned to take a walk in the 1990s.

As I stop for the day and set up camp in the dunes near the river's mouth, I wonder if John Steinbeck came back to contemplate both his beloved Salinas River Valley and his beloved Monterey coast, which he would find the more (or less) inspiring.

The next morning I walk toward what looks like a child's cartoon of a power plant, so out-of-scale is it in relation to its surroundings. Moss Landing Power Plant, with its twin five-hundred-foot-high cement boiler stacks, may be only the *second*-largest fossil-fuel thermoelectric power plant in the world, but I can't imagine anything larger.

"How does the town look to you now?" is the question Santa Cruzians ask visitors. Now presupposes the visitor knew Santa Cruz then—before the Loma Prieta earthquake devastated downtown. I am somewhat embarrassed to say I don't see much difference between pre- and postquake Santa Cruz. What I remember of the pretemblor town was a disorganized downtown, miles of pleasant sandy beaches, a slightly seedy boardwalk, and a shopping mall. The slow-paced commercial district, frequented by Santa Cruz's special mixture of surfers, college students, pony-tailed men, young families, old hippies, university professors, and more than a fair share of homeless people and alienated youth, is being rebuilt slowly, without a grand master plan, one vegetarian restaurant at a time.

Natural Bridges State Beach, just north of Santa Cruz, could use a name change. Its one remaining offshore sandstone bridge was a casualty of the '89 quake. Perhaps the state park system is attempting to preserve the memory of this once-popular sight. A better name would be Monarch Beach; just inland is a eucalyptus grove that hosts the largest concentration of monarch butterflies in America.

A few more miles up-coast, at Wilder Ranch State Historic Park, I get the feeling that not one stone has gone unpreserved. Brussels sprouts fields are in an agricultural preserve, a former dairy farm is a cultural preserve, and Wilder Beach is now a natural preserve for the benefit of nesting snowy plovers.

All of these preserves add up to more places where walking is forbidden than permitted and, as I walk along the edge of the bluffs, signs warn me away from the brussels sprouts fields because of pesticides use and away from the beach because it's a bird refuge.

A long day's walk along the Santa Cruz coast brings me to the San Mateo county line and to the state's premiere coastal preserve—Ano Nuevo State Reserve—the domain of the elephant seal. Visitors (those who have made reservations through the park system's computerized ticket agency far in advance, anyway) come from all over the world for a close-up look at the largest mainland population of elephant seals. From December through April, a colony of the huge creatures visits Ano Nuevo Island and Point in order to breed and bear young. Male elephant seals, some reaching lengths of sixteen feet and weighing three tons, arrive in December and begin battling for dominance. Only a very small percentage of males actually get to inseminate a female; most remain lifelong bachelors. The females, relatively svelte at 1,200 to 2,000 pounds, come ashore in January and join the harems of dominant males.

I've enjoyed the wildlife drama at Punto del Ano Nuevo during past winters, but now, at summer's end, I view a more peaceful scene: harbor seals sunning themselves on the beach.

Sometimes I wonder, long-distance coast walker that I am, if I am not some endangered species myself, as rare as the El Segundo blue butterfly, California legless lizard, or Guadalupe fur seal. And as such, should I not be entitled to a coastal preserve of my own where I may feed, breed, and bask in the sun as nature intended?

The next day, a sunny one, I cross from San Gregorio State Beach to San Gregorio Private Beach, where I find a nudist preserve. Hundreds of times have I been the only one on the beach with a backpack on, but this is the first time I've been the only one on the beach with clothes on. I suppose I could, in deference to the sun worshipers, strip to my birthday suit and walk a naked mile, but this seems kind of silly, so I walk briskly along the surf line, clearly conveying my intent to pass through quickly.

I'm spotted by the only other clothed human in sight—the beach's fee collector, who abandons his position at the parking area and walks briskly over to inform me that this is a private beach, known locally as Bare Bottom Beach, and that there's a fee for using it.

I tell him that I will be on Bare Bottom only another ten minutes—or as long as it takes me to walk north to the next, public beach. After his question, "Where are you walking?" and my answer, "Oregon," conversation lags; he regards me as one would a lunatic and dismisses me with a curt "Just be sure you don't hang out around here." It appears I'm the only one around here who's *not* "hanging out," but I keep this thought to myself and walk on.

Along Half Moon Bay's fine, seductively named beaches—Venice, Naples, Miramar—is a fine path over handsome, eroded bluffs and through dunes dotted with wild radish and sea fig.

Beyond Half Moon Bay the walking is worse because the highway crowds the coast, but before I become too traffic-tense I reach Montara Lighthouse Hostel. Next to the historic lighthouse is a large Victorian house that sleeps thirty vagabonds. A mixture of Belgians, Germans, Iowans, and Californians provide company as warm as the outdoor hot tub. Ahhhh.

The next morning I pass yet another nude beach at Gray Whale Cove (it's far too early for any naturist gatekeeper to demand admission and far too cold for clothing to be optional) and approach the infamous Devil's Slide. Here an eight-hundred-foot rock slide from the highway to the surf tells of the area's unstable geologic history. On the inland side of Coast Highway is McNee Ranch State Park, a destination suggested by the hostel keeper, who insists that a climb up the park's Montara Mountain will yield a stunning view of San Francisco Bay.

No signs indicate the state park, and no signs suggest which of several paths leading up the huge hunk of granite I take to be Montara Mountain actually reach the top. (Perhaps the California Park Service used up its sign quota warning us away from all those preserves to the south.) I ask directions of the only other walker around—a spry elderly woman. Clad in straw hat and sturdy walking shoes, she looks like a formidable trail companion.

"Just keep walking up—all the trails meet at the top," she informs me. "Better enjoy it while you can," she adds tersely.

Alas, she relates, the future looks grim for this park. What is a beautiful park to locals is an ideal location for a multilane highway to the California Department of Transportation. Caltrans wants to build a Highway 1 bypass through the park to replace the landslide-prone stretch of highway known as the Devil's Slide.

Caltrans and its building plans have been fiercely contested by environmentalists such as herself, who fear the highway bypass will destroy the ambience of the park and lead to further development in the area. The two sides have been battling in court for years.

Intrigued by her story, I pull pen and notebook from my pocket and ask her name.

Immediately she clams up. "You look like a reporter [Ouch!] and I'm not talking to them anymore. They always get the story wrong."

I promise I won't get the story wrong, but she tells me nothing more, except to bear left at the next trail junction and follow the ridgeline to the peak.

From lower elevation, my first view up the coast is not so inspiring. Just north lies Daly City, row upon row of identical stucco houses on uniform streets terraced into the coastal slopes, built in that "ticky-tacky" look that inspired songster Malvina Reynolds's hit tune "Little Boxes."

But the view from atop Montara Mountain is magnificent: San Francisco Bay in all its glory, the Marin headlands, and the Farallon Islands.

J O I N I N G   M E on the last leg of my journey to San Francisco is my longtime friend Jon Toste, who's offered me lodging and a little R & R at his home in San Rafael. We stash my backpack in his pickup truck and set off for the big city with not much more than lunch in our daypacks.

We ignore the WARNING: DANGEROUS CLIFFS signs, as we have innumerable times before, and begin following a path up the bluffs above Thornton State Beach.

Jon Toste and I met a decade ago at a state trails conference in Monterey. (If the beatnik, Maynard G. Krebs, on the old TV show *Dobie Gillis* had a responsible twin brother, he would be Jon Toste. He's a skinny long-legged fellow with a mop of dark hair and a beard.) He is a founder of Coastwalk, a nonprofit group that took Sonoma County residents on a weeklong summer hike the length of that county's coast in order to educate the citizenry about coastal access issues. At the conference, we found that we were talking the same talk and walking the same walk, and from that meeting, a friendship has grown.

When Coastwalk met for the first time, Toste recounts, its primary motivation was fear. Sea Ranch, a private, second-home development, had closed off many miles of county coastline, and Sonomans were worried that they might lose even more if they didn't act quickly. One problem was that the group didn't even know what Sea Ranch had. So the first walk was something of an inventory of what was public and private, what was safe and what was threatened.

"A decade later," Toste says, "I can still remember how we felt after our first walk—exhilarated! Until you walk the coast, you don't know what's in your own backyard. Walking all of it ties it together for you as a whole."

The Sonoma County coast walk was so successful that the following year more people signed up. Even more the year after. During the first year, walkers brought their own food, but in succeeding years cooked communal meals with the help of a chuckwagon towed from one coastal campground to the next.

At Toste's suggestion, Coastwalk added a Marin County walk. Each year thereafter, the group added a county or two until it now leads walks in all fifteen coastal counties. At first, Coastwalk leaders like himself shared what they knew about the coast's nature and history, but in later years the group convinced park interpreters, historians, and naturalists to share their knowledge with walkers.

"What I've learned from dealing with government and with the public is that we need to come at this California Coastal Trail situation from a positive can-do position. We need to say, 'here it is, it exists. Look at all these miles of trail that are walkable.' Let's sign it, let's promote it."

High above the beach, we pause for a breather. Besides, Toste is Italian and likes to move his hands, not his feet, when he talks.

"We need a strong advocate, someone who knows all the players, someone who could pull it all together. And you know what? I think I could be that person, get caught up in the crusade for the California Coastal Trail."

"Jon, is 'caught' the operative word?"

Toste sighs, resumes walking. Ignoring a path meandering down to the beach, he waves me into the lead, directing me onto a zigzagging path high on the bluffs.

"Getting caught up in detail is the problem. See, I guess I'm like an entrepreneur, someone who starts a new business. But the one who starts a business isn't always the same one who can manage it. And maybe the same is true with a trails organization."

I understand Toste's dilemma. I reached a similar crossroads several years ago. I wanted no more to do with grant applications, board meetings, and working with bureaucrats. I saw too much money wasted. And too much time. I simply couldn't stomach the process and keep my spirits up. So I opted out of the role of coastal trail spokesman. Whatever it was I wanted, I was getting it from walking about, not talking about, the coast.

The other Jon is now at that crossroads too, caught between the desire to do good deeds and the desire to have a calm life.

We reach the top of the bluffs. We can see a couple miles up-coast, but not far enough to see the city.

"I could be the one to develop—I hate that word—the trail, but I get frustrated with the system. The problem is, I'm not any better than you in putting on a suit and hiding my true beliefs."

He's being modest, I think. Toste is much better at hiding out. He served as a Public Information Officer for the Coastal Commission and worked in the trenches to launch the state's big beach clean-up day, and California's very successful Adopt-a-Beach program.

After observing the government bureaucracy from the inside out, he knew that Coastwalk would have to change, get more professional, in order to get respect and cooperation from the governmental agencies with whom it had to work. But was this possible to do while still maintaining the eco-activist spirit that motivated the group? At first, his fellow Coastwalk boardmembers thought Toste's suggestions—making an annual budget and keeping records—bordered on heresy. But after a time, they adopted these suggestions. Now the organization has evolved from an all-volunteer organization to one with some paid staff, from a loose-knit hiking club to a kind of adventure travel agency with complex logistics. The State Coastal Conservancy gives Coastwalk money for publications, and even for building sections of trail.

"The coast is always where I go to get back to nature, which is kind of strange because I was brought up in Thoreau country in Massachusetts, not too far from Walden Pond. Everything is woodsy around there."

I don't mean to drift away from my friend's story, but there's suddenly something more urgent to consider. A landslide has eroded away all but an eighteen-inch ledge in the cliffs. Only the narrow band of dirt beneath our feet is between us and the beach five hundred feet below.

"Uh, Jon, have you walked this trail lately?"

"To me, nature is a religious concern; my spirituality comes from worship of nature. If God is anything, he's the overseer of the ecosystem."

"Earth to Jon, earth to Jon. What are we doing up here with the hang gliders and cliff swallows?"

"What?"

"You don't mean to tell me you take this route with Coastwalk?"

"No way, it's too eroded and unsafe. We walk the beach. I thought you'd want a little adventure."

"Thanks."

"Anyway, where was I? Yeah, nature. We worship—or should, what sustains us. I get tears in my eyes sometimes when I'm on the top of the mountain overlooking some ocean vista."

The trail goes from bad to worse. Newspaper headlines flash before my eyes: Last Trail of Coastal Pioneers, with a tearjerker sidebar, The Life and Death of Two Johns. And the TV news tease: "Hikers take a big fall . . . film at eleven!"

"Jon, when's the last time you walked this stretch?"

"I don't remember, but I guess it was before the earthquake."

"The *earthquake?*"

"I heard the quake knocked hunks of these cliffs into the surf way down there. You knew we were hiking right on top of the San Andreas Fault, didn't you?"

I am thinking how nice it would be to get off the cliffs and walk the beach when the trail narrows to hiking-boot width, then disappears into space.

Toste looks over my shoulder as we take stock of the terrain ahead. In front of us looms a fifteen-foot-wide fissure in the cliffs. It's a five-foot drop into the fissure, which seems passable if we don't look down or get nervous. What looks to be the worst problem is clambering up the far side of the fissure to get back onto the trail, which appears to resume on the other side.

Although I promised myself not to look down, I do, and see a small crowd gathered on the beach below the fissure. They appear to be pointing at us, but so tiny are they from this height, I can't be sure.

After a brief discussion, during which we discard the notion of retreat (obviously we two coastal trailblazers are motivated by testosterone, not common sense), we make a plan. We tie our two lightweight parkas together and proceed. Skinny Jon with the longer legs

will go into the fissure first, while the heavier John with the lower
center of gravity will belay him down. Getting into the fissure proves
to be no problem; however, as we walk across it, disturbingly large
quantities of soft, sandy earth slide down the cliffs beneath our feet.
Leaving what seems like a half-ton of soil in our wake, we make it to
the other side. We seem to have dislodged what little ledge there was
across the fissure; even if we wanted to retreat, it's now impossible.
Getting up the other side of the fissure to where the trail resumes
looks doubtful too. Two good handholds—a rock outcropping and a
root—are visible, but they're very high. I boost Toste up halfway, and
with some wriggling and digging on his part, get him a foothold. The
next foothold is atop my shoulder, from which he springs up onto the
narrow trail. He then belays me with our jacket-rope up to join him.

   We look down. The crowd, apparently disinterested in our success,
disburses.

   We smile at each other, walk along in silence for a little while. The
trail improves considerably, climbs to the very top of the bluffs and
serves up a glorious view of San Francisco and the Golden Gate.

   A bit shaky in the knees, we stop for lunch. We laugh at our folly,
happy to be out coast walking, happy just to be.

   "You know," says Toste, "I got a degree in environmental studies,
but I've always said I learned a lot more about the environment from
walking the coast than I did from any book."

I WALK OVER "The Bridge Over the Edge of the Continent"—the Golden Gate—and follow an officially designated Coast
Trail through Golden Gate National Recreation Area, Mount Tamal-
pais State Park, and Point Reyes National Seashore. The trail is a gem,
one of the great footpaths of the world, a ramble over densely forested
ridges, wild and open coastal bluffs, and deserted beaches.

   With its moors, weirs, glens, and vales, Point Reyes Peninsula calls
to mind the seacoast of Britain. When the fog settles over the dew-
dampened grasslands, I imagine I'm stepping onto a Scottish moor, or
wandering England's Dorset coast. No wonder Chase liked it here.

   And judging from the number of visitors I meet from around the
United States and other parts of the world during my week of walking,

the coast trail here is a true world-class footpath. It's Euro-walking with a California flavor: wandering one of the West Coast's wildest coastlines by day and relaxing at a comfortable inn at night.

When Jon Toste, Coastwalk spokesman, gives his coastal trail stump speech, he talks about the great parklands of Point Reyes and Marin headlands that have been connected by a coastal trail. California's other parks could be connected by the coastal trail too, he suggests. "The great landscape architect Frederick Olmsted envisioned greenery—a string of pearls around a city. We have pearls along our coast. We just need to string them all together with a trail."

SEVENTEEN

Mendocino Bluffs

N O T   M U C H   to celebrate, I think, as I regard Vista Trail. I keep such thoughts to myself, for I'm quite sure I'm a minority of one amongst the brigade of bureaucrats assembled at the trailhead to dedicate the just-completed trail.

The three-quarter-mile-long, paved trail called Vista Trail (as dull a name as could ever be conjured by a committee), loops around a grassy blufftop. From the handrails at the edge of the bluff, a walker gets a good southern vista (or would on days less foggy than this one) of Sonoma County's beaches.

Yesterday while walking north I enjoyed close-up vistas of these very beaches: Salmon Creek, Miwok, Schoolhouse, Portuguese, Shell, Blind, and Goat Rock. I viewed the colorfully named pockets of sand from a blufftop trail that was part officially signed state park trail, part former cattle path.

Master of ceremonies is Penny Allen, chair of the State Coastal Conservancy. Clad in a denim jacket and designer jeans, she charts the five-year path taken by the trail through the bureaucratic maze. She gets a big laugh when she summons forward Richard Nichols, Vista

Trail project manager and executive director of Coastwalk, and presents him with an "Honorary Bureaucrat Award."

Besides giving out awards, Penny Allen gives out money. Lots of it. The State Coastal Conservancy is the funding arm of the much more political, policy-making California Coastal Commission. I've attended the Conservancy's monthly meetings and seen the agency, with little or no debate, disburse a half-dozen, a dozen grants, several hundred thousand dollars per, to rebuild old piers, conduct studies, restore estuaries, and buy land. Some projects—restoring the Nipomo Dunes, for example—look like monies well spent; others, such as the quarter million dollars a year the Conservancy gives itself to publish the terrible triannual *California Coast & Ocean Magazine,* complete with articles about where to walk your dog on the beach, hardly seem justifiable. However, it's not the size and scope of the projects, but the speed at which six- and seven-figure sums are awarded, that astonishes me. All of a sudden $5 million is spent. Without discussion. Before boardmembers break for lunch.

Vista Trail was not cheap. The Coastal Conservancy coughed up $2 million to buy 272 acres for it. Then the Conservancy paid the nonprofit trail-advocacy group Coastwalk $233,000 to build less than a mile of trail.

At the dedication of Pecho Coast Trail near Diablo Canyon, I had been astonished that PG&E spent $100,000 per mile to construct a coastal path, and had deduced that at such a rate PG&E could build the 1,600-mile California Coastal Trail for $160 million. But PG&E does low-budget trail work compared to the government. If Vista Trail at $233,000 per mile is any indication, the state of California would require $362.8 million to build the complete coastal trail. Make that $3.5 billion if the state intends to purchase the land lying beneath the trail.

I fall into step with the Coastal Conservancy chair as we walk the new trail, juggling our paper cups full of white wine. "Why, of all places, build a trail here?" I ask.

"You have to pick up property when there's opportunity," explains Penny Allen. "This was an opportunity."

"Excuse me for saying this, but it seems like a lot of money for a little trail."

"Property is expensive on the California coast. We have to acquire the land a little at a time. It's the only way we'll ever have a California Coastal Trail. I don't know if you know anything about the coastal trail, but there's a lot of private property en route. I mean, you can't just walk over somebody's land."

I do my best to keep a straight face. "I had some thoughts about that I'd like to share . . ."

Several officials want a word with Penny Allen and crowd close to her, signaling my time's about up. "What's the Coastal Conservancy's timetable for completing the trail?" I ask.

"Let's put it this way: the California Coastal Trail won't be completed during my lifetime or my children's lifetime. Right now, and in the foreseeable future, it's simply impossible to walk the coast from Mexico to Oregon."

Richard Nichols, a rough-edged fellow of forty, is a little more optimistic. Professionally speaking, he has to be. He is the executive director of Coastwalk, an organization dedicated to promoting the California Coastal Trail. "We're really rolling now. Next year we'll be leading walks in all fifteen coast counties. And while those walkers are having a good time, we'll be telling them that they're walking a small part of the whole California Coastal Trail, and that they need to help us work for its completion. Some of our walks book up fast. We'll have to get an 800 number or something. No. Never mind. That'd make us as bureaucratic as everybody else."

"Your organization has such a good time leading people on beach walks, why did you get into the trail construction biz?"

Nichols sighs. "You can't believe what we went through to get this trail built—the Sonoma County building department, Planning Department, Water Agency, Trails Advisory Committee, and board of supervisors. And state parks, Caltrans, the California Fish and Wildlife Service, the U.S. Fish and Wildlife Service . . .

"You know, when you're out walking the coast, you can get past any geological barrier. But when you're trying to build a trail, you find that the head of some local agency, some little official who doesn't know squat about trails, can fuck you up for months—or permanently."

Nichols grips the steel guardrails in anger. I am glad his hands are not around some bureaucrat's neck. "The delays were awful. We had to do a native plant survey and found some endangered plant. Then we found a peregrine nest and had to deal with this endangered or threatened or whatever bird."

"After this experience are you going to build any more coastal trail?"

"I don't know. When we started, we thought Vista Trail would be good practice for developing the rest of the coastal trail. If we did build the trail, we'd have to deal with thousands of bureaucrats and jurisdictions, make all kinds of deals. It's complicated. It's too damn complicated."

"Oh Saints of America, pray to God for us."

H I S   H O L I N E S S , Patriarch of Moscow and All Russia, Aleksi II, leads a service celebrating the two-hundredth anniversary of Orthodox Christianity in America.

It's my second celebration of the day, and altogether different from the trail dedication that took place a few miles south. I stand outside the small redwood chapel in Fort Ross State Historic Park among five hundred Russian Orthodox Christians who have assembled this foggy autumn day to celebrate their faith. From a nearby monastery have come skinny, bearded, black-cassocked monks, their long, dark hair tied back with rubber bands. Crowding the courtyard in front of the chapel, and peering out the windows of the blockhouses, are nuns, old women in babushkas, and parishioners from several Russian Orthodox churches in San Francisco.

"Saints of America, we are subject to sorrow, help us against adversity."

Fort Ross, like Sutter's Fort and many other forts in California, was an industrial, not a military, complex. To be sure, it had the look of a fort, including log architecture similar to Siberia and Sitka fortresses, as well as the standard accouterment of a fort—stockade, sentry posts, and a couple of cannon; however, from 1812 to 1841, when the fort was occupied, never was a shot fired in anger.

Fort Ross was built by the Russian-American Company. Organized like other European joint stock companies, it was a czar/private
sector endeavor launched to increase trade with, and exploit the natural resources of, North America. (At a time when Russia struggles to
reverse eight decades of state control and learn the ways of capitalism,
it's interesting to note that its people were once quite entrepreneurial.)
   While the Russian-American Company was keenly interested in
enterprises such as otter hunting, cattle raising, and wheat growing, it
was most certainly not in the business of saving souls. Unlike the
Spanish colonists and military, who were accompanied every step of
the way by proselytizing padres, the Russian pioneers' emphasis was on
rubles, not religion.
   But religion was not ignored in the new land. The Russian Orthodox faithful built a chapel at Fort Ross. Services were held sporadically
because a full-time priest was never assigned to the remote outpost. A
few Aleuts and Pomo converted to Christianity, but not many, because
the Orthodox Church requires a good working knowledge of church
teachings.

"Saints of America, hear our prayer.
Saints of Joy and Gladness, renew our spirits."

   The church's first foothold in North America was actually in
Alaska, and the priests flanking the Patriarch sing praises of the dedication of St. Peter the Aleut, Father Herman the Wonder Worker, and the
other men of the cloth who came to Alaska in 1794.
   In Russia, two hundred years later, it is not just capitalism that is reborn, but the Orthodox faith. A Greek Orthodox, it is a faith I share,
and while awaiting the Patriarch's arrival I can't help but feel some of
the excitement of Orthodox Christianity's rebirth as I talk to a Russian priest. After the fall of godless communism and the rise of a new
democracy guaranteeing religious freedom, congregations of ten thousand in Moscow are now common, he tells me. Holy icons have been
taken out of hiding; churches closed for eighty years have reopened.
But the political situation is most unstable in Moscow. Die-hard com-
munists are revolting against the reformist government of Boris Yeltsin.

And rumor at Fort Ross has it that Patriarch Aleksi has been summoned back to Moscow to try to keep the peace.

"Oh flowers of paradise who have bloomed in this land,
   help us persevere."

Some of the Russians stationed at Fort Ross were very much interested in the "flowers of paradise," as well as the wondrous array of plants and animals they discovered along the coast. Learned men from the Imperial Academy explored the coast and coastal mountains south to Bodega Bay and made detailed studies of the area's botany, zoology, and geography.

"Let us praise our American martyrs
   Oh Saints of America, pray to God for us."

With the double-barred Russian Orthodox cross etched dramatically against the sky behind him, Patriarch Aleksi offers a final prayer and walks across the fort parade ground to a cannon. Park rangers ask us to cover our ears. A slight, boyish grin lights up the Patriarch's face as he touches off the gunpowder and the cannon roars. He claps his hands in delight as the acrid smoke pores over his flock. Prayer may be a far better defense against evil than cannon, but it's not nearly as much fun.

I step forward to receive an autographed postcard of the Patriarch, and his blessing, then hike north.

I MARVEL at the sheer sandstone cliffs and sandy coves of Salt Point State Park as I follow a fits-and-starts blufftop trail to my evening camp near Stump Beach Cove. I am glad to learn from a park ranger that the cove is not named for the remains of redwoods logged nearby; instead, the cove honors Sheriff Stump, law and order in these parts.

The next day I reach Sea Ranch, a community infamous in the annals of coastal access history for its twenty-year battle to keep out the public. According to my map, there is now a footpath leading along the north side of it, but that doesn't help me, approaching as I am from the south.

A former sheep ranch, Sea Ranch became the site of second homes designed and built in the 1960s and 1970s to fit into the environment. The homes, with very steep shed roofs, are done in a style of architecture called Condominium I. This "Sea Ranch style" has been much imitated along the West Coast. Called "Bauhaus-inspired" by its fans and "Grain Elevator Modern" by its critics, its reception has been mixed. Some architects believe this severe style blends in with the surroundings; some of us walkers have our doubts.

Because Sea Ranch beaches are impossible to walk, and because I don't wish to retreat to the Coast Highway, I decide to traverse the community itself and soon find myself stepping onto a golf course, past the usual NO TRESPASSING sign and a most unusual WATCH FOR FLYING GOLF BALLS sign. The links, designed and landscaped to resemble a Scottish course, are dotted with deer and golfers. It's not long before I run into two old duffers in tweed pants, carrying the United Kingdom golf theme a bit far I'd say. I'm pleased to see they're not using an electric cart, but are walking the golf course.

They, however, are not pleased to see me walking the course. The shorter and redder-faced of the two steps into my path, brandishing a nine iron. "You're on our golf course," he declares.

"A golf course? Are you sure? I thought this was the trail to Gualala."

"This isn't a trail, it's a fairway. Anybody with any sense can see that. Didn't you read the signs?"

"Yes. And I'm being very careful."

"Careful of what?"

"Flying golf balls. Just like the sign said."

He regrips the iron in impatience. "The other sign: NO TRESPASSING."

"Those deer ever get on the green?" I ask, pointing to the doe and two fawns browsing nearby.

"Not much. The grass is too short for them there. They like the woods and . . . what the hell am I doing talking to you about deer?" He waves his nine iron north. "Get your butt out of here."

I cross Sea Ranch without being struck by any golf balls or clubs and reach the Sonoma-Mendocino county line at the Gualala River. Unlike most California coastal rivers, which cascade west from the slopes of the coastal mountains, the Gualala flows south to north— along the San Andreas Fault.

In the beginning there was no Sonoma County. It was part of Mendocino County when California's founding legislators established the original county lines. California's second legislature changed the boundaries and transferred the area south of Gualala River to the new county of Sonoma.

The Mendocino and Sonoma County coasts, particularly the length from the Russian River on the south to the Navarro River on the north, are sometimes combined for tourist purposes by area visitor bureaus, who refer to the co-mingled coastlines as "Mendonoma." The moniker has not caught on, perhaps because of pride displayed by locals in their respective counties, or perhaps because the name sounds like a form of skin cancer. For me, a south-north traveler, I'd amend the name to Sonomend.

Much of Mendocino County's 100-mile-long-plus coastline is given over to the works of man; they're mostly gentle works—agriculture in the form of grazing cows and sheep, vacation homes—but relatively speaking less is given over to parkland. In other counties, there's more public land than private; not here on the Mendocino coast. Mendocino County is a nice place to live, but you wouldn't want to visit there—particularly if your visit consists of walking the coast. The Coastal Conservancy could spend all of its annual budget for the next twenty years just buying up land on the Mendocino coast. No, clearly what is needed here for coastal trail purposes is the adoption of the English footpath system—that is to say, hikers are allowed right of passage over private land in exchange for civilized behavior by all parties.

Geography also conspires against the walker. The steep shoreline cliffs are cut by coastal rivers—the Gualala, the Garcia, the Greenwood, the Navarro, the Salmon, and the Albion, plus many more creeks and creeklets—that flow through steep gorges.

The land between the coast and coast highway is not extensive and what there is is precipitous. With dismal regularity I'm forced to re-treat to the highway, a sinuous route carved into the steep slopes.

Before the highway, the way to reach this coast was by sea. But there were no ports, not a single natural harbor of any size along the length of Mendocino County. And that was a problem because the county had trees, lots of them, and markets for timber if a way could be found to ship it. The shipping solution from the 1860s to the 1920s was the use of "doghole ports"—so-called because schooners would anchor in little bays only a dog could fit into. The dogholes weren't much: anchorages in the lee of eroded headlands at the mouths of creeks. The doghole designation was particularly pejorative when used by captains of larger vessels, who looked down their big bows at the little, two-masted wooden schooners.

Even in the calmest of water, a schooner had to moor so close to shore that a sudden swell or the slightest misjudgment by the captain could cause the ship to be swept onto the rocks. Usually the ship loaded the timber, not from any wharf, but from chutes perched pre-cariously on the bluffs.

Even in later years, with more maneuverable steamships, dogholes were a supreme test of seamanship. Approaching a doghole, a captain could rely only on his intuition and his copy of *United States Coast Pilot, Pacific Coast,* published by the Department of Commerce. Ac-cording to the *Coast Pilot,* here's what faced a doghole schooner cap-tain approaching the hamlet of Westport about the time Chase rode by it in 1912:

> There are few houses on the small flat at the foot of the hills, but little or no business is transacted. Mooring buoys are in place for warping into position and a wire cable used for loading. There is from 24 to 26 feet at the mooring but this is subject to change, depending on the prevailing winds and swell; at times there are 3 to 4 feet less. Communication may be had northward by wagon and telephone, and southward by stage and telegraphy and telephone. The buildings in the village, especially a yellow hotel and white church are the most

prominent features from seaward. No supplies of any kind are available.

A doghole rarely lasted more than a few years in any one spot; once the timber was cut, the logging company packed up its mill and moorings and a "port" was abandoned in favor of another a few miles north or south.

As I walk past the one-time dogholes of Gualala, Anchor Bay, Point Arena, and Saunders Landing, and see for myself what dinky holes they really are, I marvel at the considerable courage of the schooner captains. At Bowling Ball Beach, I spot more obstacles. Visible at low tide are some weird concretions, five- to ten-foot spheres formed by chemical processes from the cliff. The balls "weathered out," as geologists say, and fell to the beach below. Beyond the bowling balls are more dogholes—Schooner Gulch and Flumeville—as well as ominous, mostly hidden Arena Rock. From shore the rock is not visible, but its presence parts the waves breaking over it and is an awesome hazard to navigation. I camp near the mouth of Greenwood Creek where there was another doghole port, where schooner captains docked at the less-than-welcoming Casket Wharf.

Near sunset, I gather driftwood for my campfire. Some of the wood I gather looks mill-shaped; I wonder if I am gathering the bleached bones of a ship that long ago tried, but failed, to tie up at Casket Wharf.

I look up-coast. Some nice walking awaits me at lush, redwood-filled Russian Gulch and along Ten Mile Dunes and Ten Mile Beach. And there'll be fine sights to see, too—the bizarre dwarf pines and cypress in the Mendocino Pygmy Forest, and the town of Mendocino itself, resembling a New England village. At the very northern end of Mendocino County coast is the state's wildest coast, the Lost Coast.

I'm just about done eating my chicken 'n rice dinner when a strange green glow falls over me. I look westward for the origin of this green light, but this is no sunset glow and besides, the sun has long since disappeared into the water. I look heavenward, but there is no unusual planetary alignment or celestial activity causing a green light.

It's my driftwood fire. Burning green! Baffled, I stare into the green flames. Very mysterious. After a few moments of puzzlement, I recall high-school lessons learned from both California history and chemistry to solve this mystery of the universe. By somewhat remarkable coincidence I have picked up a timber that was once part of a copper-skinned ship. The vessel's wood was impregnated with copper crystals, which, I now remember, burn green.

After a few more moments, the green light fades, there's a hiss, and this bit of history from doghole days is reduced to ash.

EIGHTEEN

Lost Coast

IT DOESN'T GET any wilder than this.

California has a very long coastline, and millions of acres of wilderness, but it has only one wilderness coast.

The Lost Coast.

A day's walk north of Fort Bragg I'm greeted by towering shoreline cliffs, rising abruptly like volcanoes from the sea. I get just a glimpse of the two-thousand-foot-high cliffs before the morning mist turns to heavy fog and the coast is lost to my view. The Lost Coast is so rough—rougher even than Big Sur's coast—that it even thwarted California's highway engineers; much to their frustration, they were compelled by geography to route Coast Highway inland more than twenty miles.

The Lost Coast is black sand beaches strewn with patterns of driftwood and the sea's debris, a mosaic of small stones. On grassy blufftops, sheep and cows turn tail to angry winds blowing in from Siberia and the Bering Sea. Canyon mouths fill with fog, nourishing the redwoods within.

Abandoned barns and fallen fences record the efforts of settlers who tried, but failed, to tame this land. Nowhere is the Lost Coast blighted by transmission lines, oil wells, power plants, RV parks, or fast-food franchises.

As traced on the map, the Lost Coast's northern boundary is the Eel River in Humboldt County, its southern boundary Usal Beach in Mendocino County. Much of the Lost Coast is in public ownership as part of the King Range National Conservation Area in the north and Sinkyone Wilderness State Park in the south.

But "Lost Coast" is not a place name found on any map.

Except mine.

One January, a few years back, I served as volunteer ranger/campground host for Sinkyone Wilderness State Park. I cared for a couple of horses, gave directions to the very few visitors who braved the rains and miserable park road to get to the coast, read and wrote in the ranch house that serves as the park's visitor center on those days when it rained hard, and wandered the trails on those days when it rained less. I hiked all the Lost Coast's trails, mapped the territory, then supervised production of a map called "Trails of the Lost Coast."

The word *lost* on a map has long been a call of the wild to me. Lost Palms Oasis and Lost Horse Mine in the Mojave Desert, Lost Valley in Big Sur and Lost Lake in the High Sierra are just a few of the lost places I've found.

A fifty-five-mile footpath—Lost Coast Trail—traverses the Lost Coast. To reach the trailhead, from Wages Creek Beach outside of the hamlet of Rockport where I camped in a private campground, I must walk seven miles along the beaches and bluffs, then another seven miles up Usal Road. The road, a muddy thoroughfare not pictured on most maps, hasn't changed much since Jack London and his wife, Charmian, drove it in a horse-drawn carriage on a trip to Eureka in 1911, or since J. Smeaton Chase rode it in 1912. I'm not surprised that after two hours of hiking the road, not a single car has passed me.

Usal Road, with a couple of name changes, follows the crest of the ocean fronting Lost Coast peaks. It doesn't offer much in the way of coastal views, but winds through some wild country. Chase followed roads the length of the Lost Coast. He and I will part company, so to speak, at Usal Beach, where I will join the Lost Coast Trail, a pathway of late 1980s' vintage.

On my way to Usal I spy foxgloves, flowers spread from the gardens of pioneer homesteaders. Chase also saw foxgloves alongside Usal Road and couldn't contain his excitement over the thimblelike flowers.

"Actual, rosy, purple-blotched foxgloves, such as I last saw in the lanes of Surrey and Devon," he exults.

Chase, two decades removed from an England he would never see again, was understandably nostalgic. But for what exactly? The Britain of his youth? Would Chase have enjoyed a 1912 ride around Britain's coast more, or less, than his ride along California's? Would he have been inspired by Mother England's tidy fields and hedgerows or appalled by the motorcars, mines, mills, and other manifestations of the Industrial Age?

As I walk Usal Road, maybe there's a better question to ponder: Would I—or a reborn Joseph Smeaton Chase—better enjoy a modern-day adventure along land's end in Britain or in California?

These days about 80 percent of Californians and a like percentage of Brits live within thirty miles of coast. But while sharing a common proximity to the ocean, we do not share a common coastal view. In England, the coast is where one gets rid of things—power plants, resorts, gun emplacements, oil refineries, sewage plants—presumably to keep the interior looking pastoral. We Californians, while guilty of placing (more than) our share of horrors on the coast, attempt to locate the worst of our architectural and ecological atrocities some distance inland.

In Britain, the Countryside Commission, so successful at preserving the nation's hills and dales, has not had similar success along the coast. In California, the Coastal Commission has waged a foot-by-foot battle for public access and the preservation of beauty, but its legal powers end a quarter-mile inland.

At several locales along Britain's coast, I've felt myself a witness to the last gasp of an empire. Fortress Britain, whose castellated coast has long been a defense against barbarians, is still repelling invaders, this time with ramparts of uglification. Walking Britain's coast left me with the impression of a nation looking inward, determined to take care of its own.

We Californians, by contrast, appear worried what people sailing in from the Pacific Rim will think when they see our coast. And we seem to care not a whit what other Americans, or anyone arriving from the East, will see as they cross the interior on their way to the coast.

After his brief look backward to Britain, Chase looks ahead. He tells us for the first time that he always planned to finish his ride by November 1, and that he has but ten days or so to make the Oregon line.

Despite the rude and crude Californians met during the latter part of his journey, despite witnessing the great tracts of land laid waste by lumbermen, Chase is as plucky, as indefatigable, as ever as he rides the Lost Coast. His "There-will-always-be-a-California" point of view is unshakable as the "There-will-always-be-an-England" held by generations of traveling scribes.

I arrive at Usal Camp on the banks of Usal Creek, select a campsite (I can choose from among fifteen sites in the fifteen-site camp) and set up my tent. Sunset draws near though I know this only by consulting the moist face of my watch, not by any glimpse of the day star that has been absent all day.

I follow Usal Creek to its mouth at Usal Beach, a dramatic, dark sand-and-gravel strand backed by tall cliffs whose tops are lost in the fog. Scattered at the base of the eroded cliffs are huge boulders. Such rocks falling from the bluffs make me glad Lost Coast Trail stays atop the bluffs rather than below them.

Usal Beach is not a friendly place. Not only do huge rocks rain on the beach, huge rogue waves frequently surprise-attack the shore. The surf pounds offshore rock pillars, socks Usal Creek in the mouth. However, these adverse conditions that discourage even walking Usal Beach, did not discourage capitalists of a hundred years ago.

During the 1890s, Captain Robert Dollar regularly navigated his steamship, *Newsboy,* in and out of the treacherous doghole port of Usal in order to transport logs sawn by the Usal Redwood Company. The aptly-named Dollar went on to greater fame as founder of the Dollar

Steamship Line, later the President Line. The sawmill closed in 1900, and Usal became a near-ghost town, largely because the timber in these parts was inferior. The redwoods' timber prospects looked good to the loggers, but the tall trees never yielded board feet commensurate to their great size, and produced a lesser grade of lumber. Nevertheless, Georgia Pacific Company resumed logging after World War II and continued until 1986 when, after cutting down most of the trees, sold its land to the park. In 1969, the company burned Usal to the ground, to avoid what it termed "liability problems."

I lug some driftwood back to my camp and, after much coaxing, get the wet wood to burn. When the fire offers more heat than smoke, I put my pot of macaroni and cheese on the fire. As my hands and face warm and my damp clothes dry, my thoughts turn from California's wettest land to its driest.

After Chase finished his long coastal ride, he began exploring the desert, wrote desert books, moved to Palm Springs and married. No doubt after an upbringing in the England damp, and his excursion along this coast, he was ready to live out his remaining days where it was warm and dry.

THE LOST COAST is said to have two seasons: six months of rain and six months of fog. It's very foggy again today. The ocean below and the sky above are a single shade of gray. The tall grass covering the coastal slopes and the Douglas fir that border the meadowland are dripping. Lost Coast Trail is muddy, and populated by so many earthworms that the earth itself seems alive and wiggling.

I enter Dark Canyon, a rainforest-like environment of bay laurels draped with moss, maple, and alder. The fog lingers in this canyon, so that the land never seems to dry. The fog tarries too in Anderson and Northport gulches. The Lost Coast's canyons and gulches, from Usal to Bear Harbor, were logged not so many years ago, but the fog softens the scars, hides the stumps. Wrapped in mist, the forest is healing.

Along Little Jackass Creek grows one of the few surviving old-growth redwood groves, the Sally Bell Grove, named for the last full-blooded Sinkyone. She survived a massacre of her people to become a woman of strong will and strong medicine.

Near the grove, I hail state park ranger John Jennings, an easy-going mustachioed fellow who has patrolled here almost since the beginning. Here is Sinkyone Wilderness State Park; the beginning was in 1975 when the state park opened.

He spent the afternoon finding and cleaning up a marijuana garden, he reports. The grower had harvested his plants, but not his trash and Jennings hauled away beer bottles and a hammock. "A lot of trash for just two plants."

While the marijuana industry here is small-scale compared to elsewhere in Humboldt County, the weed and its growers nevertheless invade the state park.

The Lost Coast is part of the so-called Emerald Triangle, the name given to an area of Humboldt, Mendocino, and Trinity counties where many a marijuana garden grows. Indeed, the sinsemilla flourishes.

In the good old days of the 1960s and 1970s, big growers harvested huge fortunes—crops of hundreds of plants grew along the Lost Coast in such places as the banks of the Mattole River near Ettersburg. But growers have fallen on hard times, particularly on the coastward side of the isosceles. The CAMP (Campaign Against Marijuana Plants), complete with helicopter surveillance and trucks full of heavily armed men running through the woods, has been effective in reducing the number of growers. So have stiffer jail sentences and fines, not to mention confiscation and forfeiture of their land.

Now growers have taken up guerrilla gardening—cultivating a half-dozen, sometimes only one or two, plants in dispersed locations on public land. Still, a single sinsemilla plant is a cash crop of several thousand dollars, making it worth the risk to many.

As a peace officer—a term that better describes his job than that of his city cop counterparts, he must protect the Lost Coast from the locals, who, like the native Sinkyone who preceded them, could be said to be a family-oriented, loosely organized tribal group that lives off the land. But many locals are attracted to the Lost Coast because it's long been a place for people to escape tax collectors, the criminal justice system, and most conventional forms of personal and social responsibility.

"John, there are three seasons," Jennings tells me.

"No way, John. You told me *two* the last time I was here: the foggy season and the rainy season."

"That's the weather. The humans around here observe three seasons: hunting season, fishing season, and growing season."

These three seasons make it rough for Jennings in a park designated "wilderness." A wilderness is by definition off limits to vehicles, which severely restricts what locals call "traditional uses" of the land.

"Traditional uses" is a motto that plays well with the conservative board of supervisors and county government, but in practice is quite different. Traditional wood gathering is four-wheeling it up to a tree and chainsawing what you need. Traditional fishing is backing up to the river and fishing off the back of a truck. Traditional hunting is blasting at critters from a pickup truck. Traditional agriculture is planting pot on public land.

In the minds of many locals the gun is an integral part of the coastal system and they want to solve their traditional problems in their traditional manner.

Problem: Too few steelhead
Solution: Shoot the sea lions
Problem: Too few trout
Solution: Shoot the merganser ducks
Problem: Too few quail to shoot
Solution: Shoot the bobcats
Problem: Too few deer to shoot
Solution: Shoot the mountain lions

Near sunset—or more precisely *about* when the sun sets since I have not glimpsed the orb all day—I reach Wheeler, where some cement foundations mark what was a company town, from 1950 to 1960. Near the ruins grow spearmint, alyssum, and other domestic plants gone wild. During the Lost Coast's logging decade, diesels hauling 120,000 pounds of logs thundered along Usal Road from Wheeler, a modern town of thirty families, with electricity and phones.

Wheeler, one of the last company towns (and maybe the newest ghost town) on the California coast, was established by the Wheeler family. The Wheelers renamed Jackass Creek "Wolf Creek," probably so they could call their business Wolf Creek Timber Company rather than Jackass Creek Timber Company, no doubt preferring to name their company after a predator rather than a nitwit.

One of mapmaking's great joys is choosing geographical names among contenders. I figured that Jackass Creek was so named before the Wheelers and their timber company came, so Jackass Creek it should be henceforth, and Jackass Creek it is on my Lost Coast map.

I pitch my tent by Jackass Creek beneath two large redwoods. The redwoods remind me that tomorrow I will visit a very special stand of the tall trees—the J. Smeaton Chase Grove, a grove that I named for my trail companion.

FROM WHEELER, I ascend steep switchbacks, then wind through a grassland at the edge of a forest. Among the blue-eyed grass and monkey flowers are the foxgloves so beloved by Chase.

I reach Duffy's Gulch, a garden of rhododendrons, head-high ferns, and vines climbing redwoods to the sky. Splashing color about the gulch are Indian paintbrush, dandelions, huckleberry, Douglas iris, Calypso orchid, and some bright, red poison oak. The trees in J. Smeaton Chase Grove are towering thousand-year-old redwoods, some ten feet in diameter, surrounded by a multitude of ferns—sword, lady, five-finger, and woodwardia.

Doubtless Chase would have frowned at me for naming a grove for him. He was a modest man (far more photographs of his horse survive than of him) and in *California Coast Trails* wrote of the vanity in naming groves of the tallest living things for men of questionable stature.

But Chase also wrote of the rest that comes with an eternal sleep in the woods: "Every good man loves the woodland, and even if our concerns keep us all our lives out of our heritage we hope to lie down at last under the quiet benediction of slow-moving branches."

Chase is buried far from any woodland. Sentinel palms watch over his plot at the oldest Palm Springs cemetery. If he were to wake after his seven-decade sleep, he would see the same contradiction between the wild and the developed that plagued him his whole life. Behind him is mighty, snow-capped Mount San Jacinto and below him the

great expanse of the Colorado Desert. But to his left is the Alejo
O'Donnell Golf Course and to his right is a downtown Palm Springs
that has changed beyond all comprehension.

He knew he would be buried in Palm Springs, but he left handwritten instructions that he be remembered in England as well: "Out
of that strong love I bear to my dear native land I ask that subject to
the equal claims of my brothers, my name might be put on the grave-
stone of my father and mother in the old Bexley Churchyard, Kent,
England. There is space, I think that though my body will—as I now
expect—lie in California ground, there will be the slight record of my
name as an Englishman remaining in an English churchyard."

His wife, Isabel, carried out his wish. A photograph of the grave-
stone shows Joseph Smeaton Chase's name, date of birth, and death
etched beneath the names and dates of his parents, thus linking him
forever with England and California.

What did he want from California? Wealth? Happiness? Curiosity?
Certainly he never became wealthy as a result of the modest sales of
his books. His happiness is hard to judge; if we agree that humans are
social animals and that happiness is a quality that must be shared, it
would appear that Chase spent too many days alone in the saddle, too
many days alone at his typewriter, to have been truly happy. But if
Chase came to California out of curiosity, he must have been a very
satisfied man. He rode and wrote his way into *Who's Who* by exploring coastal trails, desert trails, and Sierra Nevada trails; by visiting every
lighthouse keeper, Mission friar, and octogenarian with a story to tell
from El Centro to Gasquet. He found the love of the land, the love of
a woman, the love of writing.

I know I couldn't wish for much more than that from my life.

He sure covered a lot of ground. Most of us, even in Chase's day,
could not shuck our responsibilities and retreat to the wilderness. We
take vicarious journeys to wild places. Chase beckons us to enjoy what
he called "the thousand one things that make up the silent conversation of the trail."

His obituary in the *Pasadena Star-News* pretty well sums up his
writing career in one sentence: "A writer of wide sympathies and cul-
tured taste and intimately acquainted with those aspects of California

which he dealt, his books have an assured place in the literature of his
adopted state, characterized by painstaking thoroughness, a scholarly
purity of style, and staunch loyalty to those old-fashioned standards of
art and morals which endure from generation to generation because
grounded in truth."

IT IS A MIRACLE the redwoods of J. Smeaton Chase Grove
escaped the ax and saw I think as I tramp under ever-gloomier skies to
Bear Harbor, the main port for southern Humboldt and northern
Mendocino counties from the 1860s to the turn of the century. This
onetime timber shipping point isn't much more than a mile from the
grove's virgin redwoods.

Lost Coast Trail delivers me to Bear Harbor, which from a distance
looks like it was just another doghole port with a lumber chute and a
wharf to off-load lumber onto the waiting steamer—no different from
the others I've passed on the Mendocino coast. But rusted rails dan-
gling from eroded coastal cliffs tell of a more ambitious enterprise. In
order to transport logs from Harvey Anderson's timber holdings, the
Bear Harbor & Eel River Railroad began construction of tracks from
Bear Harbor to Piercy on the Eel River. A winch lowered and raised
the locomotive and cars over the first very steep stretch of narrow-
gauge track near Bear Harbor. Past Usal Road, the train ran on its own
power. Disaster plagued the railroad from the start. A Pacific storm
destroyed Bear Harbor wharf in 1899, owner Harvey Anderson was
killed in an industrial accident in 1905, and the 1906 San Francisco
earthquake caused major damage to the tracks and trestles.

It begins to rain and I decide not to stop at Railroad Creek trail
camp, but to push on for the relative comfort of Needle Rock Ranch
House. Just offshore, a strange cloud formation, like a blackened tea-
pot, pours water from the ocean onto the land.

An hour's walk in the rain (a relief, actually, from the incessant fog)
brings me to the ranch house, a combination visitor center/hostel,
where I unpack my things. During the 1920s, a dairy operation, complete with large stockyards, stood on these bluffs. Around the stockyards stood a store, a hotel, a school, and living quarters for the families
of the dairymen. The Calvin Cooper Stewart family were the main

residents of Needle Rock, and today their ranch house serves as the park's visitors center.

There I am angered to discover that my Lost Coast map is no longer offered for sale; displayed instead is a brand-new map of Sinkyone Wilderness State Park, this one published by the state parks public relations office in Sacramento. It is a smaller map, a near-duplicate of mine except for one heartbreaking omission: J. Smeaton Chase Grove.

I'm furious: not because my work was copied, resulting in lower sales (I made the map for a nonprofit group and never expected a profit of any kind); not because state park bureaucrats have, at enormous taxpayers' expense, duplicated the work of a private effort that required no tax dollars (the government squanders money like this every day); but because the state park mapmaker substituted a blank spot on the map for the J. Smeaton Chase Grove. The map's text alludes to "a beautiful redwood grove" on the four-and-a-half-mile trek between Wheeler Camp and Bear Harbor, but does not say where one can find it.

Before I descend from anger into a major funk, the dark clouds vanish and the rain ceases. I step out onto the porch to see the sun, low over the water, struggling against the gloom. An isolated, lone eucalyptus shines ghostly white against the dark, storm-tossed sea.

It is this special, brooding light that intrigued the great Catholic theologian Thomas Merton when he visited here and talked of establishing a monastery for Trappist monks. He thought the Lost Coast shores around Needle Rock an ideal location for a life of prayer and contemplation—high praise indeed for one who believed so strongly in the power of physical silence and seclusion.

On a pilgrimage to Asia to experience Buddhist monastic life, deeper in India, Merton felt the spirit of the Lost Coast burning bright within him, and he wrote in his journal: "This deep valley, the Mim Tea Estate, above Darjeeling: it is beautiful and quiet and it is right—yet it has nothing I could not essentially have found at Needle Rock or Bear Harbor—nothing I did not find there last May."

Above the roar of the breakers I hear what sounds like the crack of a bat meeting a baseball, like someone is taking batting practice on the bluffs. I walk up-coast one hundred, two hundred yards, following my

ears until I spot an amazing sight. Two bull Roosevelt elk paw the
ground, lower their heads, butt antlers. Around them, grazing on the
bluffs are two-dozen females, by all outward appearances utterly disinterested in the result of this combat.

Again and again the elk circle, feint, clash. From a distance they look
evenly matched, but up closer it's apparent that a young bull, strong but
outweighed, is challenging an older bull. No blood is drawn. This is
more ritual, than actual, combat.

Roosevelt elk are enchanted-looking creatures, with chocolate-
brown faces and necks, tan bodies, and dark legs. The California natives look like a cross between a South American llama and a deer. In
truth, the elk are more awesome when they butt heads than when
they call. I always figured elk had a majestic call, a trumpet to arms, but
these Roosevelts have a funny little call more like the *wee-wee* of a pig
than the bugle of a powerful thousand-pound elk.

The younger bull may successfully challenge his elder next year or
the year after, but this evening the older bull, with his fuller antlers and
more clever moves, and still very much in his prime, is a sure bet to
keep his harem. Sunset (the first I've seen in days) casts an orange glow
over the clifftop combatants, like a floodlight on a stage. When the
light finally fades and darkness falls, the duel ends.

Dark shapes gather together, protection against the enemies of the
night, but if the elk intend to be inconspicuous they had better stop
eating. The ruminants tear at the grass, an aggressive munching, like a
lion ripping into a kill.

The next morning I hike up Whale Gulch on the Lost Coast Trail,
leaving behind the state park and entering King Range National Conservation Area. It's one of the wettest spots in America, with over a
hundred inches of rain annually, but today the weather seems most indecisive. Black clouds hover offshore to my left, the sun rises over the
King Range to my right. The radio in the ranch house predicted a 50
percent chance of showers.

Soon after crossing the boundary between state park and U.S. Bureau of Land Management territories, I cross another boundary, the
line between Mendocino and Humboldt counties. The county line is
another boundary of sorts—the 40th parallel of latitude.

The change in latitude heralds a change in attitude.

In the sharp morning light, this land shows its scars. The King Range is chainsaw country, Utah with fog. The magnificent coast is visible, and files of Douglas fir, but so also are clear-cut ridges, overgrazed slopes and silted streams. Some of this land looks like the "Before Rehabilitation" pictures in the Boy Scouts' Soil and Water Conservation merit badge pamphlet.

I think of yet another boundary I've crossed—this one wholly in my mind. After all this coast walking, I've decided there are three Californias: Smog Land, Fog Land, and Log Land. This beginning of BLM land, this 40th parallel, this Mendocino-Humboldt county line, this is clearly the start of Log Land.

As I climb Chemise Mountain the vegetation changes. Most of the fir have been logged, and it's tan oak and madrone that cling to the steep hillsides. Near the top of Chemise Mountain is some chemise (greasewood), as well as chaparral bushes and lots of manzanita; the presence of drought-resistant plants only a mile or so from a thick rainforest is truly bizarre. The difference in ecology has to do with elevation. Chemise Mountain, at 2,596 feet, is about 2,000 feet higher than the rainforest. I enjoy the view from atop the mountain: King's Peak, the dominant promontory to the north, a half-dozen ridges of the Sinkyone to the south, Shelter Cove on the coast far below. The view doesn't last long; it closes like a storm window.

As I descend precipitous Chemise Mountain Trail toward the coast, the weather has decided to be—indecisive. The sun warming the King Range from the east meets the storm brewing on the western horizon and the result is neither rain nor sun but a dense fog.

Here on these very steep slopes, exposed to the full fury of Pacific storms, the fir grow grotesque, their massive trunks short and twisted. Only the patter of condensed fog dripping from the branches breaks the silence.

I hurry through the dark, spooky forest. The reason for my hustle down the knee-jarring decline is that I have an appointment with Point No Pass on the beach below at precisely 2:53 P.M. and I must not be late. Such punctuality is critical because rounding the aptly named point is only possible at a rare minus tide, which, lucky for me, happens to occur this afternoon. If I can't round Point No Pass, and walk the beach to Shelter Cove, I will have to ascend this brutal slope of Chemise Mountain and hike over the crest of the King Range to continue north.

About a quarter-mile from the beach, I reach the end of Chemise Mountain Trail; it's been buried by a landslide, as if a giant bulldozer has scraped the side of the mountain. I slip-slide on feet and butt through the slide zone, hoping the mountain doesn't slide with me to the sea. When I reach the beach, I walk a mile to Point No Pass and, thanks to my watch and tide table, am able to round the point and reach Shelter Cove.

Shelter Cove is not a ghost town. Yet. As I approach I see a mountainside laced with forty miles of paved streets, with more gridded streets, an airstrip, and a golf course on the bluffs below. The labyrinth of asphalt was built to serve a subdivision of five thousand lots. By my count, only a hundred or so houses have been built—most on the bluffs.

In 1963 the Shelter Cove Development Company, a group of Los Angeles–based investors, began selling lots, and were fairly successful at it. The developers realized it was extremely expensive to bring utilities high up the steep coastal slopes of the King Range, so they tried to convince would-be Shelter Cove residents to buy the coastal lots, which they did, particularly after 1973 when a fire ravaged the slopes behind Shelter Cove, making the real estate not only unattractive, but unstable due to erosion and mudslides. But the coastal side of the development was hit even harder, by a force real-estate developers consider worse than fire and flood—the California Coastal Commission, which was established in 1973 largely to control the kind of out-of-scale development that Shelter Cove represented.

Today, Shelter Cove's commercial district consists of a restaurant (the last of several owners has been trying to sell it for years), a general store, and a post office.

Shelter Cove reminds me of one of those "living history" programs popular at missions and in gold rush towns where costumed docents pretend to be townsfolk of another era. Each member of the cast plays the role of somebody real. Shelter Cove remembers the 1960s, not as some laid-back Hippieville, but as a time of unbridled confidence in real estate and construction. And here in this Museum of Bad Development, this Resort from Hell, retirees and real-estate salespeople keep the town alive, still hoping for "an ultimate build-out of three thousand homes."

An elderly couple walks the black sand beach patrolled by swifts and swallows and . . . I can't believe my eyes, a central coast flashback, a bad dream of Pismo Beach—trucks and off-road vehicles. Perhaps Shelter Cove residents felt that if the town can't be marketed as a vacation-home resort, it can become an off-road vehicle haven. Rifles hang in gun racks in the cabs of the passing pickup trucks, fishing poles in the beds behind them. The Lost Coast locals are ever-ready to practice their traditional hunting and fishing techniques.

The beach, twenty-five miles from Shelter Cove to the mouth of the Mattole River, is the longest roadless stretch in California. Something of the thrill of knowing this, of walking this coast, is diminished when, road or not, vehicles are permitted on the beach for the first three-and-a-half miles.

Dodging cars and trucks, I walk the beach to Gitchell Creek, just beyond the boundary separating beaches that allow vehicles from beaches that forbid them. Just in case one of the locals decides to practice some traditional drunk driving on the beach tonight, I pitch my tent behind a massive log that seems guaranteed to stop even a tank.

As I gather driftwood for my evening fire, I nearly step on a rattlesnake. As lethargic a creature as I've ever seen, the timber rattler manages one flick of the forked tongue at me before uncoiling itself from a piece of wood and crawling deeper into the woodpile. I manage to work up some sympathy for a snake in such a cold and wet part of the world. The Lost Coast belongs to amphibians, not reptiles.

The next morning, I'm off into the fog, and in a few miles reach Buck Creek, where a steep trail leaves the beach and climbs into the King Range. This is my only chance to leave the beach and hike along the crest of the King Range. But now that I've left civilization—and vehicles—behind, I want to stick with the beach.

And a magnificent beach it is—rock, pebbles, and coarse black sand strewn with great logs, as if the sea, not the land, had been logged. And

water, water, everywhere: the ocean, deep and wide and restless on my
left, the fog all around me, creeks trickling, waterfalls tumbling from
the rainforest above to the beach below. High above me, at the limits of
vision, where the green slope meets the gray sky are seeps and springs
nurturing hanging wildflower gardens, scattered like Easter eggs in the
forest.

After a long day, I make another beach camp, another driftwood
fire, at Cooksie Creek. Then back to the beach the next morning.

I hear the residents of Sea Lion Rocks before I see them—two
dozen Steller sea lions. A mile beyond the big creatures is the abandoned Punta Gorda Lighthouse. In 1911, after several ships were
wrecked on the rocks and reefs off the Lost Coast, a lighthouse was
built a mile south of Punta Gorda, a name meaning "massive point."

The mouth of the Mattole River, a complication of gravel bars,
marks the northern end of the Lost Coast. Sea gulls and osprey circle
above me as I watch the harbor seals bob in the tidal area where the
river meets the ocean. I look back into the mist at the King Range, at
slopes that seem so much steeper than the angle of repose, and that are
kept from collapsing into the sea only by some hidden force deep
within the earth.

It is not really the coast that is lost, but ourselves. If we cannot find
the coast because of the smoke of our cities, the walls we build to keep
one another out, the industries we run that run us, it is surely we who
are lost.

We all need one place on the map, one place in our hearts that is
lost. In a wild place, lost from the mean streets, we can find ourselves,
our best selves. A place that is peaceful, for prayer and for contemplation, is good; a place that is wild, for challenge and confrontation, is
better; and a place that is both peaceful and wild, for the love of life
and the lust of living, is best.

NINETEEN

Faith in the Redwoods

THE MATTOLE RIVER is a living link between the mountains and the sea. On its way to the ocean, the Mattole flows through a long valley, linking redwood forests, fir forests, grassland, meadowland, and wetland. It transports sediments, nutrients, and oxygen. Life flourishes in its path.

Red-tailed hawks and golden eagles hunt along its banks. Salmon and steelhead spawn in its gravel beds.

But this river that nurtures so much life is itself half-alive. Clear-cut logging of the 1950s and 1960s all but annihilated the ancient fir forest. In the years following, the awesome Lost Coast winter rains, one hundred inches in an average year, 150 inches in a wet one, fell on a rainforest that was no longer a forest, dislodging the denuded slopes and sending millions of tons of mud into the Mattole.

Grazing, too, caused King Range slopes to erode. Sheep and cows tromp the surface until it is packed so firmly water can no longer be absorbed, and instead rushes quickly into gulches, tearing deeply into the mountainsides, gouging them until they give way and tumble into the river.

As a result of logging and grazing, millions of tons of rock and gravel slid into the riverbed. Gravel bars were formed so that the river wandered every which way. Even after a decade-long cleanup effort the Mattole has yet to heal.

Most affected of the many creatures dependent on the river are the steelhead, which depend on clear, well-oxygenated water and clean gravel beds to spawn. After braving ocean currents at the river mouth, then struggling through turbid river waters to spawn, they may find that the clean gravel riverbed in which they themselves were hatched is now buried in sediment. And, if they do manage to locate a clean gravel bed in which to deposit their eggs, the eggs might later be suffocated by additional sediment washed into the river by winter rains.

A bit inland from the mouth of the Mattole, I meet Jack, a seventy-year-old fisherman from Eureka. His pickup truck is backed up to the river and he sits on the tailgate, not reading the newspaper beside him, but studying the river. He's a healthy-looking fellow with a face nearly as red as his suspenders. He says he "fooled around" after some pan-sized trout earlier in the day, but drove to the river mostly just to get out of town for the day. Real fishing to Jack is steelhead fishing. Winter steelheaders like him start working the river in late December, or after winter rains sufficient to swell the Mattole and push through the sandbar at the river's mouth, thus allowing steelhead a way back to the river that spawned them.

"You think the river is bad now? It was worse ten years ago, and way worse twenty years ago," volunteers Jack, who says he first fished the Mattole fifty years ago.

The Mattole, after a decade of riverbed restoration, has a couple of good, clear-running spots, Jack explains, pointing them out to me. Trouble is, every local and his brother, along with guys from San Francisco and Los Angeles, all crowd into the same spots. "Most of those guys think you need perfect water to catch steelhead. You don't."

Conventional wisdom says that if the river is really fouled with sediment, both fish and fisherman are screwed. If the river is only half-fouled, then just the fishermen are screwed. But, says Jack, with a smile, he and some of his fellow anglers have figured how to fish the murky waters, which helps them escape the throngs of other steelheaders and hook a couple of fish.

"First thing you need to know," he says, putting an imaginary rod in his hand and lowering his voice conspiratorially, "is when the water's cloudy, the fish stay out of the mainstream, so you want to cast short, into three or four feet of water."

After a few practice casts, Jack launches into a peculiar dialect of fishspeak that, for a nonsteelheader like me, is hard to follow. If I get Jack's drift, what a successful steelheader needs is roe combined with an attractor—Jack prefers a brand called Spin-n-glow—something visually enticing (fluorescent colors are best) to the fish. To a lure called a Wee Wart, Jack adds a specially formulated scent. "See, first you get the fish's attention with the bright colors and then, even if it can't quite see what you're offering, it can smell it. Then with a little luck, you hook 'em."

I ask the obvious question: "Wouldn't it be easier for all parties—steelhead and steelheaders—if the Mattole River ran free and clear?"

"Yep," Jack answers without deliberation. But he pauses, regards the river a long while before elaborating. "I'm no Sierra Club member understand, and I don't like the hippies 'round here dressing up like trees and animals and protesting. And I don't like all those lawyers in their thousand-dollar suits up here arguing all the time, but I tell you, I don't want to see any more logging around here. 'Cause if they log those redwoods way up the Mattole, this river is gonna be wrecked again by all the mud and gravel that falls in. I worked all my life so's I could go fishing when I retired. I don't want to see this river go down the crapper. I don't have another twenty years to wait to go fishin' while they fix the goddamn river."

Jack's mention of the redwoods at risk prompts me to journey up the Mattole River Valley, past Petrolia and Honeydew, and a crazy quilt of meadowland and forest, to the river's headwaters above the hamlet of Whitethorn.

Here at the headwaters, where the river is in its infancy, the trees are two thousand years old. A rare virgin redwood grove—dubbed Sanctuary Forest by locals—somehow escaped more than a century of logging. Around the grove is an undisturbed mixed forest of Douglas fir and indigenous hardwooods—all mature.

I am moved by the sight of these giant redwoods, including a B.C. survivor called Big Red, for they are easily the tallest trees I've seen since I began walking the coast; however, it is the sound of this forest that stirs me this afternoon. The soft, sweet-smelling breeze swaying the branches, the trickle of the river—these are subtle sounds, quite unlike the salt-laden headwind and thunder of the surf that have accompanied me for so much of my walk.

This silent place, this redwood refuge, is not known as Sanctuary Forest by its owner, the Collins Pine Company of Portland, Oregon. It was the good sisters of the Redwood Monastery who gave this grove its name.

The Catholic Church sometimes offers sanctuary to those fleeing repressive dictators and their death squad goons. Here in the north woods, am I seeing a sanctuary movement for trees? Are the redwoods political prisoners, in need of physical and spiritual protection?

I decide to visit the Cistercian Sisters and find out just what this sanctuary business is all about.

EVEN THE DEER browsing the meadow next to Redwood Monastery appear in contemplation. The simple wooden living quarters and chapel reflect the simple, open lifestyle of the nuns, who told Thomas Merton, "We pray, we work, we live." During a 1968 visit to what was then known as "Our Lady of the Redwoods Abbey," the theologian was very impressed with the sisters' order and their surroundings as well, and figured he'd start a monastery for his brothers in Christ some ten miles down the Lost Coast at Needle Rock.

In 1962, Mother Myriam Dardenne, Abbess of the Cistercian Abbey of Nazareth, Becht, Belgium, came to California with several other Belgian sisters to begin a small Cistercian montastery at Whitethorn.

Sister Diane, clad in a sweatsuit and down vest, greets me with a firm handshake. I am somewhat surprised; I was expecting a bespectacled, old nun in traditional penguin-suit regalia, not this young woman with a warm smile, who looks like she could be out jogging on the beach.

I'm rude enough to ask why no habit, and she, apparently accustomed to the question, explains with good humor that in the 1960s the sisters did wear the stereotypical regulation habit—complete with head covering—and were known locally as "The White Ladies of Whitethorn." Subsequent Vatican decrees have allowed the nuns to exchange the habit for clothing more appropriate to habitués of a rainforest.

As we sip tea and nibble the sisters' delicious home-baked cookies, Sister Diane tells me the tale of Sanctuary Forest. The movement to save the forest arose locally—from the blink-and-you'll-miss-it hamlet of a hundred souls, Whitethorn. The Whitethornians feared that more logging would wipe out a decade of river-restoration work—and take with it not only the ancient trees themselves, but the animals that need them to survive.

Earthfirst! protesters and San Francisco lawyers working with the local Environmental Protection Information Center (EPIC) had successfully blocked other logging in the area, but these tactics didn't appeal to the townsfolk—a blend of pioneer families, Whale Gulch counterculturists, and the sisters themselves. Instead, they rallied around a suggestion from Sister Myriam Dardenne of the Redwood Monastery.

"Let's buy the forest," Sister Myriam said.

Thus, the nonprofit Sanctuary Forest, Inc., was formed, and a hundred thousand dollars of seed money raised from redwood lovers around the world for a good-faith deposit on the forest. Money begat money: another $4 million from a 1990 California Park Bond Act and some federal funds are earmarked for the forest. The future looks good for Sanctuary Forest.

"Isn't it unusual for an order of nuns to be conservationists—to rally to save some trees?" I wonder aloud.

"In Central and South America, and in Africa, various orders have helped the native people to save their land," Sister Diane explains. Our conservation work, which we probably don't think about in quite the same terms as you do, takes the form of letter writing, meetings, and nonaggressive protest. More broadly, what we seek is 'right relationships.' These are relationships that stress love of God, love for our neighbors. We also need a right relationship with the earth."

She and the other sisters deeply appreciate the beauty around them, Sister Diane affirms. The California of her girlhood was beautiful too. She was brought up in Covina, in the San Gabriel Valley of the 1950s.

She remembers the orange groves, clear-day views of snow-capped Mount Baldy. (I too remember this 1950s postcard view.) Joseph Smeaton Chase enjoyed this very view a half-century earlier from his home in nearby El Monte. Sister Diane also loves the ocean and fondly remembers the beach walks she took while a student at the University of California, Santa Barbara. She likes the daily drama of fog along the Lost Coast.

The sisters' conservation activities are real—they host Sanctuary Forest committee meetings in their community hall—but the sisters aim of saving souls is of greater importance than saving trees.

I think such conservation work, in the broadest sense of the word, must be very difficult for the nuns. For the monastic, the forest path between world refusal and world acceptance, between contemplating the glory of God and correcting the flawed governance of man, is a long and difficult one.

The so-called world refusal of the sisters is really also an acceptance of a world open to change, Sister Diane explains. The world refusal of the sisters is in itself a statement of their desire for change.

In one way, this puts the good sisters on a parallel plane with conservationists because conservationists (particularly those who reject some or most of the material world) are directing a dialectical critique of the political system with the goal of social change. The difference between nuns and conservationists is a fundamental one insofar as the conservationists' view of change is oriented to institutions, while the sisters seek to change human consciousness.

As my heads spins with more than enough to contemplate on a thousand-mile walk, Sister Diane says she has something to show me and escorts me to the chapel. Hanging here is painting of Jesus. Thomas Merton purchased the painting *Christ* from the painter Jamini Roy in India and had a friend deliver it to the Redwood Monastery. "Unusual, don't you think?" asks Sister Diane.

Truly, it is a strange painting. It has the flat, two-dimensional quality of pre-Renaissance religious painting, though Christ's triangular face, eliptical eyes and oval hands are semi-Cubist. The robed Christ, who stands with a tall cross, occupies an odd position on the canvas. At the bottom of the canvas is far too much empty space below his feet,

while the top crowds Christ's head; in fact, the artist has painted a border across the top of his forehead, implying he is ascending out-of-
frame. This is no Christ scourged or bowed by the physical brutality
that occurred just before his crucifixion. This is a broad-shouldered
Christ carrying mankind's burden with strong arms.

"I like the strength of Christ in this painting," Sister Diane comments.

What is most unusual about the painting is the cross—it's transparent, easily carried. It is Christ, not the cross, that transforms us.

"When we talk with the company who owns the forest, or we go
to a county board of supervisors meeting, we have specific goals. But
what we're really asking, with Christ's blessing, is mercy for the earth."

WHERE ARE the coast redwoods? Not on the coast between the
Lost Coast and Redwood National Park headquarters in Orick, that's
for sure. On my five-day, seventy-five-mile walk along this coast, the
only redwoods I see en route are in photos, or in partial states of dis-
memberment in logging museums.

From the Mattole River, I walk the beach and dunes until I reach
the steep, grassy slopes of Cape Mendocino. Here at the cape's edge,
I stand at the westernmost point in the contiguous United States.
Hooray! From offshore come some loud *"har-har-hars,"* as though
someone—a lot of someones in fact—is laughing at me. The har-
har-hars come from a boisterous colony of sea lions basking atop
Steamboat Island, located just west of the cape. I suppose they are
laughingly reminding me that they, not I, occupy America's westernmost point.

I walk past a multitude of sheep and cattle grazing the wide floodplain of Bear River, then across grassy False Cape (Mendocino), so
named by nineteenth-century mariners who sometimes confused it
with Cape Mendocino to the south.

After a pleasant night camped on a beach called Centerville Park,
more dune and beach walking brings me to the Eel River Delta. The
river delta is a complication of nature poorly interpreted by even my
best map, a network of levees, sloughs, and tributary streams, tangles of
black cottonwood and red alder, emerald green pasturage and neat

dairy farms, fresh water and saltwater marshes. To cross the delta I need one of those hybrid land/water craft designed by the highly creative participants of the Great Arcata to Ferndale Cross-Country Kinetic Sculpture Race, who propel their homemade, human-powered vehicles across thirty-six miles of mud, marsh, and sand; they even cross the Eel River and Humboldt Bay.

Lacking any amphibious contraption, I cross the Eel River at Fernbridge, after first detouring to visit cutesy Ferndale, a town of art galleries and gussied up Victorians recently reinstalled on their foundations after a wicked 1991 earthquake.

After crossing the mighty Eel, California's second largest river in terms of run-off, I approach Humboldt Bay, California's second-largest. The bay is nearly enclosed by two sandspits north and south. I figure I'll walk South Sand Spit and flag a ride from a passing fisherman to the north spit, thus avoiding the industrialized inland side of the bay and Eureka. (This walk-the-spit-and-hitch-a-ride technique worked well at Morro Bay and Tomales Bay.) However, after two miles of walking the sparsely traveled South Spit, and seeing nary a boat pass me, I reconsider the efficacy of this plan. I could be marooned on this spit for days without anybody picking me up.

In the fading light I retreat, taking a horeshoe hike around the bay and arriving well after dark at a slightly seedy, private trailer campground in the community of King Salmon, located across from the mouth of Humboldt Bay.

"Eureka!" is *not* what I feel like shouting the next morning when I look over the bay. Long developed for industrial and agricultural uses, Humboldt Bay looks even worse in the bright light of day, although the town does sport a spiffy new marina.

As I walk into Eureka, I pause to visit an homage to the great logging era past, Fort Humboldt State Historic Park. Rather than interpreting mid-nineteenth-century army life, the park has displays explaining how trees were cut and hauled away by ox teams and later by steam engines known as donkeys. On the very edge of civilization, such as it was in 1854, the purpose of the fort was to protect the loggers chopping down the ancient forest and the settlers who were planting the deforested land from Hoopa, Mattole, and Yurok Indians

angry about this violation of their ancestral territory. For soldiers stationed at this remote outpost, life was lonely and depressing. One unhappy soldier was a young officer by the name of Ulysses S. Grant,
who wrote to his wife, whom he hadn't seen in two years: "You don't
know how forsaken I feel here." Grant took long, solitary rides into
the surrounding wilderness and drank heavily.

Eureka boasts that it is the largest coastal city north of San Francisco. Perhaps only my single-mindedness about reaching the redwoods can explain why I am able to resist Eureka's many charming
tours: the Humboldt Bay Harbor Cruise, the five-hour Chamber of
Commerce Tour, the Coast Oyster Company processing plant tour,
the Victorian Walk past the timber barons' mansions of old, the Old
Town Tour through the boutiqued former bowery where the term
"skid row" reputedly orginated, or the Dead Mouse Marsh Bird Walk.
I do chance by a fine coffeehouse and order what is probably my last
latte of the trip. To go.

I cross the bridge over Humboldt Bay to Indian Island, a reminder
of the Wiyot Indians who lived here—that is until one night in 1860
when, while at a tribal gathering, forty of them were murdered by
Anglo-Eurekans. The murderers were never identified.

From the other side of the island, a second bridge reaches across
Humboldt Bay to North Spit, which has been industrialized since the
1880s, and looks it, a low-tech, Eastern Euro–looking agglomeration of
heavy equipment, log piles, and pulp mills. I stop at Samoa Cookhouse, an eatery that used to serve only loggers in the company town,
but has since become a cafe. My pancakes-and-eggs breakfast is good,
though the logging museum inside the cookhouse is enough to give
any redwood lover indigestion.

North of the bay, the river crossings get easier. A walker's foot-
bridge, formerly the railroad trestle of the Hammond Lumber Company, spans the Mad River. Little River proves equal to its name.

I cross the Sitka spruce–spiked Trinidad Head. The Pacific here is full
of large boulders, or tiny islands, colonized by a zillion birds: common
murres on Green Rock, storm petrels on Little River Rock. On other
rocks roost tufted puffins, gulls, and black oyster-catchers. Then it's
across another Sitka spruce–covered headland—Patrick's Point—before
descending to the sea again, and down into the fog, at Agate Beach.

The fog lingers a hundred feet above sea level, a long low ceiling over the saltwater on my left, the fresh water on my right. I walk a sandspit corridor past a series of lagoons—Humboldt, Big, Stone, and Freshwater.

Finally I arrive at the Redwood National Park Visitor Center, which, oddly enough, is not in the redwoods at all, but on the beach, at the mouth of Redwood Creek. Here in the visitor center, the logging exhibits have quite a different story to tell than the ones in Eureka, a tale of avarice and brutality, not profit and progress.

I cross Redwood National Park in two days, thirty miles of grand coastal trail, called the Redwood Coastal Trail up here. However, the redwoods I see on my way to Crescent City are limited by my route; with the exception of the tall trees thriving on the bluffs above Gold Beach, there are few magnificent groves near the ocean's edge.

While it is the ocean that protects redwoods from sun and frost by wrapping them in a blanket of fog, it is the rivers that give them life: the Mattole, the Klamath, the Smith, and especially the Eel. To view the grandest redwoods, I must follow the Eel, which I decided to do in two ways: biking and hiking. My friends Susan and Marc were kind enough to drop my bicycle in Crescent City on their way to Oregon.

I figured cycling would be a splendid way to see the big trees because most of the groves are accessible by road. But my real inspiration came from all those pretty pictures in Caltrans' bicycle touring guides. In them, there are no hills, the sun is always shining, and the cyclists are always smiling.

ON MY RIDE from Redwood National Park down to and through the Avenue of the Giants, there are plenty of hills and no sun, but I do keep smiling. I smile as I pass mist-enshrouded trees, their tops lost in the clouds. I smile through the fog. I smile through the multitude of memorial groves, named for Mather, the national park service founder, and Fleishmann, the yeast magnate, and about two hundred more about equally divided between conservationists whose good works earned them a grove and industrialists whose money bought one.

I keep smiling until I stop for lunch in Rockefeller Grove and meet Frank. Frank zooms up to me on his sparkling silver bicycle. We share a reunion of sorts. Racing along in some ridiculously high gear he has

passed me twice this morning as I labored up grades. (I have *no* idea
how I passed him.) Frank is a compact, hairy fellow. If he shaved his
face and legs, he would cut his wind resistance in half. Frank dismounts, looks from me to my rusty Japanese ten-speed, and chuckles.
"First tour?" he asks.

Without waiting for a reply, Frank begins inspecting my bicycle.
He finds the experience distressing. "What kind of bicycle is this?"

"IKI" is what it says on the frame, but I tell him there were more
letters before scratches obliterated them.

Franks suggests that if I want to get into *serious* touring, I should
exchange my hiking shorts for those cute little black racing shorts, my
hiking cap for a crash helmet, my sneakers for Detto Petro racing
shoes. He advises me to invest in a set of panniers and stop lashing my
pack to the bike with a bungie cord.

His lecturing makes me nervous. Not that I dislike talking about
outdoor gear. Choosing the right cross-country ski wax, the future of
GoreTex, and the existential nature of mummy bags are among my
favorite conversations. But this guy's a techno-freak, a real gear-head.

He wheels his bicycle over to me. It's gleaming, so brightly painted
it appears to be radioactive. I blink uncomprehendingly as he praises
the virtues of Cyclone derailleurs, the Sugino Mighty Compe crank,
the KKT Pro Ace Quill pedals. He shows me his anatomic seat with
magnesium rails and his Kryptonite bike lock.

None of this high technology impresses me. I wouldn't know a
Campagnolo brake if it stopped right in front of me. But I'm amazed
by Frank's tool kit. He has pedal wrenches, Allen wrenches, cone
wrenches, wrenches without name or apparent function, and something called a cotterless crank remover.

Before Frank showed me his tools and all the parts they could fix,
I believed that my bicycle's main virtue was simplicity: kinetic energy
transformed into mechanical energy by pumping pedals. But a number
of gears and bearings take part in this transformation and all of mine
are rusty, a condition that drives Frank crazy. He seizes a can of
WD-40 and begins spraying my bicycle. Liquid rust drips off of it.
"How can you ride this thing? The brakes! The chain!"

I try to tell him about my pedal-and-pray philosophy of cycling, but he will have no part of it. His voice rises, whining like a bad wheel bearing. "Don't you know how many things can go wrong with a bicycle?" At any moment, Frank warns, disaster could strike my headset bearings, derailleur cages, or caliper arms. We have reached an impasse. It's Zen vs. The Art of Bicycle Maintenance. With a final squirt of WD-40 he packs up his tool kit and wheels his bike away from mine. It's apparent we will not lunch together. It's as if I tried climbing the Matterhorn wearing tennis shoes and carrying a backpack full of canned spaghetti.

As Frank sits in the lush green foliage and unpacks his lunch, I explain to him my theory about Japanese products: maintenance does not prolong their lives. They come from the factory with a built-in life expectancy that no amount of tinkering will increase. They will play only so many CDs or videotapes, drive only so many miles before they self-destruct; mechanical *seppuku*. That's why I don't fiddle with my bike. I tell Frank that he too should adopt a philosophy of fatalism: when it goes, it goes.

"There's a lot to be said for the Zen approach," I conclude.

Frank is not impressed.

"It's your ass," he grumps.

"Yours, too," I answer as I pedal away. "You're sitting in poison oak."

IN THE PRESENCE of giants, the little things stand out. Poison oak climbs 150 feet up the redwoods. California huckleberry, azalea, mosses, lichen, and five-fingered ferns are everywhere—springing out of logs and stumps in a wild and dazzling profusion that I had previously associated only with the Amazon. I have the feeling I'm hiking through a jungle packed in dry ice.

I have two pages of handwritten notes from a local eco-activist intended to keep me on the trail, or what there is of it. Once I leave Maxxam Group's private road, there are only a few indistinct paths; instead, I walk across fallen trees and wade through ferns.

Perhaps the ideal way to celebrate this magnificent forest at the headwaters of the Eel River would be with flutes, drums, dancing maidens (at least two dozen would be required to encircle a redwood) cavorting among the ferns, and fairy lanterns. But bringing a dance troupe into these redwoods, bringing anybody into this forest, is strictly forbidden by its owner, the Maxxam Group. I am in Headwaters Forest, the largest grove of redwoods still in private hands. And I am trespassing. Again.

A sunbeam, a strong one, lasers through the thick fog, sending a shaft of light down the trunk of an enormous redwood. The light is like the transparent cross held by Christ in that painting hanging at Redwood Monastery. The cross haunts me as I walk among the two-thousand-year-old trees, saplings at the time of Christ. How much has human consciousness grown since then? Certainly it has not expanded exponentially, as these redwoods have. The growth of redwoods can be measured by counting their rings. By what measure can we determine the growth of human consciousness? How much more environmentally aware are we now than two thousand years ago? Perhaps in respect to the 4-billion-year-old history of the earth, and the 160-million-year-old history of the redwoods, we have not come very far very fast.

The struggle for control of Headwaters Forest is a tale of amazing greed—a financial soap opera of hostile takeovers, stock manipulation, Wall Street insider trading scandals, collapsed savings and loans, junk bonds, and Securities and Exchange Commission violations.

Back in the mid-1980s, the Maxxam Group solicited Drexel Burnham's help in raising money to buy Pacific Lumber Company. Drexel Burnham assigned Michael Milken, internationally known for his junk bond deals, to work with Maxxam. Milken bought and sold thousands of Pacific Lumber stock shares in order to take advantage of the stock price rise that would surely occur when Maxxam's takeover was revealed. Pacific Lumber stock rose as Pacific Lumber fought Maxxam's takeover.

The buying and selling of Pacific Lumber stock before and during Maxxam's takeover was illegal because Milken profited by using confidential information from his client to raise the price of stock his client was planning to buy. Milken attempted to hide his stock purchases by buying it under Wall Street trader Ivan Boesky's name—a violation of SEC regulations.

While Michael Milken received a stiff fine, a short prison sentence, and a probation term that required him to teach at the UCLA School of Business, the redwoods, without a defense attorney or a day in court, might as well have received a death sentence.

The fraudulently inflated stock prices—and resultant greater debt that Maxxam assumed when it bought Pacific Lumber—means increased pressure on Maxxam to cut lots of trees (liquidate assets) fast in order to pay off the high-interest junk bonds it used to acquire Pacific Lumber. To Maxxam, cutting old-growth redwoods like crazy is a particularly good way to pay off its debts.

Maxxam wants a couple hundred million for the 4,500-acre Headwaters Forest, a billion for all 44,000 acres in its possession. Conservationists say that figure is pure fantasy, and propose one of those Debt-for-Nature programs popular in third-world countries. United Financial Group, a Maxxam subsidiary, currently owes the federal government $548 million for the collapse of the nation's fifth-largest savings and loan. Perhaps the Federal Deposit Insurance Corporation can go after this debt, and be persuaded to accept public land in lieu of whatever bucks it can squeeze out of Maxxam.

Perhaps not.

Resource management in redwood country has a long history of doing exactly as the corporate buccaneers of Maxxam have: cut and run.

I walk back into the fog again, but the transparent cross still haunts me. To be both a Christian and a conservationist is a struggle of mine. A conservationist like me can believe in the kind of God who has ordered and given meaning to natural history, even human history, but finds it hard to believe in the Old Testament kind of God, who parted the Red Sea or extended the hours of daylight to the advantage of Joshua's Army.

None of us can duck earthly stewardship issues by shrugging and figuring that no matter what the outcome, it's the will of God. Should we not go as far as we humans can in the struggle for the environment and play our parts to the hilt in the human drama, before we call for divine intervention?

Even before Christ, men wondered when to call for spiritual reinforcements. Around 150 B.C., Greek historian Polybius opined: "Wherever it is possible to find out the cause of what is happening, one should not have recourse to the gods."

Or should we call on God first?

If prayer is the most powerful force in the universe, why do the nuns of Redwood Monastery have to raise money to save the trees?

But it's hard to be too critical of my country's Christian-capitalist environmental ethic; certainly the world's other religions haven't done any better, and have probably done a whole lot worse than Christianity: In India, Hindus have multiplied far out of proportion to the carrying capacity of the land; in Egypt, Moslems have dammed and strangled the Nile; in China, Taoism has not stopped ruthless deforestation.

I want to believe that Sister Diane and all the other good sisters and brothers, secular and divine, who work to raise and expand our individual consciousnesses are making us better stewards of the earth, but I fear our country, our society, has long ago passed a point where a change in human consciousness will resolve our problems.

More than ever we and our environment are in the hands of institutions—corporate and governmental. And it is not merely that these institutions have considerable power over our lives, but that they have evolved through common law and common use to have ideas and morality, wills and purposes, energy and inertia of their own. Far from being mere legal fictions, they have shown themselves to be resilient, adaptable, able to transcend and to survive changes in the individual humans who are supposed to control them. It is the individual human conservationist with a consciousness that is fast becoming the legal fiction.

Truly, it is the worst kind of juris-imprudence when corporations and government have standing while trees, and the individuals moved by conscience to save them, do not.

Why does nature have no standing in courtrooms? In the boardrooms of corporations? In the bored rooms of government? What does it mean for a river like the Eel, that is governmentally designated "Wild and Scenic," to have corporately owned headwaters?

We need these forests, as sanctuaries. Stories of the men and women who walked this land are not enough to pass on to the next generation; we need to pass on the land itself. These trees form a bond between the living and the dead, a reminder of the continuity of life.

We humans may be the only creatures blessed (or cursed perhaps) with the consciousness of our own mortality. It becomes a matter of some importance then, to feel that tie between the living and the dead.

It occurred to me, as I walked through logging and tourist townships and past the solemn colonnades of redwoods, that here among the ancient trees the only meaningful time distinctions are Now and Forever. Now, with its curio shops, drive-through trees, and chainsaw sculpture galleries, is sometimes disheartening. Now, in the form of clear-cut land, is best coped with by walking as quickly as possible through the eyesore. Forever is the redwoods, whose species name *sempervirens* means "everlasting." Although nothing in nature lasts forever, the redwood is as close to everlasting as any living thing can get. One hundred and sixty million years ago, great forests of the tall trees grew in Europe, Asia, and North America. Redwoods towered over the tallest dinosaur. A million or two years ago, with the coming of the Ice Age, the redwoods retreated and made a last stand along the northern and central California coast. Ninety-three percent of our coast redwoods have been chopped down; of the 7 percent remaining, 4 percent are under public ownership, hopefully forever.

There's little light on the trail now; it could be any time of day or night. Minutes, hours, and days have little meaning amidst two-thousand-year-old trees and a 20-million-year-old forest. Standing among the sorrel and the delicate redwood orchids and straining to see the top of the trees, I feel the long, joyous evolution of life on earth.

The trail stretches through the great redwood columns toward the rock-bound coast. I could walk here for a long time, maybe forever, if my heart doesn't break.

Epilogue

A LAST, VERY LONG day's walk from Crescent City to Pelican Beach on the Oregon border marked the end of a very long walk up the coast. Inviting me to continue north were all the places visited by 350 miles of the Oregon Coast Trail—Seven Devils Beach and Otter Point, Pistol River and Dragons Teeth. But beckoning me back was the sign over my right shoulder: WELCOME TO CALIFORNIA. Home. Home to Santa Barbara.

But I return to the beach almost daily, sometimes alone and lost in thought, sometimes with my family, to play. Often my thoughts return to my long walk up the coast, to a hundred towns and a thousand beaches, and to the millions of families just like my own who find something so special on the shore of the sundown sea.

I can look back now and see the change in my attitude toward the coast. First it affected me almost with an exaltation: beauty, grandeur, vastness. Next came despair, when I saw its ugliness and desecration. And then I assumed a kind of stoicism, trying to see the coast not in relationship to me, but rather as a place in itself.

What I wish to share now, with my daughter, with all who walk the beach, is the exaltation, the joy, of this coast.

Standing on the sand on one leg, much like a nearby sea gull, my two-year-old daughter, Sophia, shows me the bottom of her foot.

"Tarrr, Daddy," she declares.

"That's right, Sophia. We'll clean our feet with baby oil after our walk."

"Not boo-boo on the feet," Sophia confirms, repeating a lesson learned months before on another Hendry's Beach walk. "Tarrrr."

With a typical toddler's attention span, she soon forgets the tar on her feet and busies herself with popping the pods on a strand of kelp.

My thoughts stay with the tar. Twenty-five years ago, during Santa Barbara's disastrous '69 oil spill, I pulled screaming birds from the black tide that rolled over this beach.

Ten years after the spill I moved to Santa Barbara. I convinced Cheri, my bride-to-be, to leave Los Angeles and make her home with me in a little cottage by the beach. It is here in Santa Barbara that our daughter will grow up.

For an environmentalist, the town was just right—small enough for reflection, large enough for action. Your voice, your words, can make a difference here. You win some: Channel Islands National Park, the Dick Smith Wilderness. You lose some: Gaviota Oil Terminal, Diablo Canyon Nuclear Power Plant.

In a roundabout way, it was the spill that brought me back to stay. I had been impressed by the way energetic college students, shopkeepers, surfers, parents with their kids, all joined the beach clean-up; I saw a Montecito matron transporting oily birds in her Mercedes.

"Daddy!" Sophia calls. "Play sand now."

The spill was a conservation consciousness-raiser. Yet a quarter-century after the blowout, new wells have risen in the channel next to the old capped one. They say the new wells have deeper casings so they can't spill. And the oil tankers passing through the channel are double-hulled—not like the infamous *Exxon Valdez* that so befouled the Alaskan waters—so they can't spill either, you see.

It isn't reassuring, but perhaps it is a good reminder—that the price of living in paradise is constant vigilance.

"Daddy! Make a castle. Now, please."

I don't want the spill ever to be forgotten, but I don't want to remember any more now either, not on this postcard-perfect beach, not with a little girl pulling on my hand and reminding me of the important work to be done—building castles in the sand.

"Dig, Daddy. Dig!"

We must not forget what we have. We must not forget what we could lose. We owe the next generation no less.